Crash Course in dBASE® 5.0 for Windows™ Programming

Christopher R. Green

Crash Course in dBASE 5.0 for Windows Programming

Copyright© 1994 by Que® Corporation

All rights reserved. Printed in the United States of America. No part of this book may be used or reproduced in any form or by any means, or stored in a database or retrieval system, without prior written permission of the publisher except in the case of brief quotations embodied in critical articles and reviews. Making copies of any part of this book for any purpose other than your own personal use is a violation of United States copyright laws. For information, address Que Corporation, 201 W. 103rd Street, Indianapolis, IN 46290.

Library of Congress Catalog No.: 94-67945

ISBN: 1-56529-938-8

This book is sold *as is*, without warranty of any kind, either express or implied, respecting the contents of this book, including but not limited to implied warranties for the book's quality, performance, merchantability, or fitness for any particular purpose. Neither Que Corporation nor its dealers or distributors shall be liable to the purchaser or any other person or entity with respect to any liability, loss, or damage caused or alleged to be caused directly or indirectly by this book.

97 96 95 94   8 7 6 5 4 3 2 1

Interpretation of the printing code: the rightmost double-digit number is the year of the book's printing; the rightmost single-digit number, the number of the book's printing. For example, a printing code of 94-1 shows that the first printing of the book occurred in 1994.

Publisher: David P. Ewing

Associate Publisher: Don Roche, Jr.

Managing Editor: Michael Cunningham

Product Marketing Manager: Greg Wiegand

Associate Product Marketing Manager: Stacy Collins

We'd Like To Hear from You!

As part of our continuing effort to produce books of the highest possible quality, Que would like to hear your comments. To stay competitive, we *really* want you, as a computer book reader and user, to let us know what you like or dislike most about this book or other Que products.

You can mail comments, ideas, or suggestions for improving future editions to the address below, or send us a fax at (317) 581-4663. For the on-line inclined, MacMillan Computer Publishing now has a forum on CompuServe (type **GO QUEBOOKS** at any prompt) through which our staff and authors are available for questions and comments. In addition to exploring our forum, please feel free to contact me personally to discuss your opinions of this book.

Thanks in advance—your comments will help us to continue publishing the best books available on computer topics in today's market.

Kathie-Jo Arnoff
Product Development Specialist
Que Corporation
201 W. 103rd Street
Indianapolis, Indiana 46290
USA

Credits

Publishing Manager
Nancy Stevenson

Acquisitions Editor
Jenny L. Watson

Product Directors
Kathie-Jo Arnoff
Lisa D. Wagner

Production Editor
Kezia Endsley

Technical Editors
Charles Miedzinski
Gordon Padwick

Acquisitions Coordinator
Deborah Abshier

Editorial Assistant
Jill Stanley

Book Designer
Paula Carroll

Cover Designer
Jay Corpus

Graphic Image Specialists
Clint Lahnen
Dennis Sheehan

Production Team
Stephen Carlin
Karen Dodson
Joelynn Gifford
Dennis Clay Hager
Kaylene Riemen
Caroline Roop
Mary Beth Wakefield
Donna Winter
Jody York

Indexers
Charlotte Clapp

Composed in *Stone Serif* and *MCPdigital*
by Que Corporation

About the Author

Christopher R. Green is the principal of *Colorado Springs Technical Consulting Group*, a technical and computer support services company located near Colorado Springs, Colorado. Formed in 1986 after the demise of the Space Shuttle *Challenger*, the company offers a well-developed range of specific computerized services suitable for small- and medium sized companies. Effective project management is provided for technical project management; all facets of technical writing; software and hardware product documentation; training seminars and product support programs; technical marketing, advertising, and sales programs; database design, data input, query, and printing; technology management.

Mr. Green earned his undergraduate degree from Grand Valley State Colleges (Michigan) and an MBA from the University of Phoenix (Arizona). He has been involved in data-processing activities for 15 years. *Colorado Springs Technical Consulting Group* may be reached at 719-481-9476.

Trademarks

All terms mentioned in this book that are known to be trademarks or service marks have been appropriately capitalized. Que cannot attest to the accuracy of this information. Use of a term in this book should not be regarded as affecting the validity of any trademark or service mark.

Screen reproductions in this book were created using Collage Complete from Inner Media, Inc., Hollis, NH.

Contents at a Glance

Contents

16 Working in a Shared Environment   249

A Using dBASE III and dBASE IV Applications   263

Index   273

Introduction

Crash Course in dBASE 5.0 for Windows Programming will help you develop your knowledge of dBASE 5.0 for Windows, Borland International's latest offering for the database language market. dBASE for Windows is a quantum leap into an improved way of managing data. The software moves you from character mode into a graphical user interface (GUI—pronounced *gooey*); from static views into interactive and customizable data objects; and from a more formalized, procedurally oriented methodology (which you may be used to) into the developing world of object-oriented programming (OOP) and event-driven application programs.

The dBASE language is a structured fourth-generation language (4GL) designed for database-management tasks. A 4GL language is one that allows multiple database files to be open, and on which you can perform independent querying, sorting, and indexing tasks.

Who Should Use This Book

You may already be familiar with the concepts of programming, from design through coding and the implementation of your programs. This book provides a crash course in a better way of implementing that data; employing a broad range of skill levels, from novice to expert, the book guides you through the interfaces of menus, dialog boxes, and SpeedBars. The interface also includes an interactive Command window where you can enter and then execute your dBASE commands directly.

You can use the menu commands or the Command window to design and run tables, queries, forms, and reports. dBASE for Windows provides full compatibility with older, DOS-based versions of dBASE: dBASE III PLUS and dBASE IV. There is complete implementation of source code for programs written in these older versions.

How This Book Is Organized

Crash Course in dBASE 5.0 for Windows Programming is divided into 16 chapters and one appendix.

- Chapter 1 covers the dBASE for Windows environment, including what hardware/software combinations you need for minimum performance.

- In Chapter 2, the creation of database tables, along with some information about database design guidelines and concepts is offered.

- Chapter 3 builds on the information presented in Chapter 2 by showing you how to enter and edit data. Database sessions are covered here, as well as the dBASE for Windows Navigator. In addition, information about adding, deleting, and undeleting records, and browsing the database table is presented.

- Chapter 4 shows you how to create an index and then sort data according to the criteria you pick when creating your index. You learn how to create a master index, as well as how to store your index and use it later.

- Chapter 5 discusses how to go about creating queries (that may or may not use indexing routines) for data. A properly executed query shows you valuable information at a certain point in time.

- Chapter 6 covers forms. This discussion includes queries and tables screens, and how to create effective queries with different types of forms.

- Chapter 7 addresses the topics of menu creation through buttons and SpeedBars.

- Chapter 8 shows you how to build dBASE expressions with the *Expression Builder*. Once built, the expression can be executed through the Command window.

- Chapter 9 covers reporting and printing topics using the dBASE for Windows program and the Windows *graphical user interface*. You learn the methods behind creating a useful report on-screen and then sending it to the printer.

- Chapter 10 discusses the different text editors. Here, you learn how to use an initial editor, such as the editor that comes with MS-DOS; alternatively, you can use any editor you want, and you learn how to invoke that editor for use with dBASE for Windows.

■ Chapter 11 builds on the information presented in the earlier chapters by working with the Command window to execute commands directly from the keyboard instead of using the mouse.

■ Chapter 12 shows you how to create *structured query language* (SQL) data using the dBASE for Windows IDAPI configuration utility.

■ Chapter 13 explains some of the mysteries behind programming in general, and programming specifically in the dBASE for Windows methodology. This lengthy chapter covers the routine elements of programming for beginners and covers more difficult topics for those with higher degrees of discipline under their belts. Program creation, compilation, and debugging are covered in this chapter.

■ Chapter 14 covers the topic of *object-oriented programming*. This chapter shows you how to use objects and classes to reuse program code without having to rewrite it.

■ In Chapter 15, *dynamic-link libraries* are covered, first with respect to the client application arena, and then when creating and linking to your server.

■ Chapter 16 builds on Chapter 15's topic by showing you how to work in a shared environment by using file and record locking, database table sharing, and transaction processing effectively.

■ Appendix A shows you the rudiments of converting your dBASE III, dBASE III-Plus, and dBASE IV code for use in dBASE for Windows.

Conventions

Several conventions are used throughout the book to guide you more accurately to successful learning without fruitless searching, keying-in, or icon pointing. Where appropriate, I use standard mouse actions or data-entry from a keyboard—all within a normal Windows 3.1 interface environment.

■ *Choose* means that you should select and execute a command from a menu bar or button in a dialog box.

■ *Select* means that you should take an action on your way to a final action of some type.

■ *File, Select* means that you should proceed to the *File* menu, and choose *Select* in order the accomplish the task being demonstrated.

■ When you see a key combination such as Shift+F4, hold down the Shift key and press the F4 function key.

■ When you see commands such as the **F**ile, **R**un command, you can press Alt+F; then R to activate the command. (The hot keys are in bold.)

■ New terms and emphasized words are presented in *italics*.

■ Functions, commands, parameters, and the like are set in a special `monospace` text.

■ Anything you are asked to type appears in **bold**. Responses to program prompts appear in `monospace bold`.

■ Placeholders (words that you replace with actual values) in code lines appear in `monospace italic`. For example, `filename` or `variable`.

■ Shaded boxes, labeled "Syntax," appear throughout this book. This design feature provides easy language reference to the essential elements of dBASE for Windows programming. By providing this helpful information, *Crash Course in dBASE 5.0 for Windows Programming* is not only a tutorial, but also a quick reference that serves you for a long time to come. A sample Syntax-at-a-Glance box follows:

```
SET DEFAULT TO C:\ACCOUNTING [CR]    ( [CR] = [RETURN] )

SET SYNTAX OFF [CR]
```

Tip
Tips offer short-cuts and hints to make program-ming in dBASE for Windows easier and more efficient.

In addition to Syntax-at-a-Glance boxes, you find three other types of visual pointers in this book.

Note

Note boxes provide you with additional information. This information helps speed your learning and reminds you of important information that bears repeating.

Caution

Caution boxes warn you of problem areas, including procedures that can possibly harm your data or cause your program not to run.

Chapter 1

The dBASE for Windows Environment

This chapter introduces you to different hardware and software requirements and their configurations for different installation options. As commercial software offerings become larger in scope, integrated hardware components (CPU, RAM, and so on) are obliged to execute commands faster in order to keep up. dBASE for Windows is no different in its thirst for a large hard disk and copious amounts of RAM.

Hardware and Software Requirements

You need the following hardware configuration in order to run dBASE for Windows:

- An IBM-compatible (clone) computer with at least an 80386 processor and a minimum of 32 megabytes of hard disk space for a complete installation. A minimum installation—void of any "goodies"—requires at least 21 megabytes of space.

- A minimum of six megabytes of RAM. (Eight megabytes is recommended; more is even better!)

- A VGA/SVGA monitor and appropriate graphics card.

The following software is required:

- DOS version 3.1 (or a compatible operating system). However, if you are not using at least DOS 5.0, you cannot take advantage of available extended memory architectures.

Tip
The more memory you have available, the faster your application runs. There will be more space available for you to halt execution of a program temporarily without it adversely affecting your other work.

Tip

If you have an oversized monitor, you can get more information displayed on the desktop. There isn't a great deal of difference in the cost of a 14-inch monitor and a 17-inch monitor, but a 19-inch monitor can cost almost two thousand dollars; a 21-inch monitor is considerably more expensive.

■ MS Windows version 3.0/3.1; you may use version 3.0 if you can tolerate the relative instability of that product and the UAE errors. Make sure that you run in an enhanced mode. Version 3.1 automatically runs in an enhanced mode.

Installing and Configuring dBASE for Windows

The installation program begins at the Windows Program Manager. It is a good idea to make backups of the master disks before you begin installation. Insert the first disk into either the A: or B: drive and execute the A:\INSTALL program from the File, Run command.

As the installation command executes, you are prompted for a variety of program information. A series of dialog boxes asks for the path where you want the software installed (the default is C:\DBASEWIN), your name and company, and the type of installation you want to perform.

A full installation copies and installs all files into the directory and its related subdirectories; a customized installation copies and installs only user-selected files into the subdirectories in a configuration sufficient to allow dBASE for Windows to execute.

> **Caution**
>
> You *must* run the installation program, because copying compressed files directly from the A: or B: floppy onto your hard disk doesn't expand those files properly; the software doesn't run. You also must (obviously) have a complete set of seven software disks: anything other than a complete set will also mean that key elements of the program will be missing, assuming that you are able to perform a complete installation.

After these questions are answered, the INSTALL program assumes control, prompting you for each successive disk.

Creating a Program Group

After the installation program has completed, the dialog box shown in figure 1.1 appears. The installation program allows automatic selection of icons, rather than making the user perform the addition by hand.

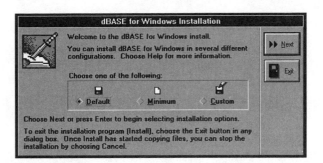

Fig. 1.1
The Installation
Request dialog box.

Choose **N**ext to create a Windows program group containing the dBASE for
Windows icons. Note that the DBASEWIN.EXE executable file resides in the
C:\DBASEWIN\BIN subdirectory, not in the C:\DBASEWIN directory, as you
may expect.

The installation program makes the following changes to your WIN.INI file:

```
[DBASEWIN INSTALL]
Location=C:\DBASEWIN\BIN\DBASEWIN.INI
```

In the same file, the following lines describe the location of your main *Integrated Database Application Programming Interface* (IDAPI) configuration file:

```
[IDAPI]
CONFIGFILE01=C:\DBASEWIN\BIN\IDAPI.CFG
```

A normal WIN.INI file is located in the C:\WINDOWS subdirectory. The
installation program automatically makes the required changes to this file.
However, if you later want to relocate the program to another drive or
subdirectory, you have to edit this file. Find the [DBASEWIN INSTALL] section
down toward the end of this file and make the desired changes. If you also
decide that you want to have the IDAPI subdirectory located in your
DBASEWIN subdirectory instead of a stand-alone directory, you have to
make the applicable changes there, too.

Caution

You should make a backup of the WIN.INI file with a different name in case you make
a mistake and the file doesn't run after you save it with the new information.

Loading Files During Startup

You may consider loading the same series of files each time you launch dBASE for Windows. If you do, edit the [SETTINGS] section of the DBASEWIN.INI file, which is in the C:\WINDOWS directory. The following example automatically loads LOCAL.PRG from the C:\ACCOUNTS\PHONE directory path:

COMMAND=C:\ACCOUNTS\PHONE\LOCAL.PRG

To use LOCAL.PRG as a file specification from the initial program launch, add the following command to the command line of the Program Manager Run dialog box:

DBASEWIN.EXE C:\ACCOUNTS\PHONE\LOCAL.PRG

If you want to open and run this file automatically, you have to alter the line that runs from the Program Manager icon.

Configuring IDAPI

If you intend to use any Paradox aliases or to connect to an SQL database such as Oracle, Paradox for Windows, or Ingres, you have to configure Borland's IDAPI database engine and then use it to integrate those programs. (As previously stated, IDAPI stands for *Integrated Database Application Programming Interface*.) You launch the IDAPI configuration utility from the Program Manager.

When the IDAPI utility is installed, the results are built into a directory (C:\IDAPI) located just below the root directory. You can change the settings by double-clicking the IDAPI icon in the dBASE for Windows program group. Note that you should make any IDAPI changes outside dBASE for Windows. Close all your open files, exit dBASE, and make the changes in the IDAPI configuration utility; then save the changes and restart dBASE for Windows.

Figure 1.2 shows the IDAPI Configuration Utility dialog box. In this figure, the Driver Name box is empty, indicating that no SQL databases are installed.

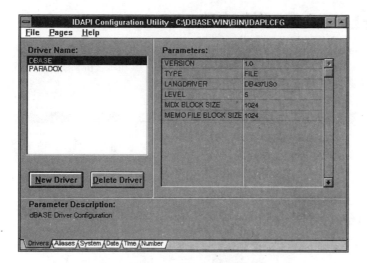

Fig. 1.2
The IDAPI
Configuration
Utility dialog box.

For Experienced dBASE Users

Experienced users who have "come up through the ranks" with earlier versions of dBASE will appreciate the ease and flexibility with which their programs are integrated into dBASE for Windows.

For example, the Command window replaces the old *dot prompt* popular in dBASE III PLUS and dBASE IV. Commands are executed in the Command window in much the same fashion as they were performed at the old dot prompt. Executed commands are displayed on-screen as they are performed by the program.

Users of dBASE IV might be sorry to see some old favorites disappear, however. The Control Center, popular as a dBASE IV frontispiece, is available as an equivalent through the menu system and catalog windows, and it is gratifying to see that the function keys now work!

Although you may still have the catalogs that show related items, it is no longer necessary to select and load them before using them. When the databases (now called *tables*), queries, reports, and forms are selected, they are automatically associated with one another without any prompting.

The commands SET HISTORY, LOAD, and CALL are no longer appropriate to the Windows environment interface; they are not included in this release.

Experienced programmers will find that their programs created in other versions of dBASE run unchanged in dBASE for Windows. The Debugger can still debug their programs; event-driven programs allow users to switch tasks; and object-oriented programs are easier to maintain, enabling you to reuse code.

Tip
The Function Keys work only if you program them. For example, the command SET FUNCTION 2 to "Colorado Springs" pastes the text "Colorado Springs" at the cursor's location whenever the F2 function key is pressed.

Parts of the Environment

After you finish installing dBASE for Windows, the program group shown in figure 1.3 appears. To launch the program, double-click the dBASE for Windows icon at the top-left corner.

Fig. 1.3

The dBASE for Windows program group.

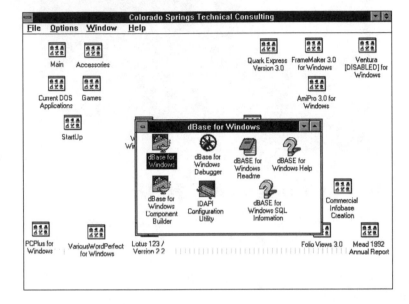

After the hard disk finishes its gyrations from your double-clicking the dBASE icon, you are presented with figure 1.4, the opening menu.

Notice in figure 1.4 that the window periphery shows standard Windows GUI material. The square at the top-left corner closes the application if you select it. The triangles at the top right corner minimize the application or allow you to size it.

A standard **F**ile, **E**dit, **V**iew, **N**avigator menubar occupies the area directly below the title bar. If you don't have the luxury of using a mouse, you can access these subheadings by pressing the Alt key, and the letter underlined (bold in this book). For example, to access the **F**ile menu, press Alt+F. Many of these drop-down menus have a right-facing triangle at the end of a subheading title. In dBASE for Windows, this means that there is a third level of menu selections available to you.

Directly underneath the menubar is a second bar called a SpeedBar. This particular bar is one of several different menubars that appears throughout the program. It permits you to make quick selections without having to go back and forth between the menubar and your desktop work session.

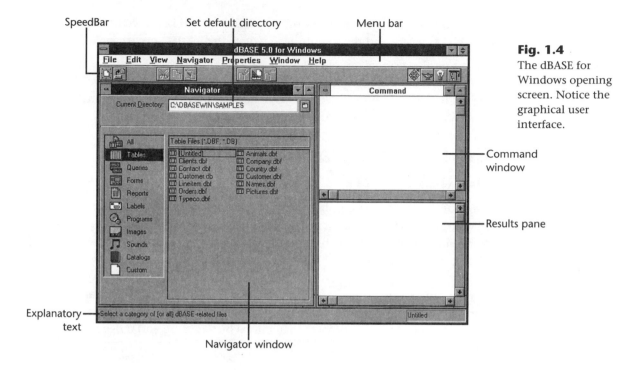

SpeedBar   Set default directory   Menu bar

Fig. 1.4
The dBASE for
Windows opening
screen. Notice the
graphical user
interface.

Command
window

Results pane

Explanatory
text

Navigator window

Although the purpose of these icons might be obvious to some, their meaning can become fairly difficult to interpret. dBASE for Windows comes to the rescue here by providing an interpreter. If you rest the mouse on one of the icons, an explanatory sentence appears in the bottom bar beginning at the left-bottom edge. For example, the first icon provides the explanatory text *Select a category of (or all) dBase-related files*.

At this point, nothing is open so the dialog box at the bottom-left corner reads untitled. After you open a table or perform some other activity that opens an entity, the *Untitled* phrase is replaced with the name of the open file. Other information, such as the record number, where the record pointer is, whether the Insert key is on, and so on, appears on this status line when you open something.

In figure 1.4, the Navigator is on. Note that you are also able to maximize/minimize this dialog box. You can set the directory that you want to use from the Current Directory dialog box at the top of this Navigator dialog box. If you wish to change the current directory, pull down the file icon, displaying the Choose Directory dialog box, and make your change from there.

You can minimize the Navigator by clicking the minimize triangle. The dialog box minimizes to a Steamship wheel, leaving the desktop area white. The Command box is the remaining open box to the right. The upper portion of this box includes the Command window (where you can key in commands from the keyboard) and the Results pane (where the results appear).

You can minimize the Command box by clicking the minimize triangle. The box minimizes to a magic lantern, leaving the desktop area white. As you progress through the different elements of dBASE for Windows, notice that the SpeedBar changes along with the menubar.

dBASE as a Relational-Database Management System

dBASE for Windows is a complete, *relational-database management system* (DBMS) that allows users to manage data as they build independent data-management applications. Thus, a user can build anything from systems that handle something simple like an address book to a more complex system, such as one that handles a relational series of information linking databases together. For example, a National Parks employee might have grizzly bear information such as banding, weight, size, height, and so on in one table, and a listing of all the sightings of that animal by township and range in another.

In the older releases of dBASE, databases were called *databases*—in this most recent release, they are called *tables*. The most common way for you to interact with them (and all other forms of the program) is through the graphical user interface (GUI). This GUI includes menus, dialog boxes, windows, palettes, and other graphical elements. It is one of the two places where you go to interact most effectively with dBASE. The other place is the Command window, where you can key in commands from the keyboard. To learn more about the Command window, see Chapter 11.

dBASE for Windows introduces a new way of working with your applications: *sessions*. When a session is on, closing a window that refers to a table closes the table as well, unless other open windows refer to that table, in which case the window stays open. This is a standard Windows-type paradigm.

When a session is off, closing all windows that refer to a table does not necessarily close the table. Using sessions can affect what happens to your application when you switch between working in the user interface and entering commands in the Command window. You can find more information about sessions in Chapter 3.

Getting Help

The online help system is automatically installed and configured during the initial dBASE setup process, unless you specifically omit it when configuring dBASE. Unless you have extremely strong programming resources and never refer to a help utility or your hard disk space is limited, I recommend that you include it in the installation process.

Online help employs the typical search engine found in all Windows applications. Each topic describes some aspect of the user interface and its language elements. When you are finished consulting a topic, you may return to dBASE for Windows or jump to another topic.

You can get a detailed description of the dBASE for Windows help system by choosing **H**elp, and then **H**ow to Use Help from the dBASE for Windows menubar.

Finding Topics

You access the online help screen in any of the following ways:

■ Choose **H**elp, **C**ontents from the dBASE for Windows menubar. Pressing Shift+F1 accomplishes the same thing.

■ Search for a topic by choosing **H**elp, **S**earch, or choose the **S**earch button from the Help system.

■ Type **help** and a phrase from the dBASE Command window (for example, typing **help sessions** gives you information about using sessions). Also, typing **help** by itself displays a list of available help topics.

Using the Interactive Tutors

dBASE for Windows features interactive tutors that help you understand the software while you remain in the program. You can artificially create database tables, generate queries, write reports, and produce catalogs using live data. Then, you can save and reuse the results after closing the tutor window.

To use the interactive tutor, choose **H**elp, Interactive **T**utors to display the opening screen. You can launch a topic by clicking the button next to its name. The interactive tutor utility is another optional installation item. However, I recommend that you include it.

Using the Sample Files

The dBASE for Windows sample files are installed in a SAMPLES directory located beneath the main C:\DBASEWIN subdirectory. The sample files include tables, queries, reports, and forms that you can use as templates or simply as learning tools. You may choose not to install these sample files because of hard disk space restrictions, although they demonstrate significant dBASE methodologies and can be useful in developing your own applications.

You can execute the sample programs by using any of the following options:

- Double-click the program icon.

- Select a program icon. Alternatively, press F2 or choose **N**avigator, **E**dit Records.

- Select a program icon and click the Run button in the SpeedBar.

- Right-click the icon and choose **E**dit Records from the SpeedMenu.

- Type **DO** *<program name>* in the Command window and press Enter. Note that you do *not* have to complete the filename extension. To run PHONE.PRG for example, type **DO PHONE** and press Enter.

You can view any of the sample file program text in the dBASE for Windows text editor.

You can execute the sample programs by using any of the following commands:

- Double-right-click the program icon.

- Select a program icon. Press Shift+F2 or choose **N**avigator, Design **T**able Structure.

- Select the program icon and click the Design button in the SpeedBar.

- Right-click the program icon and choose Design **T**able Structure from the SpeedMenu.

- Type **MODIFY STRUCTURE** *<program name>* in the Command window and press Enter.

Remember that you type your program name in the preceding examples and not the actual words, *program name.*

Using the Form Expert

Toward the right edge of the SpeedBar, between the graduate figure and the Magic Lantern icon, a light-bulb icon announces the arrival of a new feature in dBASE for Windows—the *Expert,* designed specifically and exclusively for use when you want to design a form.

The Form Expert accepts the minimum inputs from you as it creates a form for you. Controls, control properties, labels, and the capability to link data are available.

Summary

This chapter explained the installation processes of dBASE for Windows. Specifically, you learned the hardware and software requirements for running dBASE for Windows, what constitutes a minimum installation, and how to create a program group in Windows. You also learned the components of the dBASE for Windows opening screen and some of the more common menubar configuration screens. Finally, you learned how to use the IDAPI, help, and interactive tutors associated with dBASE for Windows.

In Chapter 2, you learn about creating database tables.

Chapter 2

Creating Tables

Organizing Your Information

Information, the saying goes, is knowledge, and knowledge is power. Think about the data (disguised as knowledge) that impacts your everyday life. From the time you get up in the morning until you retire at night, your senses are bombarded with inputs that control your behavior. Most of this data cannot be adequately captured, ordered, and sorted before it is represented to you in a useful format. If it was, you could probably use to it your advantage and be a little further down the road. This chapter begins the process of showing you how to channel your data into compartments through the creation of a table, or database structure. Once created, it will be used in later chapters to hold your data, and finally to sort knowledge so that it helps you with your task at hand.

Once you create a table structure, you then populate it with data. Usually a structure has names that a user can easily identify: a person's name, for example, can be a database fieldname called FIRSTNAME. A field of someone paying a bill after the due date might have a notation made against them in a fieldname called TARDY. You can add someone's birth date as a date field called BIRTHDAY. Rarely are database tables of any design cast in stone. As your requirements change, you alter the table to reflect those new changes. This chapter talks about creating database structures, making changes, and saving the table after the structure is stable.

Database Design Guidelines and Concepts

A *database* is a collection of related material organized for a specific purpose or activity. In the dBASE parlance, a database is a collection of tables created to store information and work with indexes, forms, and reports. Each table

Tip

Before you apply fingers to keyboards, give some earnest consideration of what you want your data to show you, how you want the information to be displayed, and what the relationships among the various elements will be. Incomplete design is one of the biggest reasons projects fail.

Tip

As you create, save, and copy your work, take some notes about what you did and why. Six months from now, a set of notes proves a valuable addition to your application.

begins with a maximum eight-character name followed by the .DBF extension.

A *table* is the basic unit from which you begin to build an application. A table contains at least one record, and each of these records contains fields. Fields identify other tangible pieces of each record: a customer number, client name, address, city, state, and so on. The table structure is such that all records must contain the same field in the same position.

Fields may hold many different types of data: alphabetic, numeric, and dates are perhaps the most common types. However, in dBASE for Windows, fields can also hold graphic images or sound files. Each column (vertically based data) in the table is considered a field.

A table's structure includes its table type—either a dBASE, Paradox, or an SQL type—and at least one field. During table definition, each field is presented and you define its name, its width, and its field type. The field type must be one of the following: Character, Numeric, Memo, Logical, Date, Float, OLE, or Binary. An optional keyfield allows you to create an index. Such a keyfield displays records in a unique order without having the user resort the fields.

Figure 2.1 shows a typical table view in a horizontal format. Note the record number (*Rec*) in the first column, and the remaining table fieldnames at the top of each column. The record pointer is positioned at record 21. You may expand or contract the amount of space each fieldname occupies by positioning the cursor at the intersection point of each vertical and horizontal line and waiting with your finger on the mouse button until the cursor changes to a cross. Then drag the fieldname to its new dimensions.

Creating a New Table

The Table Structure window, or Table Designer, is used to create or modify the table's structure.

Double-click the [Untitled] table icon in the Navigator or Catalog window. You can also click the Design button in the SpeedBar. Or, you can enter **CREATE** in the Command window.

Starting the Table Designer opens the Table Structure window shown in figure 2.2. The figure shows an [Untitled] table. You complete the fieldname, type, width, whether to declare it as a decimal, and index field. You can Tab to each field and type the new information.

Creating the Table Structure

The top portion of the Table Designer represents properties that apply to the entire table.

- The *Name* is the table's name. It is *untitled* until you save it as something.

- The *Type* is the type of table you're creating. It can be a dBASE or PARADOX table. (It can also be an SQL type if you installed an SQL driver). Make your selection from these two options.

- The *Updated* field represents the date that the table was last updated and saved. Note that the date represents the system date. If the system date is incorrect, you receive an incorrect date.

- The *Bytes Used* field is the total number of bytes used by the fields as defined in the table.

- The *Bytes Left* field is the maximum record size for the table, minus the bytes used for the fields. dBASE records can be a maximum of 32,767 bytes.

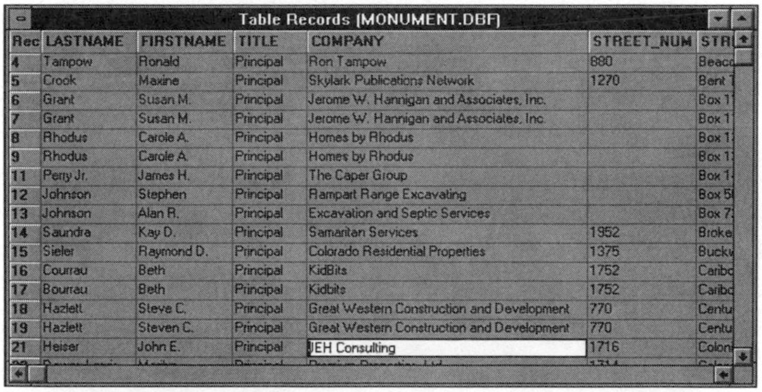

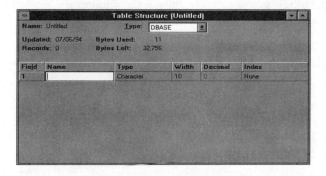

Fig. 2.1
The components of a table.

Fig. 2.2
The Table Designer.

Defining the Field Structure

The Table Designer's bottom portion lists the fields defined in the table. Each field appears in a separate row; you can use each name only once. A space is not an acceptable character to use in a fieldname; use underscores to represent spaces (for example: the field LAST NAME appears as LAST_NAME). You can, of course, use plain old LASTNAME as a fieldname.

Each field has the following properties:

- The *Field* is the field number and order in the table. They are consecutive, labeled as read-only, and automatic. In other words, you will always increment in whole numbers; 1, 2, 3, 4, etc. (Some database manufacturers allow you to add decimal increments, as in 1, 1.1, 1.2, 1.3, etc, but dBASE for Windows doesn't allow this luxury.) Similarly, if you elect to add a record between existing records 1 and 2, the added record becomes number 2, and the old record 2 increments to become record 3. You always add below, not above the record number.

  Data is always entered as read-only until the end of the record is reached. As you get to the end of each record, the lock is released from the current record and reapplied to the next record. *Automatic* means that when you reach the end of the current record, the computer automatically increments to the another record and waits for you to type the new information.

- The *Name* is the name of the field. Each name may be up to 10 characters. Alphanumerics are acceptable, but the first characters must be letters. Use short, descriptive, and meaningful naming conventions. Each field must be unique, and fields are not case-sensitive. For example, there is no difference between the fieldname Lastname and LASTNAME.

- *Type* is the field type. The field type you select from the list determines what kind of data the field contains. After the default, *Character* field, which contains only alpha charaters, the choices are Numeric, Memo, Logical, Date, Float, OLE, and Binary.

- The *Width* is the field size. You can change the field size for the character, numeric, and float fields. All others (for example, the DATE field) have a fixed width.

- The *Decimal* field is the number of digits allowed to the right of the decimal point. This field is valid only for float and numeric fields. You can set the decimal value to a number of two less than the width value you defined. However, the maximum width, including the decimal settings, the decimal point, and an optional minus sign, is 20 characters.

- The *Index* field determines whether the table is indexed by using the values in this field. You can decide whether you want the data to appear in *ascending* (A-Z) or *descending* (Z-A) order. Choosing *None* omits the field from indexing.

> **Note**
>
> As you go about creating your various table structures, you can't make many serious errors. The computer prompts you with a dialog box and a beep if you try to invoke something that is logically incorrect, or not available with a particular option. Finally, even if you force a change during the initial creation, you can't save it until the computer is satisfied with your design.

Figure 2.3 shows a dBASE table with six fields. Note that fieldname characters must be linked with underscores.

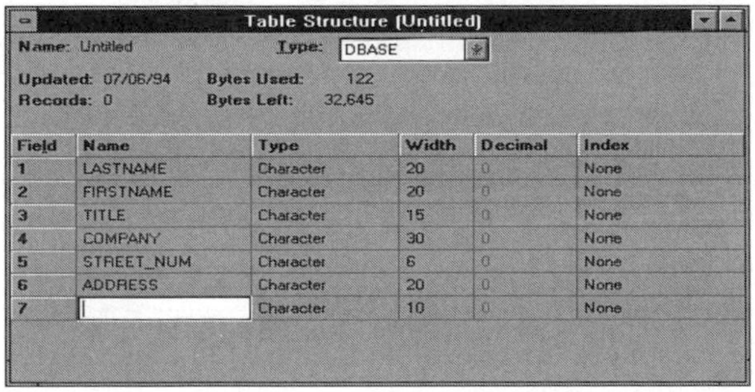
Table Structure (Untitled)
Name: Untitled
Type: DBASE
Updated: 07/06/94
Records: 0
Bytes Used: 122
Bytes Left: 32,645
Field
Name
Type
Width
Decimal
Index
1 LASTNAME Character 20 0 None
2 FIRSTNAME Character 20 0 None
3 TITLE Character 15 0 None
4 COMPANY Character 30 0 None
5 STREET_NUM Character 6 0 None
6 ADDRESS Character 20 0 None
7 Character 10 0 None

Fig. 2.3
Definable properties for each dBASE table.

Modifying Your Table

You use the Table Designer to add and delete fields from a table.

To add a new field to the end of a field list, choose **S**tructure, **A**dd Field; or right-click anywhere in the Table Structure window and choose **A**dd Field from the SpeedMenu. A new row appears as the last row in the table.

To insert a new field anywhere in the database structure, click the row above the point where the new field is to appear. Then choose **S**tructure and **I**nsert Field or right-click and choose **I**nsert Field from the SpeedMenu. The new row appears above the row you selected and becomes the current row.

To move a field—effectively changing its order in the table—point to the field number in the far left column. The pointer changes to a hand. Drag the row up or down to its new location.

To delete a field, click the row identified for deletion. Choose **S**tructure and **D**elete Selected Field; or right-click and choose **D**elete Selected Field from the SpeedMenu. The Table Designer deletes the field definition.

Figure 2.4 illustrates a field order change. Position the cursor in the Record Number field (Field), and watch as the cursor changes to a hand. Then drag the entire line to its new location.

Changing a Fieldname

Sometime in the future, someone is apt to arrive at your workspace and ask you to change a fieldname to something more appropriate. Maybe they didn't like the original name, or now they want to use a different name for that field. Perhaps the database has metamorphosed and some of the data is obsolete. Either way, you're obliged to change the offending fieldname to something more appropriate.

Caution

Before you attempt this task, make a backup copy of the database. During every interim step, you should be making additional backups of your data. This way, you always have something to fall back on if your anticipated results don't pan out. If you don't make backups, you're likely to lose precious data when the file converts from the old to the new edition.

When a table's structure changes unbeknownst to you, the Table Designer creates a duplicate copy of the old table. Then a new table is created with the revised design. When you save your changes, an attempt is made to copy all the data back into the new database from the old database. Upon conclusion, dBASE deletes the backup table.

When you have finished changing the tables structure, choose **F**ile, **S**ave, and **Cl**ose from the main menu. Once the command completes, open the restructured table by using the Table Records window. Verify that the correct changes were performed and that the data is in the condition you're expecting. If it isn't, revert to your backups.

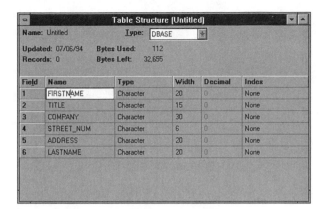

Fig. 2.4
Changing the
table's field order.

Changing the Appearance of the Table Designer

At some stage in the game, you may become dissatisfied with the existing database structure and the requisite fields. Perhaps some columns are too small, others too large. You can use the Table Designer to perform a variety of resizing, moving, and hiding columns and row grid lines.

To *resize* a column, point to the column border. When the pointer changes to a double-edged arrow, drag the border until the column resembles the size you want and then release the mouse button. Reducing the size tends to hide some of the information in that column. Resize the windows until you can see all the information.

To *move* a column, point to the column title. When the pointer changes to a hand, drag the column to its new location.

To *show* (or *hide*) the gridlines, choose **P**roperties, **T**able Structure Window; or right-click and choose Table **S**tructure Window Properties from the SpeedMenu. A Table Structure Properties dialog box appears. You may check or uncheck the Horizontal or Vertical Grid Lines.

Saving Changes

Your proposed changes are not amended to the database structure until you save the database. Whether you are saving for the first time, or you have made several modifications to the table over time, the saving option creates the table with a .DBF extension and generates any associated files, such as

.DBT (memo files) and .MDX (production indexes). You are not obliged to save your changes. An abandoned database reverts to its original format, allowing you to rethink your alterations before casting them in stone.

To save changes to a table design, perform one of the following options:

- To save a table with a new name, choose File, Save As.

- To update an existing table and keep the Table Designer open, choose File, Save; or press Ctrl+S.

- Choose File, Save and Close; or press Ctrl+W.

To save changes to a table design and close the Table Designer, perform the following:

- Choose File, Close; or press Ctrl+F4.

If you are saving for the first time or are choosing the function Save As, the Save Table dialog box appears.

In figure 2.5, a previously created table is being saved to a filename. The computer automatically saves the file with a .DBF extension. If you don't like the current directory, move to a different one before typing the table's name and saving it.

Fig. 2.5
Saving a created
table to disk.

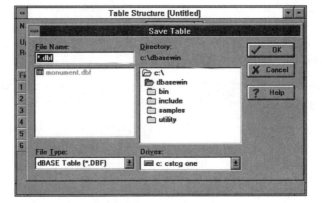

Type a valid, DOS-based filename. You do not have to type the .DBF extension. Remember that you are limited to eight alphanumeric characters. You can also choose a different drive and directory. Choose OK. dBASE creates the table and any associated files.

Note

When you save and close your changes to a database, the Table Designer uses the fieldname and field position inside that structure to determine how to transfer information to your new structure. *You must be absolutely sure that an identical, corresponding field has been created in the new table.* If this is lacking, none of the existing data from the old field is copied into the new field as the database is updated.

To get around this potential difficulty, you should always copy the database, or back it up before you begin. That way, if you run into trouble, and the results are not as expected, you have something to fall back on instead of having to find and rekey any lost data, which could be an impossible task.

Summary

This chapter began by defining what a database is, as well as why it is important to have an effective design on paper before you start to commit the work to dBASE for Windows. You also read about the important components required for the creation of a file.

The chapter talked about creating and saving a table structure; then I showed you how to change and delete the table's field orders. Finally, I illustrated the way to save a created table and any associated files to your hard disk.

Chapter 3

Entering, Editing, and Viewing Data

Data-entry activities require speed from the computer and accuracy from the user. All such data entry—editing, sorting, and their various manipulation activities—occurs within the Table Records window. After being entered, any data may be diced and sliced for viewing in any of three different field and record layouts. You can change the Table Records window properties so that fields and records display the information you want.

Many similarities—and some differences—exist between dBASE for Windows and earlier versions. For example, editing sessions allow you to edit the same table in multiple windows. This function is useful for cutting and pasting information between the two windows, where formerly you had to open and close different database tables in order to duplicate data. Now, you can use the cut/copy/paste feature to hold information temporarily.

You can import and export data from Paradox and SQL tables to the application of your choice.

Considering Data-Entry Issues

Although the topic of indexing is covered in Chapter 4, you should lend some thought to the use of indexing and how it might be applied to your data. An index both affects and supports features that your application provides: data entry, queries, and reports. Indexes affect the order in which records appear by letting users find and update information with a minimum of table searching. You can make data-entry tasks easier by using the following considerations:

What is the order that users might expect to see the data on-screen? Do they expect to see company information first, followed by a purchasing history? Indexes should reflect the expected order of information in a table.

When searching for records in a table, what type of information might users already be expected to know? Perhaps they already have an invoice number, and simply need to know who it belongs to. You should create an index that provides the most common ways of identifying demographic information.

Are calculations involved in the data contained in the table? Perhaps you might want to calculate your quarterly sales by region? A properly created index places similar records in consecutive order so that users can quickly search for the first record in the series and stop the processing after the last record in the search.

Managing Tables with Sessions

A session is the best way to manage tables and windows when performing multiple tasks. By default, *Sessions* is always *on*. This is to ensure that memory and other behavioral characteristics resemble Windows applications as closely as possible. You may disable or enable Sessions on the Files tab of the Desktop Properties dialog box by choosing **P**roperties, **D**esktop, and then clicking the Files tab.

> **Note**
>
> When Sessions is on, dBASE for Windows manages tables and windows like those in a normal Windows operating environment. When Sessions is disabled, dBASE handles table editing more like earlier versions of dBASE did. dBASE uses workareas to access multiple tables.

As you open each file with sessions enabled, each file can have a maximum of 255 workareas. The benefits can most easily be observed when using queries. Each query uses tables in workareas, beginning with one. Multiple queries can run simultaneously, even though each one uses workarea one, because each query runs its own session with its own set of workareas. Without sessions, a dBASE programmer has to go to great lengths to save and restore the operating environment when responding to events.

As previously discussed, Sessions is designed to assist those who want to handle multiple tasks (not multitasking) in the user interface. If you are

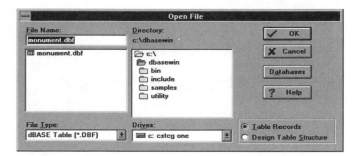

Fig. 3.3
The Open File
dialog box.

As discussed previously, you can open a table more than once. If sessions is on, each instance of the table is its own session. Moving to another record in one window does not move it in the other; the two sessions are independent of one another, although any changes made in the first are also reflected in the other.

Adding Records

Another word for *adding* is *appending*, and in dBASE for Windows, records are always added by attaching them to the end of an open table. A table must be open, although it can be empty before you may use it.

To append a record—or any number of records—into the table, choose **T**able, **A**dd Records. An empty record appears. You can then enter your data.

Figure 3.4 shows a new record suitable for data-entry activities. You can tab to each successive field, or position the cursor at the beginning of each field.

Rec	LASTNAME	FIRSTNAME	TITLE	COMPANY	STREET_NUM
208	Brown	Bill G.	Principal	Preconstruction Services	1155
209	Richards	Neil A.	Principal	Rampart Custom Cedar Homes	2565
210	Kannmacher	Larry J.	Principal	Lamacher	8234
211	Mabry	Esther J.	Principal	Esther J. Mabry	4465
212	Kittell	Richard	Principal	Business Technology	2613
213	Swain	Wilton G.	Principal	Forefront Computers	7620
214	Street	John W.	Principal	Rockey Mountain Long Distance	1155
215	Hubbard	Richard P.	Principal	Professional Resources Company	3415
216	Hicks	Rebecca R.	Principal	Two Designers	7410
217	Fosha, Jr.	Charles E.	Principal	Challenger / Desktop Training Systems, Inc.	7271
218	Christofferson	Elizabeth F.	Principal	Integrated Success Systems, Inc.	7633
219			Principal	Assault Defense Products, Inc.	1710
220			Principal	Chapel Hills Subway	8029
221					

Fig. 3.4
Adding records
to a table.

If you have added records to a table with an active index, you already know that each record appears at the end of the table. After you finish entering new data, dBASE for Windows updates the index and moves the record in the table to its correct location according to the index criteria. For editing purposes, the last record you add remains the current record.

Moving to a Different Record

Tip
If you are uncomfortable using the GOTO command in the Command window, select Table, and Go To Record Number. Alternatively, the key combination Ctrl+G provides the same dialog box. Either type the record number you wish to go to, or press the key in the record number box until it shows the physical number you want.

A complementing command for the various browse options described previously is the GOTO command. When you use GOTO from the Navigator or Command window and then link with a browse command, you can quickly snap to any record number in your table.

If you choose to work within the Navigator, choose **T**able, **G**o to Record Number. A dialog box appears. Either type the number of the record you want, or select the number by incrementing/decrementing the record pointer.

Alternatively, you may use the following command in the Command window: GOTO *n*, where *n* is the record number. GOTO BOTTOM positions the pointer at the end, or bottom of the table; likewise, GOTO TOP positions the pointer at the top of the table. Then, to browse records at that record number, enter **BROWSE** or **EDIT** in the Command window.

Deleting and Undeleting Records

You can delete records from a table when you are satisfied that you don't need that record, or a series of records, again.

You must perform two tasks to delete a record or a series of records. You first delete the record; then you must pack the resulting database. First, dBASE for Windows marks the offending record as deletable. Then, upon your command (PACK) the table is packed, the deleted records are indeed deleted, and the table is reorganized to reflect those deletions. Thus, until a table is packed, a deleted record may still be undeleted (or recalled from being deleted).

Note

All PACKing really does is make sure that the records that you marked for deletion are actually deleted. After the table is packed, you cannot recover those deleted records from the table. Unless you are very sure about what you are about to do, it is a good idea to make a copy of the table before proceeding.

Deleting a Record

To mark a record for deletion, select the record and then choose **T**able, **D**elete Selected Record. The record disappears from the screen. If you wish to see those records marked for deletion, choose **P**roperties, **T**able Records Window to display the Table Records Properties dialog box. Then click the Records page and check the Dele**t**e checkbox.

Figure 3.5 shows a record marked for deletion.

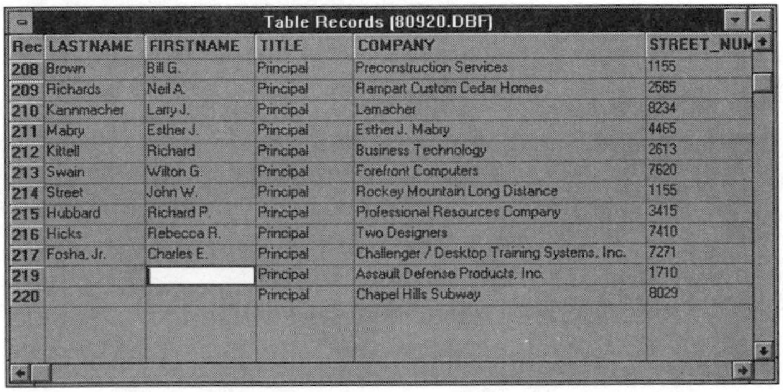

Rec	LASTNAME	FIRSTNAME	TITLE	COMPANY	STREET_NUM
208	Brown	Bill G.	Principal	Preconstruction Services	1155
209	Richards	Neil A.	Principal	Rampart Custom Cedar Homes	2565
210	Kannmacher	Larry J.	Principal	Lamacher	8234
211	Mabry	Esther J.	Principal	Esther J. Mabry	4465
212	Kittell	Richard	Principal	Business Technology	2613
213	Swain	Wilton G.	Principal	Forefront Computers	7620
214	Street	John W.	Principal	Rockey Mountain Long Distance	1155
215	Hubbard	Richard P.	Principal	Professional Resources Company	3415
216	Hicks	Rebecca R.	Principal	Two Designers	7410
217	Fosha, Jr.	Charles E.	Principal	Challenger / Desktop Training Systems, Inc.	7271
219			Principal	Assault Defense Products, Inc.	1710
220			Principal	Chapel Hills Subway	8029

Fig. 3.5
The table reflecting a record marked for deletion.

You also can use the Command window to delete and pack a table. For example, to delete record *n*, type **`DELETE RECORD`** ***n*** into the Command window. To delete a series of records, type **`DELETE NEXT`** ***n***. To recall those same records, issue the command `RECALL RECORD` *n*. The command `RECALL NEXT 40` recalls the next forty records from the pointer position. Issue the `PACK` command from the Command window to purge data, and then create a new one void of your deleted records.

Tip
To recall a record that has been marked for deletion (before packing the table), select the record, and then choose **T**able, **T**able Utilities, and **R**ecall.

Editing Data

After you enter your data into a table, you may need to change it. In the Table Records window, you can edit one field at a time. You must first select the field you want to modify from the record number, making it the *current field*. To do so, click the field that you want to change.

Table 3.1 lists the keyboard keys needed to move between fields.

Table 3.1	Keys for Moving Between Fields	
Go To	**All Layouts**	**Form and Column Layouts**
Next Field	Tab or Enter	Up-arrow key
Previous Field	Shift+Tab	Down-arrow key
First Field	Ctrl+Home	
Last Field	Ctrl+End	

The selected field is highlighted. To display the contents of memo, OLE, or binary fields, select the field and press the F9 key.

> **Note**
>
> Character fields accept any combination of alphanumeric, punctuation, spaces, and characters in a left-aligned mode.

Editing Number Fields

Because number fields are either numeric (usually fixed point) or float types, the field accepts other characters such as numbers, periods, commas, and the minus sign. Numbers are right-aligned (in contrast with alphanumerics, which are left-aligned). dBASE ignores any leading zeros you enter. Other characters that you force into a number field receive an error message.

Editing Date Fields

Date fields accept dates only in the format MM/DD/YY. After you declare a date field, the computer is interested only in the numbers: the field automatically enters the front slashes for you. If you type an invalid date, such as an incorrect leap year or a month with too many days in it, an error message appears.

Editing Logical Fields

A logical field is one that accepts only Boolean logic: the operands true (.T.) and false (.F.). True values may include the characters *Y*, y, *T*, and *t*. False values, as you may suspect, include *N*, *n*, *F*, and *f*. Other characters that you attempt to enter receive a beep.

Editing Memo Fields

Memo fields contain free-form text that you type into a text editor look-alike. This information is stored in the .DBT file. You may enter as much text as you want, subject only to the limitations of your hard disk.

You must first open the memo field (after declaring it as such from the Table Structure) before you enter data or view its contents. To open a memo field, perform one of the following options:

- Choose **V**iew, Fie**l**d Contents.

- Double-click the Memo icon.

- Move to the field and press F9.

Figure 3.6 shows the results of clicking an already defined MEMO field. The text editor appears, allowing you to type information into the field.

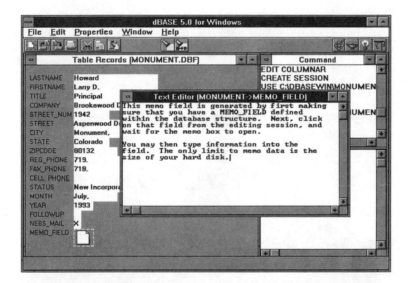

Fig. 3.6
A Memo field in
the text editor.

The Editor Properties dialog box controls memo editing. Options in this dialog box include Word Wrap, Auto Indent, Spacing, and Font. You can use these settings once the Memo Field is open. Click Properties, Text Editor and make the changes from the defaults.

Editing Binary Fields

Binary fields accept stored data from a standard Windows binary data format—including image files (.BMP or .PCX) or sound files (.WAV). The subsequent information that you select is stored in dBASE tables with a .DBT extension. These fields are represented as icons from the Table Records window. When you can see the picture, the field contains data.

So, first you declare the field as a binary field. Then you tell Windows/dBASE for Windows what file you want to see. Then, when you want to access it in the software, you click it, and the picture expands to reveal the file.

Adding Image Files. If you want to add an image file to a binary field, double-click the binary field you want to update. An image viewer box appears. Select Image Viewer, and then choose OK.

> **Note**
>
> Windows provides you with the option of scanning your own drawings and saving them as .BMP files. The Windows utility Paintbrush allows you to draw your own material and save it as either a .BMP, or .PCX file format. Once saved and available on your hard disk, you may insert these files into the Image Viewer.

After the Image Viewer is open, use **F**ile, **O**pen. Then select either a .BMP or .PCX file. Then close the Image Viewer and watch as dBASE for Windows saves the image in the table's .DBT file. You can then display the image by double-clicking the field or by selecting it and pressing the F9 key. Figure 3.7 shows a .BMP file extracted from a binary field.

Fig. 3.7
An image extracted from a .BMP file.

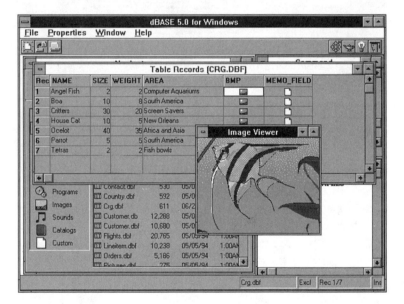

Adding Sound Files. You also can add sound files (.WAV) in a similar manner. Double-click the binary field you want to update. A Binary Type dialog box appears. Select Sound, and then choose OK. An Open File dialog box appears. Select the .WAV file you want. Then close the Image Viewer and watch as dBASE for Windows saves the sound file in the table's .DBT file.

You may then play the sound file by double-clicking the field. A dialog box appears. Choose the Play option. The sound is played once each time you click the mouse. Pressing Stop terminates it and closes the dialog box.

> **Note**
>
> Windows provides you with the option of creating your own .WAV files, as long as you have the correct soundboard and recording microphone. Although such files occupy large amounts of space, once you have recorded and saved them as .WAV files on your hard disk, you may insert these files into the Image Viewer dialog box.

Editing Object Linking and Embedding (OLE) Fields

You can use Object Linking and Embedding (OLE) data in dBASE only if the other Windows applications support OLE. OLE data include graphics, spreadsheets, and other documents. You should be aware that not all applications support OLE. If you encounter difficulties, check with the other program's documentation to determine whether it supports OLE data.

An application that does support OLE allows you to insert objects created with other applications into your table. After the link has been established, you can launch a session in the external application by double-clicking the document from dBASE for Windows.

Adding an OLE Object in an OLE Field. You can link two objects by following these steps:

1. Start the application that contains the file you want to link. Then open the object to be linked.

2. Cut the piece that you want to link and move it to the Clipboard using **E**dit, **C**opy.

3. Minimize the application and open dBASE for Windows.

4. Open the table and double-click the OLE field where the data will reside.

5. To hardwire the link, select **E**dit, Paste Link.

Embedding the OLE Object Directly into dBASE for Windows. Alternatively, you can embed the object directly in the dBASE table. Follow these steps:

1. Select the OLE field in the table. Double-click it to open the OLE viewer.

2. Choose Edit, Insert Object. Then specify the object type in the Insert New Object dialog box.

3. When the OLE server application begins, create the object you want to embed. Then choose File, Update to insert that object in the OLE field.

4. Close the server application and exit the OLE Viewer window by choosing File, Close.

Blanking a Record

Blanking out a record clears all the data from that record. Every field, including the keyfields, is empty, but the empty record is not lost. In fact, dBASE retains it as a record populated with spaces. If you want to blank a record, choose **T**able, **B**lank Selected Record. From this point, enter the new information.

If you want to undo blanking at a later time, perhaps after you have finished all the editing of a particular record, and conclude that you do not want to make the change, you must abandon the change while the table is still open. You must make two choices here: you must abandon all changes to the specific record before you move to the next record or dBASE will not peform the updating function. Secondly, if you close the table without saving anything, dBASE abandons all your choices.

Viewing Data to Be Modified

The Table Records window is primarily used to modify data held in an existing, single table. This window displays data in three styles. You may switch among them by pressing the F2 key once the table is open:

- The *Browse* layout displays multiple records in a table. Your records appear as rows, whereas fields appear as columns.

- The *Form* layout displays a single record in a table; the fields are arranged horizontally in the Table Records window with the fieldname located above each field.

- The *Columnar* layout displays single records, arranging the fields vertically with the fieldname in the extreme left column and the data to its right. The layout you use depends on your task.

Viewing Data in Browse Layout

Using the Browse layout allows you to view multiple columns and rows to see more records than you can by using the Edit command, where only one record is displayed on-screen at any one time.

After you open a table or switch from the Table Design to Table Run mode, the table appears by default in a Browse layout. You may want to switch between the various layouts and can do so from the **V**iew menu. Otherwise, select **P**roperties, **D**esktop to open the Desktop Properties dialog box. Select the Files page, and then select the Edit Records mode you want.

An original Browse layout is shown in figure 3.8.

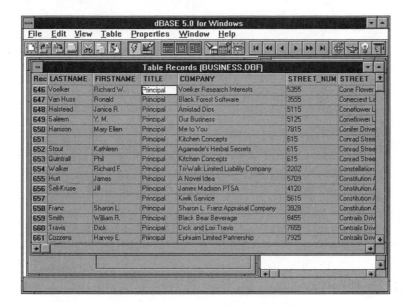

Fig. 3.8
The original Browse Layout.

Viewing Data in Form Layout

In a Form layout configuration, the data appears as a single record in a table. The fields are aligned horizontally from left to right, with the record data possibly stretching out beyond the right edge of the window. To switch to and from this layout, choose **V**iew, **F**orm Layout.

In figure 3.9, the Form layout appears.

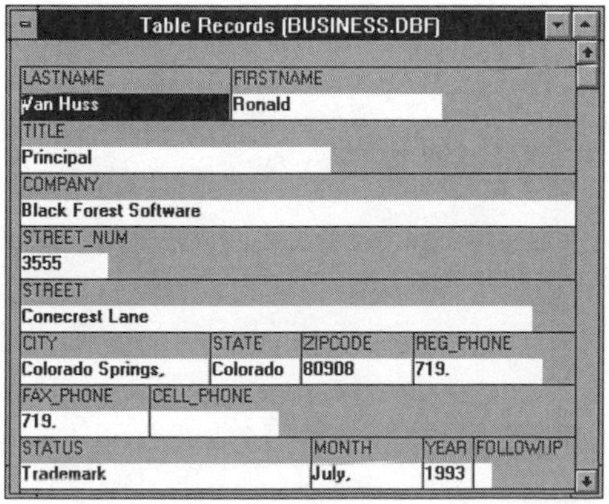

Fig. 3.9
The Form layout version of a window.

Viewing Data in Columnar Layout

A Columnar layout, as the name implies, displays the fieldnames at the extreme left column, with all the data fields to the right. In this mode, you can view only one record at a time. To switch to and from this layout, choose **V**iew, **C**olumnar Layout. Figure 3.10 shows the same data as figure 3.9, but the records are in a Columnar layout.

Fig. 3.10

The Columnar layout version of a window.

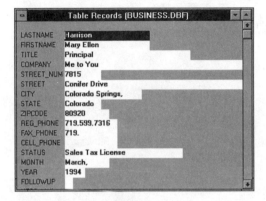

Customizing the View of Your Data with Table Record Properties

Finally, you can utilize a selection process that allows you to see specific fields in your table, while suppressing others. The Table Records Window Properties is available by either selecting Properties, Table Records Window, or by right-clicking the mouse button from inside an open table. The following options are available:

- The *Fields Tab* allows you to display or hide fields from your view.

- The *Records Tab* contains information that allows you to determine settings for editing operations, as well as the allowable range values for indexing purposes.

- The *Windows Tab* contains window title, grids, and field-width setting options. These are all fully customizable.

To display the Table Records Properties dialog box from the Table Records window, choose **P**roperties, **T**able Records Window.

The dialog box that appears provides three additional choices:

- A *Fields* page that displays the fields displayed in the Table Records window. You may elect to show or hide these fields as you work.

- The second selection, *Records,* changes the way records appear in the Table Records window. You can determine different settings and range values for indexing keys, and perform other customizable data-entry tasks.

- The *Window* page includes display options like the window title, width, and the capability to lock columns or freeze fields.

You can make these selections by clicking each tabulation setting from the Properties, Table Records Window.

Figure 3.11 shows how the Table Records Properties dialog box uses data settings for maximum user effectiveness.

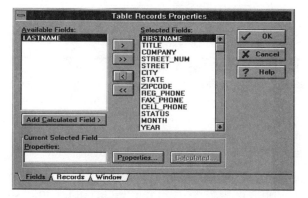

Fig. 3.11
The Table Records Properties dialog box.

Importing and Exporting Your Data

dBASE for Windows provides a relatively easy way for you to import data from other applications and to export data to other software offerings. dBASE for Windows also allows you to import spreadsheet data from such popular programs as Quattro Pro or Lotus 1-2-3.

When data is imported, the information is normally appended into an open table from another table, or from a different type of file. Table 3.2 provides ways that you can exchange imported data using different formats.

Table 3.2	Data Formats	
File Type	**Description**	**Default Extension**
dBASE	dBASE table	.DBF
Paradox	A Paradox table in which each row is a record and each column is a field.	.DB
DBMEMO3	Table and .DBT files in dBASE III PLUS. This file should be used only when exporting to dBASE III PLUS tables.	.DBF/.DBT
Delimited Text	Character fields are delimited with quotation marks or other characters; fields are separated by commas, or other characters; logical fields contain either a T or F character. Records are terminated by a CRLF code.	
System Data Format (SDF)	Fixed-length records are terminated by a CRLF code.	.TXT
Quattro Pro	Spreadsheet data (import only)	.WB1
Lotus 1-2-3	Spreadsheet data (import only)	.Wkn

When data is proposed for exporting purposes, it must be copied from one table to another or created as a different file format. Although *export* is primarily used to exchange data with other applications or to create a copy of a table with only a subset of information, the exporting opportunities for applications elsewhere are bounded only by your imagination.

Creating an export file automatically creates a destination file into which source information is poured. Keep in mind some of the following caveats when attempting to create an exported file for use in another application:

- If one or more dBASE memo fields is exported, a .DBT file is created with the same name as the destination file. The memo text is then copied to it.

- Records marked for deletion are copied unless you exclude them from processing with a FOR or WHILE condition, or unless you check the Deleted option on the Table tab in the Desktop Properties dialog box.

- If you intend to export to a Paradox table, each record in the source file becomes a row in the Paradox table; each field then becomes a column.

- When exporting to file formats other than dBASE, dBMEMO3, or Paradox, make sure that the file being created is in a format importable by the other software. Check field widths, field types, and acceptable values. If you are unsure, check the other software program's user manual.

Exporting Records

To export records to another format, select the source table. Then choose **T**able, **T**able Utilities, and **E**xport Records. The Export Records dialog box appears, as shown in figure 3.12.

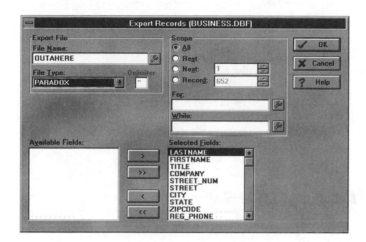

Fig. 3.12
The Export Records dialog box.

Choose OK to export the data you've selected.

Importing Data

Unfortunately, importing data is still limited to spreadsheet information from Quattro Pro and/or Lotus 1-2-3 spreadsheets.

Choose **F**ile, **I**mport to display the Import dialog box (see fig. 3.13). Then type the filename at the prompt. If the file is not in the default directory, type a complete path and filename, as in **C:\LOTUS123\ONLINE.WKn**.

Tip
An alternative method of importing is to save your Quattro Pro or Lotus 1-2-3 files as text, without the formatting information.

Fig. 3.13
The Import dialog box.

Checking the **H**eadings checkbox allows you to use the first row of the spreadsheet as a fieldname in the new .DBF file.

Undoing Changes

At some stage along the way, you may come to the conclusion that you're editing the wrong table, or that the changes you made are counterproductive. For whatever reason, you want to abandon the changes and start in a different file area.

You can undo your changes to the record as long as you haven't moved to another record in the table, or made another selection.

To abandon your changes, perform one of the following actions:

■ Choose File, Abandon Record. You abandon the changes but remain in the Table Records window.

■ Choose File, Abandon Record and Close.

■ Choose the Table Records window by clicking the Control menu dialog box. A message dialog box asks whether you want to save your changes. Choose No.

Saving Changes

Your changes are saved automatically whenever you perform any of the following activities:

■ You move the record pointer to another record.

■ You use a different layout in the Table Records window.

You can save a record by hand with any of these options:

■ Choose File, Save Record. You save the record and remain in the Table Records window.

■ Choose File, Save Record and Close. You save the record and close the table.

Closing a Table

Make sure that you always close a table correctly by following established procedures. Closing your table correctly ensures that your changes and modifications are saved and that active system resources can be used by other functions. An orderly shutdown scenario prevents (or at least mitigates) corruption of your hard-won data.

If you want to close a single table, choose one of the Close options from the File menu or close dBASE for Windows.

Summary

This chapter continued to build on the information presented in the previous section. In particular, this chapter showed you how to populate a table with data by adding records, and how to edit that data after you have keyed it into the table. You also learned how to add data into the various field types (alphanumeric, numeric, date, memo, and logical) and how to append image, sound, and binary files. You also read about the capability to link OLE files and learned the methods of exporting and importing data files from other applications into dBASE for Windows.

Chapter 4

Indexing and Sorting Data

Indexing and sorting information are only two of the many ways that you can organize your data for greater flexibility and disposition in an application. dBASE for Windows includes two additional approaches for establishing data order in tables.

Indexing your records in either *ascending (A-Z)* or *descending (Z-A)* order linked to a single, user-defined field allows you to see your data faster, and without as many read/write hits to the hard disk. Although a table may have more than one index, only one (the *master index*) is active at a time—and the records always appear in the order the active index calls for.

The natural order of records in a table is determined by one of two methods:

- Natural order—Where the physical sequence of records in a table is the order in which they were originally entered.

- Logical (or indexed) order—Where a logical sequence, rather than an ordered sequence, determines the order. The records are displayed numerically or alphabetically in either an ascending or descending order. The index tracks the record's location in the logical ordering, as well as its natural order. The logical order is independent of the natural order.

In dBASE for Windows, multiple index files are acceptable. This means that you can design and maintain multiple indexes using the Manage Indexes dialog box. Alternatively, individual index files permit a user to contain a single index. dBASE can use indexes created by Paradox and SQL tables.

Tip

Most of your applications use data in ascending order. Occasionally you will want to see information in a descending order; perhaps you're a sales manager interested in seeing who isn't making quota each month. Going from a low to a high dollar figure in a list might more easily identify those falling behind.

Indexing Versus Sorting

Tip
You should keep all of your index files in one place. If they are kept in a subdirectory within dBASE, the program will always be able to find them. When you finish with a table and want to archive it to removable media, make sure that you archive the indexes as well as the tables. Then you don't have to spend extra time rebuilding them when it comes time to employ the original table.

Creating an index to organize your data increases your ability to retrieve information without creating new databases each time you want to see the information in a different format. An index makes it faster to find the data you need, processes only required records, and lends higher degrees of organization to that information. You are not obligated to build indices to view the data, but the alternative is to build identical databases, each sorted a little differently than its predecessor.

Some key differences between *sorting* and *indexing* are

Creating Tables: The indexing process creates a file with a series of records in a logical record order. Sorting a table creates a separate table, but it is filled with data from the original table in your sorted order.

Arranging Records: Indexing and sorting both arrange records in a specified order. However, indexing changes only the logical order, leaving the natural order intact. Sorting changes the natural order of the records, as reflected in the new sorted table.

Processing Operations: You can do some operations, such as searching for data or running queries, faster by using an index. Other operations, such as linking, require indexing.

Using Functions: Indexes allow you to order records according to keys derived from using dBASE functions and operators on keyfields. When sorting, only fields are used and they must be in ascending or descending order.

Adding Records: Records added to a table are updated in an index automatically (upon saving). If you add records to an unindexed table, you must sort the data again to reflect those changes.

Mixing Field Types: You must convert keyfield values to a common field type with indexing. Sorted records may be ordering on fields with different field types.

Mixing Order: Indexes are either in ascending or descending order. With a sorting order, you can mix and sort fields in either ascending or descending order.

Figures 4.1 and 4.2, respectively, show identical data in their windows. Figure 4.1 is a natural order table, where information appears in the order in which it was entered. Figure 4.2 shows an index that has placed the information into ascending order.

Fig. 4.1
A natural order
table.

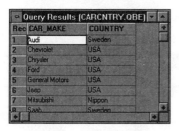

Fig. 4.2
An indexed table.

When you first open your table from the Navigator window, it is always in the natural order. You have to activate an index to tie the records together. To activate an index in the Table Records window, select it from the **T**able, **T**able Utilities, and then **M**anage Indexes dialog box.

Creating a Simple Index

A simple index is the most basic index because it contains a single field. When you create an index, an .MDX file holds the information. Such a file may hold up to 47 separate indices. An index does *not* change any data in your table: it merely orders it according to your instructions. Deleting an index merely removes the order: it does *not* delete the table. An index and a table always remain two separate entities.

To create a simple index, follow these steps:

1. In the Table Designer, choose an index order—either ascending or descending order.

2. If a fieldname doesn't already possess a declared index, choose **N**avigator, Design **T**able Structure to open that table. Then change the index field to ascend or descend.

3. Choose **T**able, **T**able Utilities, **M**anage Indexes. When the Manage Indexes dialog box opens, click **C**reate to create a simple index.

You can use any combination of alphanumeric characters for a total of 10 characters, but the first character must *always* be a letter.

4. Add the keyfield that you want to have indexed.

5. Determine whether the field will be sorted in an ascending or descending order: the default is ascending.

6. Click OK to return to the Manage Indexes dialog box. Then click the new index name to select it as the master index by clicking OK. dBASE saves any changes you make to an index. The index you select first becomes the master index.

Figure 4.3 displays the dialog box that manages all your created images. In this example, the indexes are named COUNTRY and STUFFER, and key respectively on the fieldnames COUNTRY and CAR_MAKE.

Fig. 4.3

The Manage Indexes dialog box.

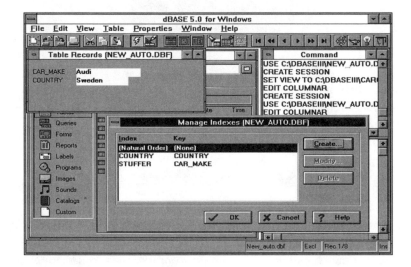

In most instances, creating an index will take some time. If the table is large or if the key expressions are long and complex, you may have to wait until dBASE is done before you can continue.

> **Note**
>
> Just because your monitor shows little activity doesn't mean that the program has died. Be patient; creating indexes sometimes take some time as information is copied into and out of temporary files.

Figure 4.4 shows an index allied with AUTOS.DBF called NEW_AUTO.NDX that indexes on the field CAR_MAKE.

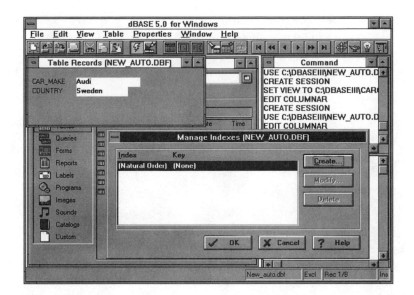

Fig. 4.4
Creating a simple index in the Table Designer.

Now that you created one index, you can create several more, name them, and store them in one location. The next section covers creating a master index.

Creating a Master Index

When you open a table with the Navigator, the table always appears in its natural order. You must select the appropriate index if you want the table records ordered in some specific manner.

You can have many indexes populating your directories; however, you can have only one index active at a time. The active index is called the *master index*. The master index always determines the order of records in the table.

When you want to change the master index, choose **T**able, **T**able Utilities, **M**anage Indexes. In the dialog box, double-click the index you wish to use; or you can click it once and then choose OK.

Indexing on a Record Subset

In normal circumstances, an index includes all the records in a table. From time to time, you may want only a portion of the available records to be indexed. Indexing a subset of your records makes it easier to process information in that table.

To create an index that includes only certain records, you have to state which records you want to include in a valid dBASE expression. For example, in the AUTOS.DBF table, a conditional statement such as COUNTRY="USA" displays only those automobiles built in America. Chapter 8 provides additional information on conditional statements.

Creating an Index

Type the following code in the Command window to create an on-the-fly index:

```
USE AUTOS EXCLUSIVE

INDEX ON COUNTRY TAG CARS FOR COUNTRY="USA"

BROWSE
```

First, you open the AUTOS table in an exclusive mode. You then index on the COUNTRY fieldname with an index called CARS. You are interested only in those records that have cars made in the United States. Once the index is created, the BROWSE command shows you which records conform to your criteria.

As this index is being created, a copy of it is placed into the index listing. After you finish the index in the Command window, you may see the list of available indexes by accessing **T**able, **T**able Utilities, and **M**anage Indexes. The result shows you the list of indexes. In this example, the index name is CARS and the key fieldname is COUNTRY.

Reindexing an Index

Sometimes an index becomes damaged, perhaps as a result of power failure or an .MDX file corruption. Although a prudent user always has an electronic backup within easy reach, many users simply do not bother to perform timely backups of their data. In a worst-case scenario, you may have to delete a corrupted index completely and recreate the index from scratch.

To reindex an index, open the table and choose **T**able, **T**able Utilities, Reinde**x**. dBASE rebuilds the index.

Creating a Complex Index

A complex index is so-named because it uses a combination of one or more keyfields in concert with dBASE commands. A complex index is used when a single field does not adequately identify each record, or when the flexibility of an expression that defines the index condition is required.

The complexity of the key expression varies according to the way the index is used. Consider the following rules when defining complex indexes:

- The complex key must be a valid dBASE expression.

- The expression must evaluate to a character, date, numeric, or float value.

- Usually, but not always, the index contains at least one fieldname.

- When multiple character fields are being indexed, concatenate fields using a plus sign, as in *firstname+lastname*. Different fields can be concatenated by converting them to a single type.

Indexing on Logical Fields

Logical fields are an either/or proposition. They are either Yes or No (Y/N), or True or False (T/F) entities entered into the LOGICAL field during data entry activities.

You can use logical fields with other types of data in indexing activities. However, before using them, you must convert them from their logical genesis into character data.

Although no direct conversion is provided within dBASE, a function known as an *immediate if* (IIF()) is available to make your life a little simpler. The IIF() function works because a logical expression is still a condition and may be massaged.

In the following example, you open a table called AIRLINE. This table contains a logical fieldname named CALLED. In the example, the airline wants to call all their passengers who normally fly in business class and offer them the option to upgrade their tickets to first class for a small fee. The table identifies the passengers that qualify (BIZCLASS), and marketing gets the list of people to call (FIRSTCLASS). You can look at the FIRSTCLASS index to determine those passengers that were not called.

```
Use AIRLINE
INDEX ON IIF(CALLED, "Y", "N" ) TAG BIZCLASS
INDEX ON TITLE+" "+FIRSTNAME+" "+LASTNAME+IIF(CALLED, "Y",
"N") TAG FIRSTCLASS
```

To create a complex index, select **C**reate in the Manage Indexes dialog box.

Figure 4.5 shows how to create a complex index by using a key expression (COUNTRY+CAR_MAKE). You can click the Tool button if you want assistance from the Expression Builder.

> **Note**
>
> The Expression Builder helps you to assemble a dBASE expression and then insert that expression into a currently open window or dialog box. An *expression* is a series of characters that tells dBASE to perform some function. It might open a table and perform a specialized sort or index. Perhaps you want to award all your employees with a 25 percent raise, using a mathematical expression such as BASEPAY*0.25. You may want to award only those employees who have outperformed their competition (BASEPAY*0.25 for BONUSPAY .GT. 25000, and so on). A key expression can employ multiple fieldnames, dBASE functions, and operators.

Fig. 4.5
Creating a
complex index.

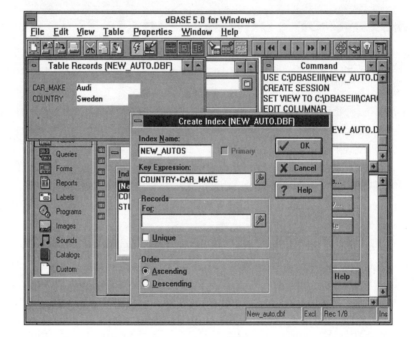

You can save a newly created index or one that has been modified by clicking OK in the Manage Indexes dialog box.

Sorting Your Data

You already know that sorting a table copies its contents to a separate table. The *source table* is the table containing the data you want to copy, whereas the *target table* is the table containing the copied data. Sorting starts with the first character in the key expression and proceeds to the right in its execution path: punctuation comes before numbers, numbers before letters, and upper-case letters before lowercase letters.

> **Note**
>
> Use sorting when you want to export data to another application, or when you want to create a separate table for reporting purposes. Use indexing when you need data-entry, querying, and reporting tasks to be faster and more efficient in the data that the table displays.

To sort data into a new table, follow these steps:

1. Open the table you want to sort. Then choose **T**able, **T**able Utilities, **S**ort Records.

   The Sort Records dialog box appears, as shown in figure 4.6. The available fields are arrayed in the first column; the listboxes allow you to select the order in which the fields appear.

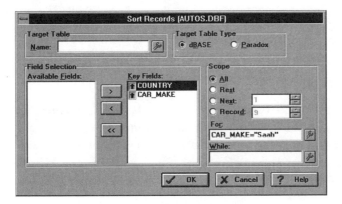

Fig. 4.6
The Sort Records dialog box.

2. Select the fields on which you want to sort your records and click the greater than (>) button to move them into the Key Fields list. The order they appear in the Key Fields list determines the order of the sort.

3. Select the sort order you want for each keyfield by clicking the arrow button or pressing Alt+down arrow. Then select the order from the menu.

4. The Scope option allows you to select the record you want to include in the target table. Note that the default is set to **A**ll, which means that every record, including the current record forward, is used. Re**s**t means that all records from and including the current record to the end of the file, are used. Ne**x**t really means next number. Any number of records,

from and including the current record to the end of the file, are used. Record means a single record selected by its record number.

The FOR and WHILE conditions specify similar activities. By using FOR, the computer sorts on information while a condition is true, sending those records to the top of the new table. For example, SORT TO CARS WHERE COUNTRY="USA" creates a new table called CARS containing all the records where COUNTRY equalled USA.

The WHILE command works in a parallel with For. It specifies a condition, and causes processing of the data to continue for as long as the condition is true. When it becomes false, the processing stops. Therefore, the command COUNTRY <> "USA" continues to work while COUNTRY doesn't equal USA. When it does, processing in this example stops.

5. Name the new table by using the Target Table dialog box.

6. When you finish, click OK. dBASE creates a new table containing all the records you selected in the correct order.

If the file already exists, you are prompted to overwrite it. The program copies the records you selected to the target table, sorting them as specified, beginning with the keyfield.

Summary

In this chapter, you learned the differences between indexing and sorting data. You also learned how to sort data in different ways. This chapter also showed you how to create a variety of different indexes, from simple to more complex ones.

Chapter 5

Creating Queries

A *query* is just what its name implies: a question to the data in order to gain an answer. By selecting data in one or more tables, you can obtain answers to questions not immediately apparent from simply looking at the table.

You can use queries also to link tables, thus establishing a *relationship* between them. For example, all client demographic data (name, address, and so on) is contained in one table, and clients' merchandise-ordering habits are contained in another. Neither table alone provides you with the information you need about that client, but a properly constructed query allows you access to both tables—providing you the information you need.

When you create a query, you access the resulting data through a *view,* or window, that displays that data. Although this view may look like a table itself, the displayed data can come from more than one table. You can select and perform calculations on the data in a view, just as you can in any editing window. dBASE stores these editing changes directly in the table or tables used to create the information.

As your queries are saved, the commands are stored in a QBE file. This QBE file contains statements that determine how to sort and select the data stored in one or more tables. The QBE file does not contain data: the data still comes from the DBF database tables.

Indexing in Queries

Although this topic was covered in Chapter 4, it is important to consider how indexing might be applied to your queries. An index both affects and supports features that your application provides: queries, data entry, and reports. Indexes affect the order in which records appear by letting users find and update information with a minimum of table searching.

Query tasks can be easier if you consider the following questions:

- What types of questions are users going to ask of their data? Will they want to know the number of inventoried items of a particular product? Perhaps an index should be created that queries either a product name or some identifying number.

- What type of information might a user reasonably be expected to know before attempting to query the table? Would the user know the product's name or identification number? You could create an index for commonly known information that assists in searching quickly for the right table data.

- An index intended solely for occasional, or on-the-fly queries might better be created at query time instead of having to maintain the index on an on-going basis. After the query is complete, you can delete the index.

Creating a Query

To create a query, first open a table; otherwise you receive an "Open Table Required" warning message. Change the current directory to the one containing the tables that you want to use. Then perform one of the following actions:

- Click the Queries icon in either the Catalog or Navigator window. Double-click the Untitled icon in the Queries panel; or right-click the Untitled icon and choose **N**ew Query from the SpeedMenu.

- Choose **F**ile, **N**ew, **Q**uery.

- In the Command window, type **CREATE QUERY**. Or type **CREATE SESSION** and then **CREATE QUERY** to use the sessions feature. The Open Table dialog box appears. You then select the table you want to query. After a table is selected, the Query Designer window opens.

Figure 5.1 shows a query screen with the 80920.DBF table in use.

Fig. 5.1
Creating a query.

If you are already browsing a table that you want to use in the query, click the Design Query button on the SpeedBar; or choose **T**able, Create **Q**uery.

The Query Designer opens in a new window and your Browse window remains in the background.

Figure 5.1 shows an [Untitled] query design, called a *skeleton*. The cursor sits in the first field (LASTNAME) of that table. In this example, an arrow pointing to the LASTNAME field indicates a query on that field name. You can move to either the left or right by clicking the arrows next to the table name.

The Query Designer presents only a skeleton of the table structure. The table's name is displayed at the left with the name of each field. If you add more tables to the query, their skeletons appear in the Query Designer window.

If the skeleton is too long to fit in the window, click the scroll arrows to see more fields. You can see more of the skeleton by dragging the right and left edges of the window.

Opening an Existing Query

A checkbox appears beneath each field name in the table skeleton. Here, you can specify the fields you want to include in the view. Simply click the appropriate field to include it; deselect the checkbox to exclude it.

You can select all the fields by clicking the Select All checkbox beneath the table name. You can then deselect individual fields by clicking their boxes again. To deselect all the fields, click the Select All box again.

In figure 5.2, the COMPANY, TITLE, and LASTNAME fields are checked. The cursor is positioned in the TITLE field, awaiting more data entry.

Fig. 5.2
Defining a
table's view.

If you foget to complete any fields, dBASE displays all of the fields when you run the query. You may go back and complete any that you forgot.

When the data is viewed, the fields appear in the order shown in the query skeleton. You can change the order by dragging fields to their correct positions. The mouse pointer changes to a hand when it is over the field names, indicating that you can drag them to another location. When the query runs, you can drag the fields the same way they are ordered in the view.

> **Note**
>
> Regardless of the order in which the field names appear, the screen pointer always lists the order that the fields appear in the query structure.

Selecting Record Order

When you initially open a table or display it in a view, the records always appear in their natural order. On occasion you may want to change the order of records in a view. Order boxes in the query skeleton are the quickest way to specify record order. Sometimes the order boxes create a Read-Only view of the data.

To specify the record order, point to the order box and hold down the left mouse button. Then drag the selection up or down, releasing the button when you are satisfied with the order.

In figure 5.3, the records are organized in the order defined in the Query box. There are five ordering options for character fields: no order, or *none*, which is the default; *ascending; descending; ascending and ignore case*; and *descending and ignore case*. You can see this ordering and set it according to your wishes by selecting the small-arrowed box to the left of each field name title in the Query Designer box. In figure 5.2, these may be the COMPANY, TITLE, LASTNAME, or STREET_NUM boxes. All other field types have either ascending or descending capabilities.

Fig. 5.3
Table results from the previous query.

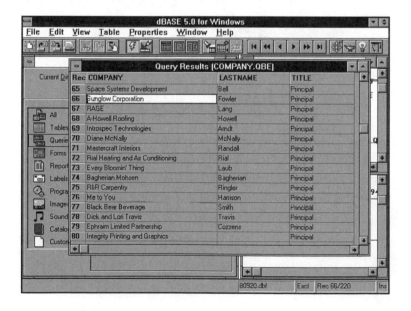

The order box in figure 5.4 illustrates that sometimes you may want to order records based on more than one field. Perhaps you want the information to be ordered by LASTNAME, alphabetically by STREET, and within each CITY. You can accomplish this ordering by checking the order boxes in two or more fields. The record order is determined by the left-to-right order of the fields in the query skeleton.

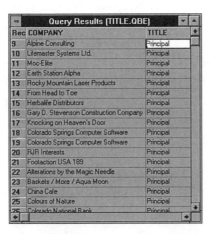

Fig. 5.4
Ordering records on more than one field.

> **Note**
>
> You must either specify an index or add a new index to arrange records in a query.

Filtering Data with Conditional Statements

You can enter query conditions so that only those records that meet your conditions are selected. This process, by definition, selects some records and eliminates, or suppresses, others. The field name in the table must be a logical field before you are allowed to exercise a Boolean operation on it.

Type the condition in the space beneath the field name in the file skeleton. To enter a condition, click once in the space below the field name or use the Tab or Shift+Tab to move to the field you want. Then type the condition.

When you press Enter, the condition is checked for a valid structure and syntax. If dBASE finds an error, it highlights the condition and gives you an error message on the status bar. As you type the condition, check the fields

Tip
A *Boolean operation* is a condition that can be only one of two possible choices. For example, a choice may be either ON or OFF. It cannot be both.

you want to use and click the Run button to execute the query. dBASE uses those conditions to examine the table, displaying only the records meeting the criteria.

The example shown in figure 5.5 shows a query of all those automobiles that have a left-sided drive system. That would seem to include the big four manufacturers of the United States (which are marked *.T.* for *true*), at the expense of those in Japan, and Sweden, who have right-sided drive vehicles. The results of this query appear in figure 5.6.

Fig. 5.5
A query to find all automobiles that have a left-sided drive steering system.

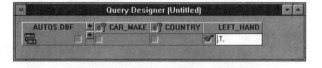

Fig. 5.6
The results of a .T. condition match.

Data may also be filtered with relational operators. Table 5.1 lists the relational operators. The default is = (equal). The syntax for a filter is *<relational operator><expression>*. Examples of relational operators are shown in Table 5.2.

Table 5.1 Relational Operators	
Operator	**Description**
>	Greater Than
<	Less Than
=	Equal
< > or #	Not Equal to
>= or =>	Greater than, or equal to
<= or =<	Less than, or equal to
$	Contains
Like	Pattern Match

Table 5.2 provides some relational operator examples that you can use in a command line.

Table 5.2 Examples that Use Relational Operators	
Expression	**Purpose**
>=[06/02/94]	Matches the dates on or after June 2, 1994.
>="S"	In a character field, this command finds all records that begin with "S". The characters between the quotation marks are case-sensitive.
$"Supplies"	Matches all records that include "Supplies" somewhere in the field.
<>"CO"	Matches records that do not equal "CO".
Like "Associates"	Matches records that include text-ending with "Associates".

The syntax for using the dollar sign ($) in a field filter condition is different from that for an expression. For a *field filter* condition, the dollar sign means "contains", and the syntax is $"Supplies". In an *expression*, the syntax is reversed, and the dollar sign means "is contained in...", such as "Supplies"$<*fieldname*>.

Some additional requirements apply to query conditions that have certain field types:

- *Character text* must be couched between double or single quotation marks. To find all cars made in the USA, you enter "USA" or 'USA' in the COUNTRY field. To find all COMPANY entries after MasterCraft Interiors through the end of the file, type the condition >"MasterCraft Interiors" in the COMPANY field. If you want to find only empty fields, type two apostrophes without any information between them (' '). To locate only those records that are not empty, use the <>"" syntax.

- *Numeric information* must be entered exactly as it is stored. This includes the appropriate decimal point and the negative sign. To find all numbers greater than 3.165 within a numeric field, type the condition **>3.165** in the Numeric field.

- A *Date field* is one that must be enclosed in braces ({}). For all records that are dated before 2, June, 1994, enter **<[2/06/94]** in the DATE field. If you are looking for fields that have no date, enter the empty braces in the field. If you are looking for records that have a date, no matter what that date is, enter **<>{}** in the DATE field.

- *Logical fields,* or Boolean operators, always use the either/or qualification. From the previous tip, you know that a Boolean operator is one in which a condition can be only one of two possible choices: it is On or Off. It cannot be both. Your choices must be couched between periods (.T., .F., .Y., .N., etc.). Figure 5.5 is looking for all left drive cars. The condition is TRUE, or .T.. The computer searches for that condition, capturing all those that meet or exceed the requirements, and supressing those that do not.

- *Conditional statements* in memo fields allow you to find text in those fields. The request must be used with the dollar sign operator ($).

Saving a Query

After creating your query, you can save it and run it again whenever you need to. Saving a query creates a .QBE file containing the dBASE commands executed when the query runs.

To save a query as a .QBE file:

1. If the query has already run, change to the Query Design mode by clicking the Design button on the SpeedBar.

2. Choose **F**ile, **S**ave.

If you close the query window without saving it, dBASE gives you a chance to save the query before the window closes. You are better off saving the query itself, instead of saving the query results. If the view is saved, a new table is created that duplicates at least some of the data in the original table, even though the new table's data is not updated when changes occur in the original tables.

Running a Query

After creating a query, you should run it to create a view of the data. The results should be as you arranged and selected them. When a query is executed, dBASE closes all the open tables to remove any temporary sorted tables, indexes, as well as any tables that have been removed from the query. Then the tables used in the query are reopened. (If you have sessions turned on, this process has no effect on the other open windows.)

Nothing is cast in stone here: if you don't like the results, simply delete the view and re-create the data.

To run the current query, click the Run button on the SpeedBar, or choose **V**iew, Query **R**esults.

You can manipulate query results just as you can the Table Records window in the Browse layout. You can scroll through the results using the scroll bars or use the SpeedBar buttons to see the *next*, *previous*, and so on, records.

Opening an Existing Query

Queries that you previously saved to disk appear as icons in the Queries panel of either the Catalog window or the Navigator. The number of tables in a query is limited to the number of workareas, the default is 255. The number of lines in a condition is limited by a filter-generated statement that must be less than 4,000 characters.

To open an existing query, find the icon that represents the query. Then perform one of the following actions:

- Right-click the query icon and select the action from the SpeedMenu. Choose **R**un Query to run the query; or choose Design **Q**uery to open the Query Designer.

- Click the query icon and then click either the Run or Design Query button on the SpeedBar.

- Double-click the query icon to run the query and view the data.

- Double-right-click the icon to open the query in the Design mode.

- Click the query icon and press F2 to run the query.

- Type **MODIFY QUERY** *<queryname>* in the Command window.

Using Multiple-Table Queries

As previously discussed, much of the power within dBASE for Windows is derived from multiple tables linked with common fields. This type of design optimizes performance and efficiency and minimizes redundant information.

To query a database with two or more tables, you have to open the tables and define the relationship by linking common fields. You must specify the information you want to send by using the table skeletons. When the query is executed, the results appear in a view that lets you work with the data as if it were a single table.

Opening Multiple Tables

To create a multitable query, follow these steps:

1. Open the Query Designer. Then choose Queries from the Navigator. Double-click the Untitled icon or type **CREATE QUERY** in the Command window.

Tip

To switch to a different layout to view one record at a time, choose **V**iew, **F**orm Layout; or choose **V**iew, **C**olumnar Layout.

2. The Open Table Required dialog box opens. Select the first table for the new query and choose OK. A table skeleton showing the structure of the table appears in the query window.

3. When the Query Designer is open, click the Add Table button on the SpeedBar; or choose **Q**uery, **A**dd Table to specify additional tables.

Figure 5.7 presents two table query skeletons: CUSTOMER.DBF and ORDERS.DBF. Any tables you create must have identical field names in order to link them.

Fig. 5.7
Using the
order box.

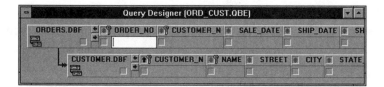

The following table shows the structures that make up the two example tables as shown in figure 5.7:

ORDERS.DBF	CUSTOMER.DBF
ORDER_NO	**CUSTOMER_N**
CUSTOMER_N	NAME
SALE_DATE	STREET
SHIP_DATE	CITY
SHIP_VIA	STATE_PROV
TOT_INV	ZIP_POSTAL
AMT_PAID	COUNTRY
BAL_DUE	PHONE
TERMS	FIRST_CONT
PAY_METHOD	YTD_SALES
MONTH	CREDIT_OK SIGNATURE NOTES

Note: The only identical field name in each table is CUSTOMER_N, as shown in bold.

Once the tables are open in the Query Designer, set a relation by defining the common field that links each pair of tables. The table that the link is being created from is referred to as the *parent table*; the table to be linked is the *child table*.

You create a link by dragging the icon of the parent table to the icon of the child table. When the cursor is over the table icon, a special *Create Link* pointer appears. You can create a link also by clicking the parent table and then clicking the Link Tables button on the SpeedBar; or, choose **Q**uery, **S**et Relation.

Once you have linked the tables, the Define Relation dialog box appears. Specify the fields to link and the relationship in the dialog box.

Figure 5.8 illustrates that after you identify your links, you must define a relationship between them. In this example, a relationship between the parent (CUSTOMER.DBF) and child (ORDERS.DBF) tables exists with a common link (CUSTOMER_N).

The identification of links is a two-part process. First, you identify the tables that are to be linked. Then you tie them together with the create link that starts with the parent (upper) and finishes with the child (lower). When you've done that, you have to define the relationship between them. This is accomplished with the Define Relation dialog box, shown in figure 5.9.

Fig. 5.8
Selecting records that match a condition.

If the *parent* and *child* table have a field of the same name and type, this field appears as the default linking field. Use the selection lists if you need to specify a different field. The relationship you define between the tables appears in the skeletons in the Query Designer.

Figure 5.9 shows links from the customer table to the orders table, based on the customer number field. A second link joins orders as the parent.

After establishing the link, check the fields and enter the expressions just as you do with a single-table query. Click the Run button on the SpeedBar when you are ready to execute the query. The results appear in figure 5.10.

Fig. 5.9
The Define
Relation
dialog box.

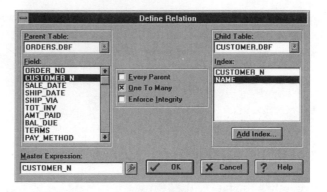

Fig. 5.10
The query results.

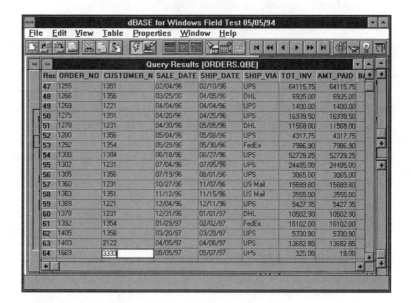

Understanding Relationships among Different Entities

Relationships exist among a series of linked tables in a database. For each
record in the first table, a corresponding record exists in a second table. For
example, a single customer may have many orders: this represents a *one-to-
many relationship,* because each order consists of one or more items for the
same customer.

Tables can enjoy a *one-to-one relationship,* too. For example, a query can search
for guests who attend an event. A single ticket is sold to a single person (who
may or not be married!) for a single seat.

Generally speaking, you can assume that two linked files have a *many-to-
many relationship.* In a group of sales representatives, their customers are

probably linked to a table of customer accounts. Each sales representative serves many customers, and larger accounts might use more than one sales representative.

Summary

Information in dBASE comes to you in two forms: information useful to you now, and information useful to you later. You use queries to make these determinations, and this chapter illustrated several methods for creating questions to locate and classify useful information.

You can use conditional statements also to create filters after initial data has been displayed. A conditional statement allows you to apply more focused questions to your data in order to define specific questions.

Chapter 6

Creating Forms

Forms employ windows that you can use to display and edit data. You can use a form on a single table, or with two or more linked tables linked.

You can design forms that contain objects such as pushbuttons, scroll bars, checkboxes, and listboxes. Once created, these objects allow you to view data and manipulate the way it is displayed.

To create a form, you need to display its components. Forms are essentially objects that contain other objects; typically they contain *controls* (push buttons and entry fields); *properties* (window size, location, and color); *events* (occurrences such as mouse clicks or key presses); and *methods* (subroutines, procedures, and code blocks).

The dBASE for Windows Form Designer shows tools and objects in a visual manner so you can see the form on-screen as it is created.

> **Note**
>
> The Form Designer in dBASE for Windows is a window in which you can display and edit information. A form can based on a single table or on multiple tables linked together. As a form is designed and assembled, you may include objects such as pushbuttons, scrollbars, checkboxes, and listboxes that, when implemented on your form, allow the user to view and manage data. Forms can provide the entire user interface for custom applications created in the dBASE for Windows environment by using programming tools or by utilizing the Form Designer.

Designer Tools and Techniques

The basic form-building utility is the Form Designer—it helps you complete your form design. Two views help you work with forms: Design view and Run view.

Form Designer is the Design view. The form's appearance and behavior are designed here. Two internal views are available: Layout view and Order view. Use the Layout view when you begin to design the forms on-screen. Use the Order view to specify the visual layers and the tabbing order of the form. The Run view is used at runtime: Controls are activated and any data linked to the form is available.

To design a new form with the Navigator, select Forms in the file type list, and perform one of the following:

■ Choose **F**ile, **N**ew, **F**orm from the Form Designer menu.

■ Double-click Untitled in the fields list.

■ From the Command window, type **CREATE FORM** and press Enter.

The Form Expert appears. You may elect to have expert assistance provided by dBASE or wing it yourself with a blank form. Click whichever choice you want. Here, you read about both scenarios; an expert assistance method and a blank form method. The results are the same—arriving at a final screen that shows the Controls palette on the right side of the screen and your selected form on the left.

Figure 6.1 shows the opening screen after choosing the [untitled] choice from the Forms file type list.

Fig. 6.1
The Form Expert screen with two choices.

The Expert Assistance Sequence

What follows is a series of screens that helps you to pick your way through the maze of selections before reaching your objective.

Figure 6.2 shows how Expert Assistance first asks you to select a file for the Queries and Tables that you are going to use in the remainder of the design work. Make a selection from the Available Files list and click **N**ext to continue.

Fig. 6.2
The Form Expert
Queries and Tables
screen.

After you select the database, a series of available fields appears (see fig. 6.3). Click each field in the Available listbox that you need, and then click the greater-than (>) sign to paste your selection into the Selected listbox. If you make a mistake, click the less-than (<) sign to take a field out. You can select every field by clicking the (>>) sign; likewise, you can deselect every field by clicking the (<<) sign. When you finish, choose **N**ext.

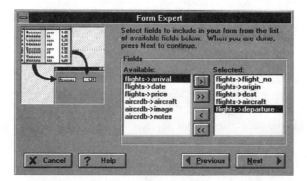

Fig. 6.3
The Form Expert
screen that allows
you to select your
fields.

Figure 6.4 asks you to determine what type of layout scheme you want the fieldnames to appear in initially. Make your selection and click **N**ext to continue.

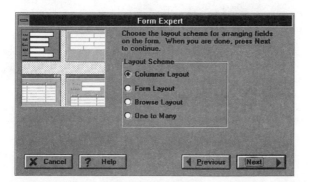

Fig. 6.4
The Form Expert
screen that allows
you to pick a
layout scheme.

In figure 6.5, dBASE asks you to select fonts and colors for each of the items that appears on the form. dBASE provides default values and colors: if you don't like them, click the icon to the right of each entry and make the necessary changes. This is the penultimate screen; choose **C**reate to produce the form containing your selections.

Fig. 6.5
The Form Expert screen that allows you to change properties of the screen.

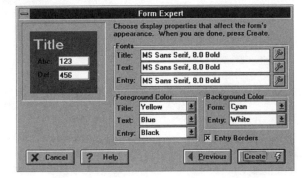

Finally, as shown in figure 6.6, the [untitled] Form Designer box appears. The basic design is located on the left portion of the screen, with the Controls palette to the right.

Fig. 6.6
The Form Designer (Expert Assistance) final screen.

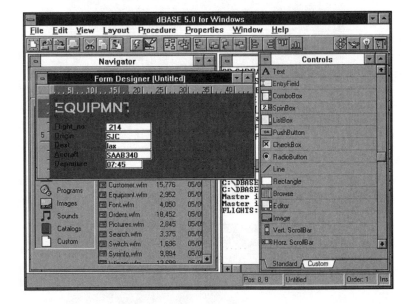

The Blank Form Sequence

This method of creating a form design is considerably more simple, because the only action you have to take is to click the Blank Form selection and then choose **C**reate.

Figure 6.7 shows the results of clicking the Blank Form selection.

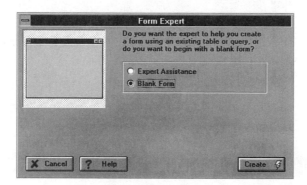

Fig. 6.7
The Form Expert
Blank Form screen.

Figure 6.8 shows the [untitled] Form Designer box that appears. The basic design is located on the left portion of the screen, with the Controls palette to the right. Note that here, you asked for, and received, a blank Form Design.

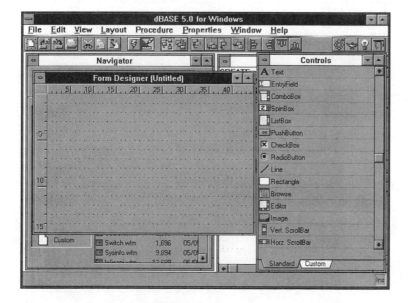

Fig. 6.8
The Form Designer
(Blank Form)
opening screen.

Working in the Design Window

An important part of the designer surface includes the *main window,* where the form is designed. You can change the default parameters by modifying the height, left, top, and width properties—an interior grid is used mainly to align controls, and vertical and horizontal rulers provide you with an ongoing look at your progress.

To alter any of these properties, choose **P**roperties, **F**orm Designer. Then right-click the form object or control, and choose **F**orm Designer Properties from the SpeedMenu. The Form Designer Properties dialog box appears.

To the right of the Form Designer window is a Controls palette, used as a main editor for Forms Design. Table 6.1 shows the icons and their meanings in the Controls palette with the Standard setting.

Table 6.1	Controls Palette Icons	
Icon	**Name**	**Use**
A	Text	To input text into the form.
	Entry Field	To enter a single value.
	ComboBox	To enter a number of values.
	SpinBox	To enter a single number or date value.
	ListBox	To enter a number of values.
	PushButton	To enter a single, interactive task.
	CheckBox	To toggle between two values.
	RadioButton	To enter one of many possible values.
	Line	To draw a line on the form.
	Rectangle	To draw a rectangle on the form.

Icon	Name	Use
	Browse	To view table records.
	Editor	To view memos, character fields, or text files.
	Image	To view a bitmapped image.
	OLE	To view another application.
	ScrollBars	To select from a set of values.

Creating Value for Your Form

Once you decide on the basic form design and create the initial outlines, your form probably needs to be populated with text, boxes, and other items.

A Form Designer is intended to help you configure your form to fit your particular needs. To see it, click the right mouse button anywhere within the Form Designer area. Then click the first title, Form Designer Properties.

Figure 6.9 shows a default Form Designer Properties dialog box. You can set the following properties from this dialog box: Form Settings, which govern the grid and ruler characteristics; Controls Palette Draw Mode, which specifies how controls are displayed on the Standard page of the Controls palette; Form Expert, invoked for new forms; Grid Settings, used to determine the size of the grid units; X and Y Grids; and Mouse (Revert to Pointer), used to return to default properties when you choose the Controls option in the Controls palette.

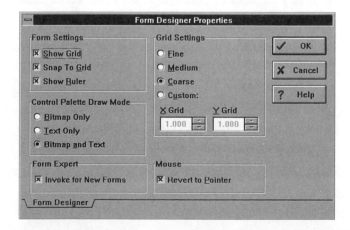

Fig. 6.9
The Form Designer Properties dialog box.

When you create a form, the default view is Design view. The two menu items specific to Design view are *Layout* and *Procedures*. Layout is used to align objects on the design surface, whereas Procedures is used with the Procedure Editor.

Creating Text

Text objects create read-only attributes on a form. That is, they accept no keyboard input, and they cannot be linked to another object. You can use them when providing labels and display titles.

To add new text, click the text control on the Controls palette and move the pointer to where you want to place the text. Then click or press and drag the text to the size you want.

Figure 6.10 shows a text box placed on the Form Designer.

Fig. 6.10
Placing a text box on the untitled form.

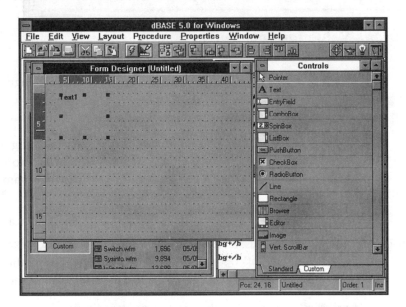

Creating Entry Fields

To add an entry field to a form, click the entry field control on the Controls palette and move the pointer to where you want it.

Figure 6.11 shows the Entry Field box placed on the untitled form.

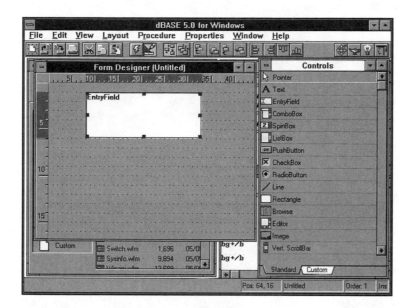

Fig. 6.11
The new entry
text field.

Once you place this text field on the form, you can move, resize, and align it as needed.

Linking an Entry Field to a Field in a Table

When the form runs, oftentimes you want to have data already appearing in a form. For example, a link might be created with a NAME field in a customer table with a specific entry on the form. When you type the customer's name on the form, that information is appended to the table.

To link an entry control, display the Data Linkage Properties. Then enter a fieldname in the Data Link Property, preceded by its table name, or *alias*.

Click the Tool button in the DataLink property to select the field using the Choose Field Dialog box. When the link is completed, the field data in the current record appears in the entry area of the entry field.

Creating Lines

Lines are really little more than graphics that also accept no keyboard input. They should be used sparingly on a form to add appeal. Use too many, and the form looks cluttered. Lines are typically used to separate or associate controls on a form.

To add a line, click the line control on the Controls palette, move the pointer to where you want to place it on the form, and then click or press and drag the line to the size you want.

You can set the line width to thicker or thinner than the default, or you can break the line into long or short dashed lines. To change the line style, select an option from the Pen property.

Figure 6.12 shows the effect of placing a line on a form.

Fig. 6.12
A line drawn on the Form Designer.

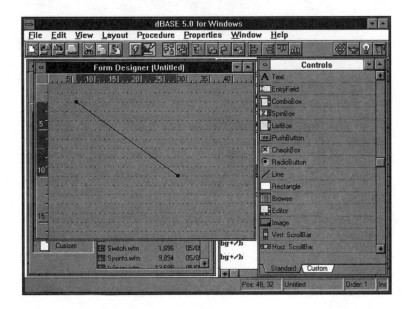

Creating Rectangles

Tip
You can place rectangles or boxes over existing material. To display any underlying controls on the form, select the rectangle (or box), and then choose **L**ayout, **S**end to Back.

Rectangles, like lines, are also graphically inclined and accept no keyboard input. Again, their main purpose in life on your form is to add appeal or highlight certain areas. Like lines, too many clutter the form, detracting from its appeal.

To add a rectangle, click the rectangle control on the Controls palette and move to where you want the rectangle to be. Then click or press and drag the rectangle to the size you want.

Figure 6.13 shows a rectangle drawn with two radio buttons on the Form Designer box.

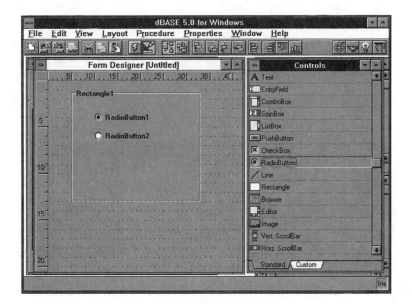

Fig. 6.13
A rectangle with
two radio buttons.

Creating Borders

A rectangle always has a border with a normal style. You may want to expose
this border, but sometimes it looks better to hide the border completely, or
raise or lower it. To hide a border, display the Visual Properties and set the
Border property to *false*. To change the border style, select one from the list in
the BorderStyle property.

Preventing Users from Typing Values

By default, the Form Designer allows you to type values in the text box portion of a spin box. Sometimes, however, you might want users to select items
rather than type them. To disable the editing area of a spin box, set the
SpinOnly property in the Controls palette to true.

Creating Editor Controls for Memo Fields and Text Files

Editor controls display and manage long lines of text strings. These strings
can be linked to text fields and memo fields. An editor control uses either the
dBASE text editor (see Chapter 10), or another editor that you specify in the
Files page of the Desktop Properties dialog box.

Adding an Editor Control to Your Form

To add an editor control, click the editor control on the Controls palette and move the pointer to where you want to place it on the form. Then click or press and drag the editor control to the required size.

You can link an editor to a character or memo field in the table. To link an editor control to a character or memo field, display Data Linkage Properties and enter the character or memo fieldname in the DataLink property, preceded by the table name, or alias. For example, if you wanted to link the editor control to the LASTNAME field in an 80920.DBF table, enter the phrase `80920->lastname`.

If you want to link an editor control to a text file, display the Data Linkage Properties. Type the keyword **FILE** followed by the name of the file. For example: **FILE C:\JEKYLL\HYDE.TXT**. After the link is complete, the contents of the text file appear in the entry area of the editor.

Figure 6.14 shows the results of such an addition. First, add the editor control to the box. Then open the Properties dialog box and choose the Datalink option. Clicking this box provides access to the Data Link dialog box, where a link between the editor control box and an actual text file occurs.

Fig. 6.14
The new editor control.

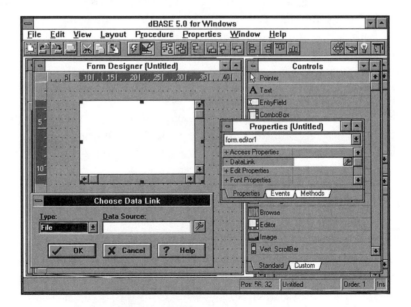

You may also want to make the contents of an editor control read-only—the default is editable. To make an editor control read-only, display the Edit properties, and set the Modify property to false.

Other properties can restrict users from any editing operations. To prevent users from adding records, set the Append property to false; to prevent users from changing records, set the Modify property to false; and to prevent users from deleting records, set the Delete property to false.

Creating and Using Listboxes

Listboxes display choices for the user. To add a listbox, click the listbox control on the Controls palette, move the pointer to where you want to place it on the form, and click or press and drag the listbox to the required size.

Five types of data are available as prompts in a listbox:

- *Files* located in a current directory

- *Tables* located in a current directory

- *Elements* in an array

- *Values* in a table field

- *Names* of fields in a table

To specify which type of data you want to use, set the DataSource property from the **V**iew, **O**bject Properties dialog box. Once you get to the Object Properties, set the Methods tab. Then find the Data Link Properties section. If this has a + sign to its left, click it to expand the title. Find the DataSource section, and insert the data to be used. Figure 6.15 shows the result.

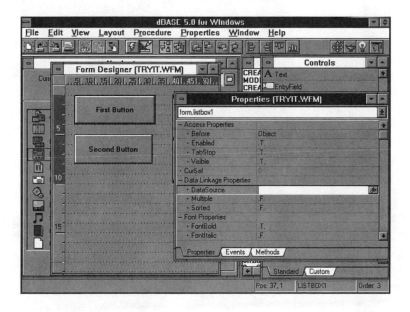

Fig. 6.15
Specifying which type of data to use.

Creating Browse Controls

A browse control displays records in a row-and-column format. It simulates the Browse layout in the Table Records window. Browse controls are especially useful for displaying records of a child table when the form is based on a multitable query.

To add a browse control, click the browse control on the Controls palette and move the pointer to where you want to place it on the form. Then click or press and drag the browse control to the required size.

You may link a browse control to a table so that the contents are displayed and changed when the form runs. To link a browse control, display the Data Linkage Properties and enter the alias name of a table in the Alias property. Then click the Tool button in the Alias property to select the field using the Alias dialog box. Once the link finishes, the correct table appears in the browse control.

Figure 6.16 shows the results of a browse control creation.

Fig. 6.16
The newly created browse control using ORDERS.DBF.

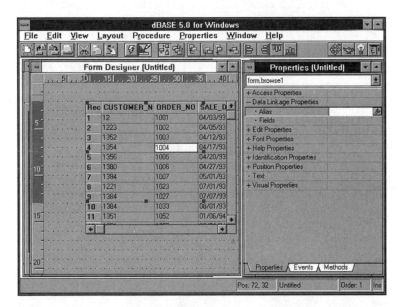

Note

Note from the Data Linkage Properties box that those options preceded with a plus sign (for example, +Access Properties) have other options nested below them. To see those options, double-click the main title.

Creating Scroll Bars for Numbers and Dates

Scroll bars accept values from a known range of numbers or dates. You may want to use the scroll bar to show something graphically: for example, a percentage representing completed tasks or changes to a project status.

To add a scroll bar, click the vertical or horizontal scroll bar control on the Controls palette and move the pointer to where you want to place the scroll bar. Then click or press and drag the scroll bar to the required size.

Figure 6.17 shows vertical and horizontal scroll bar placements. The Data Linkage Properties dialog box is exposed in a manner already described in other examples.

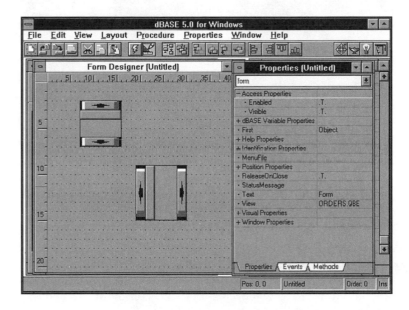

Fig. 6.17
New vertical and horizontal scroll bars.

Once you create a scroll bar, you can link it to a numeric, float, or date field in a table. This is so you can display and change the field when you run the form. To link a scroll bar, display Data Linkage properties and enter a fieldname in the DataLink property, preceded by its table name or alias. When the link is complete, the thumb on the scroll bar reflects the value in the linked field in the current record.

Scroll bars possess valid data ranges for their values. To set a valid range for a scroll bar, display Edit Properties and set the RangeMin property to the minimum property value greater than 1. Similarly, set the RangeMax property to the maximum property value, whose default is 100. When you run the form in the future, the thumb on the scroll bar does not exceed the selected boundary values.

Adding and Linking a Browse Control to a Table

To link data to a browse control window, access the **O**bject Properties dialog box from the **V**iew main menu. Pull down the Data Linkage Properties by setting the Methods tab. Find Alias, and enter the name of the table that you want to link in that box. In figure 6.18, the COMPANY table has been added to the box. The results of this action are shown in the black-handled boxes at the bottom of the Form Designer, TRYIT.WFM.

Fig. 6.18
Adding a control to a table.

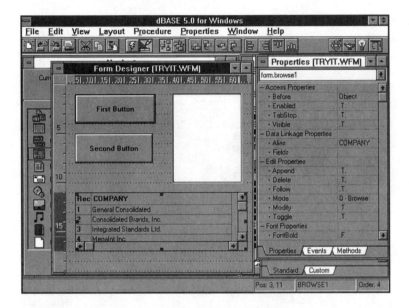

Creating Image Controls

Forms can also have images embedded in them. You can link an image control—typically a .PCX or .BMP file—from a directory on your hard disk, or you can select a file from an external source. You can also include scanned images, such as employees' photographs linked with their textual data.

Adding a New Image Control

To add an image control, select the image control on the Controls palette and move the pointer to where you want to place it. Then click or press and drag the image control to the required size.

Figure 6.19 shows the Form Designer box with an image control box embedded in it.

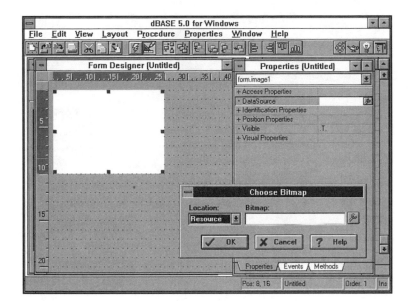

Fig. 6.19
A new image
control box.

Linking Images to Data

You can link images from any of three sources: a binary field located in a table, an external graphics file that has either a .PCX or .BMP file extension, or a resource within the dBASE file DBASERES.DLL. To link any of these sources, display the Data Linkage Properties and double-click the Tool button in the DataSource field. The Choose Bitmap dialog box appears.

In figure 6.20, the Choose Bitmap dialog box shows that the bitmap image number 641 (a *book*) is selected. The dialog box shows an effigy of the image in the graphics area.

Finally, as figure 6.21 shows, the book image identification is embedded into the DataSource portion of the DataLink box, and the image is displayed in full size inside the image box.

To use an external file, select the Filename in the Location list. Enter the filename of the .PCX/.BMP file or double-click the Tool button to select it from the File Open dialog box.

To use a binary file, select Binary in the Location list. Enter the filename or click the Tool button to select it from the Choose Fields dialog box.

To use a resource from the DBASERES.DLL dynamic-linked library file, select Resource from the Location list. Double-click the Tool button and watch the Bitmaps dialog box appear. Select the graphic you want and choose OK. The graphic appears on the form after the link is completed.

Fig. 6.20

The Bitmap dialog box with a book image.

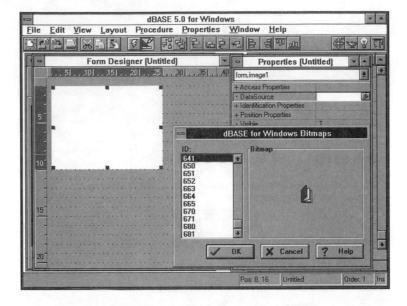

Fig. 6.21

The image located inside the Form Designer.

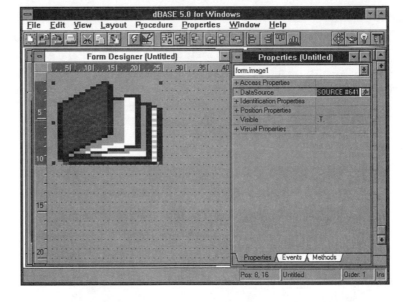

Having done all this, you may find that the image is larger (or smaller) than the space you have to hold it. Perhaps it also abuts textual information, and each crowds the other out. If this is the case, you may elect to align it along the left border, center it in the middle of the frame, or stretch it.

To set the alignment, display the Position properties and select the alignment from the list under Alignment property.

Creating OLE Controls to Display OLE Data

OLE objects display OLE documents that were previously stored in OLE fields in a table. When the form runs, you may see the OLE object. Double-click it to launch the server application and change its contents.

To add an OLE control, click the OLE control on the Controls palette and move the pointer to the place where you want to place it on the form. Then click or press and drag the OLE control to the required size.

Figure 6.22 shows the embedding of the AMT_PAID field from the ORDERS table (ORDERS->AMT_PAID).

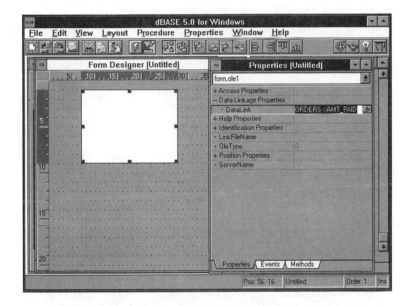

Fig. 6.22
The OLE control.

You may also want to link an OLE control to an OLE object stored in an OLE field. When the form runs, you see the image; double-click it to perform any editing tasks.

To link an OLE control, display the Data Linkage Properties. Enter a fieldname in the DataLink property, preceded by its table name, or alias. When you complete the link, the field data in the current record appears in the OLE field. The control features store information about an OLE object in the LinkFileName, OLEType, and ServerName properties. If you want to see additional information about any of these properties, press F1 when the property is highlighted.

Printing Your Form

You can print your form at any time by selecting either the Print SpeedBar button, or choosing **F**ile, **P**rint. The form is delivered to your printer.

Running, Changing, and Saving Your Form

Once you create a form and it is ready to have data appear in it, you must *run* the form.

Choose **F**ile, **O**pen, and then select the form you want. Then select **R**un Form, followed by OK. The form appears in Run Mode. You may print the form by clicking the Print SpeedBar button, or choosing **F**ile, **P**rint.

After you create a form and complete its initial design, you should save it. Choose **F**ile and Save **A**s to save the form with a new name, or to overwrite an existing form name. To resave an existing form, choose **F**ile, **S**ave.

You may decide that the changes you made are not worth saving, or that you edited the wrong form. In this case, choose **F**ile, A**b**andon and Close.

The Form Designer abandons any changes made to that form design, allowing you to begin fresh with the correct form.

Figure 6.23 shows the Open File dialog box. Once you save the form, it is available for massage. Note the **R**un Form and De**s**ign Form radio buttons at the bottom-right corner of the screen. To perform either function, first select and file's name and paste it into the **F**ile Name box. Then click the appropriate form designation.

Fig. 6.23
The Open File dialog box with the optional Run Form/Design Form buttons.

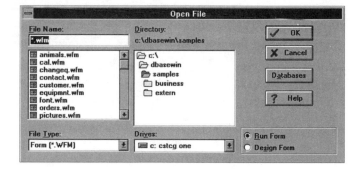

Writing Event Handlers

There are three generic types of user interfaces: a command line, where the user types commands in at a dot prompt; menu-driven, where the user selects choices from available options; and event-driven, where the user interacts with visible options such as forms containing pushbuttons or listboxes. This section concentrates on writing event handlers.

In the two examples that follow, two event handles are portrayed as individual lines of code. In the example, the event handler is coded with hard-coded references. The second example shows a generic reference. The only difference between the two is that the first example executes only when assigned to a button named MyButton in a form named EventTest. Its counterpart, the second example, executes with any button on any form.

Example 1

```
PROCEDURE ClickAlert
EventTest.Text = "Go Ahead! Punch my Button!"
EventTest.MyButton.Text = "Oh Well..."
RETURN
```

Example 2 ·

```
PROCEDURE ClickAlert
form.Text = "Go Ahead! Punch my Button!"
this.Text = "Oh Well..."
RETURN
```

In the dBASE for Windows environment, you attach code to event handler properties of controls that correspond to specific events. For example, you want some activity to happen when the user presses the mouse button, or when the mouse button is double-clicked. In an event-driven application, the following generic activities apply: the application is automatically launched by displaying a startup form or something happens, such as a button clicked or key pressed. In turn, an event handler executes. Finally, the application waits for the next input to occur.

The Form Designer helps you to develop event-driven programs. Once the Form Designer and its tools have been used to build data entry forms, dialog boxes, and the other pieces of an application, the Procedure Editor, which is a Form Designer tool used for entering and editing program code, ties the components together by writing procedures that execute when events occur. Your code no longer executes in a sequential manner; that is, it starts at the beginning and finishes at the end. In between, it branches out to subroutines and performs loops while, or until, certain conditions are met. The new methodology executes based upon events (*called event-handlers*) attached to a form. The event handlers control the events.

Example 3 shows a modification of the *this* and *form* references shown in in the previous two examples. These references are available *only* for procedures linked directly into event properties. They are *not* used in any subsequently called procedures.

If an event-handling procedure calls another procedure (in an activity similar to subroutine calling), and that procedure uses either the *this* or *form* reference, *this* or *form* needs to be passed as a parameter to the called procedure.

Example 3

```
PROCEDURE ClickAlert
form.Text = "Go Ahead! Punch my Button!"
this.Text = "Oh Well..."
DO Retaliate WITH form
RETURN

PROCEDURE Retaliate(FormRef)
                LOCAL 1Counter
                DO WHILE 1Counter <10
                        FormRef.ColorNormal = "r/w"
                        FormRef.ColorHighlight = "w/r"
                        FormRef.ColorNormal = "w/r"
                        FormRef.ColorHighlight = "r/w"
                        1Counter = 1Counter + 1
                        ENDDO
                RETURN
```

Chaining Events Together

Events, as described, do not always execute based upon the what the user does—the so-called user interface. Some events cause other events to occur. For example, if you click a pushbutton that is not activated, it becomes activated. As that occurs, the image changes from a cold grey image to an image with contrast and (hopefully) some color.

A sequence that causes this event to occur can become considerably more complex if another control is already activated when the user clicks a pushbutton. The control losing focus might have its own event handlers that used to fit into the execution sequence.

Now, a single mouse click can create havoc if the correct event-handlers aren't assigned to each control in a multiclick environment.

The following example illustrates a method for experimentation with different event handles and their execution methods. Codeblocks are assigned for each event; when the event that codeblocks handle is executed, a notification message is presented in the Command window.

Example 4

```
LOCAL f
f = NEW SHOWEVNT ()
f.Open()
```

```
CLASS SHOWEVNT OF FORM
                  this.OnSize = {;? "OnSize"}
                  this.OnMouseMove = {;? "OnMouseMove"}
                  this.OnRightMouseUp = {;? "OnRightMouseUp" }
                  this.OnRightMouseDown = {;"OnRightMouseDown"}
                  this.OnLeftMouseUp = {;? "OnLeftMouseUp" }
                  this.OnLeftMouseDown = {;? "OnLeftMouseDown" }
                  this.OnLostFocus = {;? "OnLostFocus" }
                  this.OnGotFocus = {:? "OnGotFocus" }
                  this.OnOpen = {;? "OnOpen  "}
                  this.OnSelection = {;? "OnSelection" }
                  this.OnClose = {;? "On Close "}
                  this.OnMove = {;? "OnMove" }
                  this.Text = "These Form Events Work pretty
                            Good!"
                  this.Width  =  30.00
                  this.Height =  10.00
                  this.Top    =  21.17
                  this.Left   =  31.00
                  DEFINE PUSHBUTTON P1 OF THIS;
                                  PROPERTY;
                     OnRightMouseUp{;?"P1.OnRightMouseUp"},;
                     OnRightMouseDown{;?"P1.OnRightMouseDown"},;
                     OnLeftMouseUp[;? "P1.OnLeftMouseUp"},;
                     OnLeftMouseDown {;? "P1.OnLeftMouseDown"},;
                     OnLostFocus {;? "P1.OnLostFocus"}.;
                     OnGotFocus {;? "P1.OnGotFocus"},;
                     OnClick {;? "P1.OnClick"].;
                     Text "First Button",;
                     Width    8.00,;
                     Height   2.00,;
                     Top      2.00,;
                     Left     2.00,;
                     Group .T.
                  DEFINE PUSHBUTTON P2 OF THIS;
                                  PROPERTY;
                     OnRightMouseUp {;? "P2.OnRightMouseUp"},;
                     OnRightMouseDown {;"P2.OnRightMouseDown"},;
                     OnLeftMouseUp [;? "P2.OnLeftMouseUp"},;
                     OnLeftMouseDown {;? "P2.OnLeftMouseDown"},;
                     OnLostFocus {;? "P1.OnLostFocus"}.;
                     OnGotFocus {;? "P2.OnGotFocus"},;
                     OnClick {;? "P2.OnClick"}.;
                     Text "Second Button",;
                     Width  8.00,
                     Height 2.00,
                     Top    2.00,;
                     Left   12.00,;
                     Group  .T.
                     ENDCLASS
```

To execute this file as written, you have to be in dBASE for Windows. Access the Forms area, and make sure that you can see the filename. I called it TRYIT.WFM. You can name it anything you wish.

From the Command window, type **DO TRYIT.WFM** and watch the show begin. As the form executes, you can see the effect that pushing on the individual mouse buttons has. Note that every move you make with the mouse while this program is running is monitored in the Results Pane, located beneath the Command Window.

Figure 6.24 shows a typical screen with the program running, including the Command window commands and the Results Pane outcome.

> **Note**
>
> If you don't like the size of the buttons or their titles, or if you are displeased with the main menu title, you can edit the file using the dBASE Editor, described elsewhere in this book, to change those attributes; you also can use your favorite line editor to make those changes. Just make sure that you save the material as a DOS, or text-only, file when you finish.

An improved method might be to try your hand at the Form Designer, physically editing the pictorial aspects of the attributes with the mouse by typing keyboard commands in an editing session.

Fig. 6.24
The results of the TRYIT.WFM file running in its own Window.

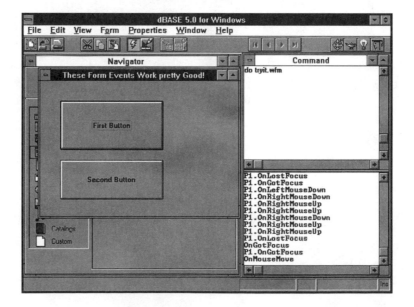

> **Note**
>
> If the file doesn't run, or blows up when you execute it, you have to edit the file—perhaps several times—in order to rid the program of errors. No one writes error-free code the first time, so check your characters. Also check the control codes, such as the braces, commas, and periods throughout the text.

Mouse events are handled through mouse clicks with the OnClick event, which applies uniformly to pushbuttons and menu items. If you require greater control, Table 6.2 should provide a way to handle mouse clicks on any form object.

These events handle double-clicks, mouse button presses, and mouse button releases for almost any control that you wish to devise. In addition, three parameters are passed to these events that control other vital pieces.

Table 6.2   Handling Mouse Clicks on Any Form Object

Mouse Button	Double-Click	Press	Release
Left	OnLeftDblClick	OnLeftMouseDown	OnLeftMouseUp
Middle	OnMiddleDblClick	OnMiddleMouseDown	OnMiddleMouseUp
Right	OnRightDblClick	OnRightMouseDown	OnRightMouseUp

The flags parameter is a single-byte value that indicates whether the Control (Ctrl) or Alternate (Alt) keys were pressed when the event occurred. A column parameter indicates the column location of the mouse pointer. Finally, a row parameter indicates the row location of the mouse pointer.

In the final example, the flags parameters BITSET() and BITDO() interpret the single-byte value.

Example 5

```
PROCEDURE ShowMouseFlags (nFlag,nCol,nRow)
                nShiftKey = 4
                nCtrlKey = 8
                IFBITAND(nFlag,nShiftKey)=nShiftKey ?
                " Shift Key "
                ENDIF
                IFBITAND(nFlag,nCtrlKey)=nCtrlKey ?
                " Control Key "
                ENDIF
    RETURN
```

Program Launching Activities

An event handler's most common event is to perform an action in response to a mouse click. These are most commonly connected to OnClick events when applied to pushbuttons or menu items. Such handlers may be any type of procedure, although many are designed to handle simple actions such as opening or closing a form.

In the example that follows, an OnClick event closes, and then releases a form.

Example 6

```
PROCEDURE CloseForm
                    form.Close()
                    form.Release()
RETURN
```

OnClick events in forms are handled most elegantly by assigning subroutines, of which the one in Example 5 is displayed.

Data Validation and Responding to Data Changes

Data entry forms usually require that the programmer create a piece of code that validates the user's response. Among other reasons, the chief reason for this is to make sure the user *zigged* or *zagged* when s/he was supposed to. Three main properties are employed to conduct this check. A Valid executes when the user makes a change to the control's value and then tries to leave that control. The event handler should evaluate the new value and return a true (.T.) response if it is valid, or a false response (.F.) if it is invalid. A ValidRequired determines whether the Valid event handler executes every time focus leaves the control, even though the control contains a default value, or only when the user makes a change. Finally, a ValidErrorMas specifies a message displayed on the status bar when the Valid event handler returns a false value.

In the following example, the user is prompted to enter a time. Your job is to evaluate that a valid time has been entered.

Example 7

```
DEFINE ENTRYFIELD Time OF TimeForm;
            PROPERTY
                                Left 15,;
                                Width 5,;
                                Picture "99:99",;
                                VALID ValTime,;
                                VALIDREQUIRED .T.,;
                                VALIDERRORMSG "That is an
                                Invalid Time"

            PROCEDURE ValTime
                                LOCAL 1Hours,1Mins
                                1Hours=VAL(LEFT(this.Value,2))
                                1Mins=VAL(RIGHT(this.Value,2))
                                IF hrs<0 .OR. hrs>23 .OR. min<0
                                .OR. min>59
                                                  IsValid=.f.
                                Else
                                                  IsValid=.T.
                                ENDIF
            RETURN IsValid
```

Creating On-Line Help
for an Application

Most successful applications provide some degree of on-line help for the user
when s/he gets stuck or needs bailing out. The simplest type of help is a Text
object that labels the contents of another object, such as "Enter a Name" that
is positioned next to a name entry field. Messages may also be located in a
status bar using a device called a StatusMessage property.

If a deeper level of support is required, you can display information through
Windows using the OnHelp event. This piece of code executes when the user
presses the F1 key.

In the following example, a table is created containing Help text with a
record for each form in the applications, and the help text that has been

previously stored in a memo field. The following code should be assigned to the OnHelp event for context-sensitive help for each form.

Example 8

```
PROCEDURE DisplayHelp
CurrentWORKAREA = WORKAREA()
SELECT HelpFile
SEEK(this.Text)
IF FOUND()
OPEN FORM HelpWindow
ENDIF
SELECT (CurrentWorkArea)
RETURN
```

Ordering and Relating Records

Ordering records is accomplished through the configuration of indexes tied to the table that contains those records. Some degree of ease must be available for organizing and using data so that useful information can be extracted from that which is not currently useful. The mechansim is database tools—such as queries, forms, and reports—that use indexes to visually display information.

Ordering records is a dynamic, ongoing process that takes into consideration the logical order versus the physical order of records. At first glance, sorting appears to be the most natural way that data should be organized, because most of our modern-day tools—telephone books, dictionaries, and other reference data—are organized according to alphabetical order. Similarly, tables have logical indexes that allow the ordering of data in dynamic tables. This aspect of database sorting makes the physical order of the table obsolete.

Joining Two Tables Together

In dBASE for Windows, you can use the command JOIN to join two tables together. The outcome is a large table, consisting of two smaller tables that have their fields arranged in a new order.

The JOIN command may be used to create a temporary table so that a subset of useful information is available to a user.

Index Tags and Their Files

There are two succinctly different types of indexes that you can create upon your command within the dBASE environment. The first is a multiple index file that has an .MDX extension. The second is used with a single index file, and has an .NDX extension. A single index file is one that provides direct compatibility with older dBASE III Plus files. In order to create an index, you must first open an appropriate table with the USE command in the Command window, or click the Table icon from the Navigator window. Decide which fieldname you want to index. In the previous line, I chose to use the CUSTOMER table and to index on the LASTNAME field. Type the following commands in the Command window:

```
USE CUSTOMER
INDEX ON LASTNAME TO LASTNAME.NDX
```

When the indexing has concluded, your LASTNAME fields are sorted alphabetically by last name.

Any single index file used on a regular basis should be converted to a production .MDX file to take advantage of automatically updating data in the table.

In the following example, I convert an .NDX index file into an .MDX file by typing the following commands into the Command window:

```
USE EXCLUSIVE CUSTOMER INDEX LASTNAME.NDX, COMPANY.NDX
COPY INDEXES LASTNAME.NDX, COMPANY.NDX
USE
```

You may also decide that a single index should be created from an .MDX TAG. This feature allows you to provide backward compatibility to dBASE III. Perhaps at some stage in the future, you will want a dBASE III index; this method of index creation allows this luxury.

In this example, I again use the CUSTOMER table. For the sake of argument, assume that it contains thousands of key accounts, and the production .MDX file has a few tags in it. I want to update customers' records by their identification number (CUST_NO) and copy that number into an .NDX file:

```
USE CUSTOMER
COPY TAG CUST_NO to CUST_NO.NDX
SET INDEX TO CUST_NO.NDX
```

Index Maintenance

As was suggested in the last section, it is not a good idea to keep thousands of indexes around forever. Your bottom line, I suspect, will be that you use a small percentage of the available indexes on a regular basis; most of the others are used infrequently.

You can delete indexes that have lost favor with a standard delete command. From the last example, assume that you decide that you no longer need the LASTNAME.NDX or the CUSTOMER.NDX files. Use the following command in the Command window to rid yourself of them:

Tip
Try not to create too many .NDX files. Doing so only fills up your hard disk and makes it harder to find files that enjoy regular usage. Bear in mind that .MDX files are automatically updated as changes are made to your data; consequently, you need fewer open files from which to reference.

```
DELETE FILE LASTNAME.NDX
DELETE FILE CUSTOMER.NDX
```

You can similarly delete unused tags. Here, however you do not need to name the .MDX file when it is open in the current work area. For example, if you no longer need the CUST_NO index from the previous example, simply delete it:

```
DELETE TAG CUST_NO OF CUSTOMER.MDX
```

Sometimes, of course, you need an index tag for a special one time only search. You can do this by using the NOSAVE command with the phrase SET ORDER TO. With the NOSAVE option, a temporary tag is created in the production file. When the index is closed, the tag is deleted:

```
SET ORDER TO CUST_NO of CUSTOMER.MDX NOSAVE
```

Caution

Be careful not to delete tags with the NOSAVE option. If you don't have a handy backup from which to restore your material—and most of us don't—you'll likely be obligated to spend copious amounts of time recreating them.

Corrupted Index Files

With some practice, it is possible to unsynchronize index tags after you have performed many updates! To prevent indexes from being unsynchronized with the data, you should make it a habit to reindex those tables that enjoy heavy usage.

You may reindex your files by following these steps:

1. Open each table separately in a different work area.

2. Open all indexes besides the production index that you want to update.

Tip
In a multiuser environment, use the EXCLUSIVE command to open single usage.

3. Type the following commands in at the Command window. Note that these are examples. Your table and index names will be different:

```
USE CUSTOMER in 1 INDEX LASTNAME.NDX EXCLUSIVE
USE CUST_NO in 2 INDEX CUST_NO
REINDEX
```

Opening Your Index Files

You can open index files independently and close them according to your needs with each table. You may open an .MDX file at the same time you are naming the tag you want as the master index.

```
USE CUSTOMER INDEX NAMES.MDX ORDER [TAG] FIRSTNAME OF NAMES.MDX
```

You can swap an active tag with another tag from the same, or another multiple index file with the command: `SET ORDER TO TAG LASTNAME`.

You can open several indexes at any one time with this command:

```
USE CUSTOMER INDEX NAMES.MDX, CLIENT.MDX, SOIUNDS.NDX
```

> **Note**
>
> Memo, Binary, or OLE fields do not accept indexing on their fieldnames.

Closing Your Index Files

You can close index files by using any of the following commands without an argument:

```
SET INDEX TO
SET ORDER TO
```

The command `CLOSE INDEX` closes all open index files except for the production .MDX file. In order to close the production file, you must close the table.

The commands to close or quit closes all files, including your index files, as the dBASE application is closed in an orderly, precise manner. Alternatively using the word `USE` without an argument, or `CLOSE DATABASES`, automatically closes all tables and their associated files.

> **Caution**
>
> Under no circumstances should you physically turn off the computer as a method for closing the program or terminating an application. If you do not corrupt your information the first time, you will the second or third time you use this method. If you use this method on a regular basis, make sure you have excellent backup data... you're gonna need it!

Searching and Summarizing Records

Search commands and related functions locate and change specific data that you stored in database tables. You are *not* obligated to use indexes in order to see your data, although an index is a faster method of getting to the good stuff. A number of dBASE commands can quickly and efficiently find your data.

The LOCATE command searches through the entire length of your table, looking for the string you identified.

The following example shows how LOCATE finds a customer account in a table:

```
CUSTACCT.PRG
USE CUSTOMER
LOCATE FOR LASTNAME="Perron"
IF FOUND()
DISPLAY CUSTACCT
ENDDIF
```

The commands FIND and SEEK use a key order to search through any indexed tables to find specified data quickly. SEEK is the most flexible command, whereas FIND has been relegated to the dBASE III camp.

The FIND command is not fussy. It accepts a character, date, or numeric index to look for literals that you supply. However, it is case-sensitive. You may get around this by using the UPPER() function for uppercase or the LOWER() function for lowercase characters.

The SEEK command uses indexes based on expressions that include one or more fields, operators, combining characters, numbers, or dates. Like FIND, it is case-sensitive.

The SEEK() function contains all the characteristics of the SEEK command, displaying a TRUE or FALSE result for the search it has been asked to conduct.

The SEEK function is used in the following example to find a customer and display a phone number and account number:

```
USE CUSTOMER
SET ORDER TO CUSTOMER
SEEK("Colorado Springs Technical Consulting Group")
DISPLAY PHONE, CUST_NO
```

Tip
Use the SEEK() function instead of FIND or SEEK. It provides you with better overall performance.

When there is no open index, the LOOKUP() function behaves as LOCATE and performs a record-by-record search. LOOKUP() should be used only with an indexed file to search for an expression in one field, and to retrieve the data from another field.

In the following example, the SEEK command finds a specific client by account number. Once found, the outstanding balance is displayed. Then the client name appears.

```
USE CUSTOMER
INDEX ON CUST_NO TAG CUST_NO
SEEK 36586
Amount=LOOKUP(BEGINBAL,CUST_NO,CUST_NO)
? BALANCE
Name=LOOKUP(CUSTOMER, CUST_NO, CUST_NO)
```

Performing Field Calculations

Individual commands such as SUM(), AVERAGE(), and CALCULATE() do an admirable job of calculating numbers. The CALCULATE() command is the best, however, because it processes through the records only once to get the figures upon which it will calculate. The two former functions, SUM() and AVERAGE(), perform the same type of calculation, but you must keep calling them each time you want them to perform.

The command CALCULATE AVG(Cost), STD(Cost) TO mavgcost, mstdcost performs calculations on average and standard, storing the results in *avgcost* and *stdcost*.

In the following example, the program counts the number of orders one of your customers has placed. The CUSTOMER table is indexed by the CUST_NO field. Then a customer number is requested by the program, which is entered by the user. By using SEEK(), the program looks for the customer number in the file, and when it finds it, counts the number of orders that have been placed by your client. Finally, the average quantity of parts ordered by this client is determined.

```
mCUSTOMER = SPACE(6)
INDEX ON CUST_NO TAG CUST_NO
@10, 10 Say "Enter the Customer Identification Number :";
GET mCUSTOMER
READ
SET KEY TO mCUSTOMER
SEEK mCUSTOMER
CALCULATE CNT(), AVG(Part_qty) TO MORDER_CNT, mAVG_QUANT;
WHILE mCUST = CUST_NO
```

In the following table, the use of CALCULATE() is shown by defining the task and the CALCULATE() equation that should be used.

Job	Equation
Averaging Values	CALCULATE AVG(Cost) TO mavg_cost AVERAGE Cost to mavg_cost
Compute Maximum Value	CALCULATE MAX(Date_trans) TO mMax_Date ? MAX(mhired,mfired)
Compute Minimum Value	CALCULATE MIN(Cost) TO mMin_Cost ? MIN(mDate1,mDate2)
Count Items	CALCULATE CNT( ) to mCount COUNT TO mCount
Standard Deviation	CALCULATE STD(mCost) TO mStd_Cost CALCULATE VAR(mCost) TO mVar_Cost
Sum a Value	CALCULATE SUM(mCost*mQuantity) TO mTotal SUM mcost*mQuantity TO mTotal

---

Caution

The computation of the maximum and minimum values in the previous table using the MIN( ) and MAX( ) functions always returns the smallest or largest value in the named field. As stand-alone functions, they return the smaller or larger of two values.

Summary

This chapter showed you a variety of methods that you can use to create forms in your applications.

You also learned to create utility for your form by adding text, boxes, rectangles, lines, and spin boxes. Then additional linkage information that allows you to link boxes with independent data was presented.

Chapter 7

Creating Menus, Buttons, and SpeedBars

This chapter describes how to create and design menus; how to create and place pushbuttons on a form; and how to create *SpeedBars*, which are pushbuttons with special properties. You should review Chapter 6 before working with this material if you have not read that chapter.

This chapter is an extension of Chapter 6. Here, you use the Form Designer and Menu Designer to create utility for a variety of different forms. Because these principles have broad application for the remainder of the dBASE for Windows software, they deserve a section of their own.

Creating Menu Titles

Two types of menu titles are available for you to use: drop-down and cascading. As you begin to decide which one of the two you will use, consider the following points:

The title should always describe the action that occurs when the selection is made. It goes without saying, of course, that the item performed actually happens. For example, Save should really save a file! A parent menu should describe the generic activities of all the items in the child menu. When you click File, for example, you expect to see activities relating to files. If you select Edit, you expect to see items such as Cut, Copy, or Paste, and so on.

If a menu opens a dialog box, ellipses should be used within the child menu to indicate it does so. The most common example is the Save As... function popular in most File parents. The ellipsis indicates that when the choice is made, a dialog box is opened.

Ideally, a menu item should also have a *mnemonic device*: a letter that, when used in combination with either the Control, (Ctrl), Alternate (Alt), or Shift

(Shift) keys provides the same results as if you used the mouse. Again using a common File menu example, you can use the Alt+F combination to pull down the File menu. Other popular combinations are Ctrl+O to Open a file and Ctrl+S to Save a file. Be careful not to duplicate key combinations and try to make the combination intuitive. For example, it might be obvious that Ctrl+O opens a file, but Ctrl+P might not make the cut.

Creating Menu Separators

Sometimes it is useful to employ a separator in a file menu system. This is little more than a horizontal line that separates subchoices from one another. A typical File menu uses separators to segregate generic choices. For example, in the File menu, separators appear between Close and Save, Save All and Find File, and Print and Exit. Some users feel that the appearance of a separator across the board makes it easier to see the choices.

Creating Menus

Tip

In order to use the Menu Designer, you should be working in the Form Designer and be actively creating or changing a form.

Generically speaking, menus created with the Menu Designer present a list of choices with an active default. When you make a selection, a menu item initiates that task—it can start a process or display a dialog box. Choosing a menu triggers an event that causes a piece of code to execute. Almost all applications have at least one menu: it can appear within the form windows or replace the dBASE for Windows menu.

As you saw previously, dBASE provides several types of menus in the Menu Designer:

■ *Menu bars* are top-level menu objects that appear on the form. Each form has only one menu bar. Menu bars are created automatically when a new menu is created.

■ A *drop-down* menu, as the name suggests, drops down when the cursor enters its boundaries.

■ *Cascading menus* appear to the right of drop-down menus to display another depth of options. They normally have an indicator (in dBASE, a right-pointing triangle) embedded toward the end of the line on which the option is available.

The Menu Hierarchy

Menus are organized in a hieriarchy of top-down orders that are known as *objects*. The top object is the menu bar, which is positioned across the top of the screen from left to right. At the next level, menus that drop down are those that appear immediately beneath the menu bar. Any subsequent level of menus always emanates from the second level menu bar.

Menus are always associated with one another in a *parent-child relationship*. Top-level menus are always the parent menus; whatever drops down from those are always known as the child menus. As in real life, a child menu always belongs to a parent menu, although a parent menu may have many child menus.

Think about the menu choices that appear at the top of each Windows GUI screen. Their order is standardized in the File, Edit, View... order. Underneath any File menu—no matter which software program it is, you always expect to see New, Open, Close, Save As..., Save, and so on. Consider these standardizations as you go about designing your own menu system.

> **Note**
>
> The most important and frequently used menus should be as accessible as possible to users. Those that are not used as much should also be easy to find. A good menu design takes both of these options into account.

Tip
You will find that simplicity in menus pays dividends to the user that uses them. A menu system jammed with useless choices appears cluttered—often falling into disuse. A simple menu system has users gravitating toward it.

Creating a New Menu Object

To add a new menu object, you should first be in the Form Designer. Choose **L**ayout, T**o**ols, Design **M**enu. The Menu Designer appears.

To open an existing menu, from the Navigator or Catalog window, choose **F**ile, **O**pen. When the Open File dialog box appears, select the Menu File **T**ype. Select the Design **M**enu option, and then choose OK. The Form Designer opens, and the Menu Designer appears with the menu you selected.

Figure 7.1 depicts an [Untitled] Menu Designer with the cursor positioned in a box, waiting for text-entry from the user.

Creating Drop-Down Menus

You can add a drop-down menu to the menu bar as well as to individual menu items on the drop-down menu. To add a new drop-down menu, begin typing the text for the menu title at the cursor position in the menu bar. To create a second menu to the right, choose **M**enu, I**n**sert Menu Item. Then type the text of the menu title inside the newly created textbox.

Figure 7.2 shows two titles, *Edit* and *File*, as part of a new drop-down menu. This drop-down menu is saved as an .MNU menu file.

Fig. 7.1
The Menu
Designer.

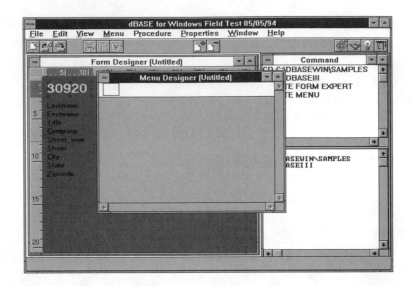

> **Note**
>
> As a menu is created and saved, the Menu Designer saves the file, complete with the
> embedded program code that defines the menu with an .MNU extension. Unless you
> save it elsewhere, the file is always saved in the default DBASEWIN directory.

Fig. 7.2
Adding a new
drop-down menu.

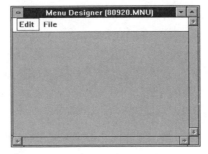

To add a menu item to a drop-down menu, choose **M**enu, **In**sert Menu Item.
A new item appears below the selected menu, as shown in figure 7.3.

Next, type the menu title text. You can add an almost limitless number of
drop-down titles. If you run out of space, expand the window boundaries
until you have more room.

In figure 7.3, a series of new items, *save as...*, *close,* and *open,* appears in the
parent file.

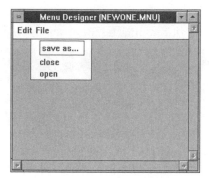

Fig. 7.3
A series of new
items in a drop-
down menu.

Creating Cascading Menus

You can add cascading menus to a drop-down menu or to another cascading menu. To add a new cascading menu, select the parent drop-down menu or cascading menu; then choose **M**enu, **In**sert Menu Item. A new cascading menu appears. Type the text item that you want to access from this section. Again, you may continue to add cascading titles until you have exhausted your allotted space. If this occurs, you may want to take a long, considered look at what you created. Usually, less is more.

Figure 7.4 shows a cascading menu addition to open (*new file*). Note the arrow pointing to new file—it indicates that additional items are available from the *open* menu choice.

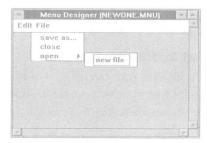

Fig. 7.4
A new cascading
menu.

First, type the menu title. Then add those items to a cascading menu by choosing **M**enu, **In**sert Item. A new item appears below the selected menu item. Then type that menu title.

Deleting a Menu

You can delete any menu if you no longer need it. To delete a menu, select the menu you wish to delete. Then choose **M**enu, **D**elete Selected. Menu Designer removes the menu and any subordinate data. Note that the only way to get a menu back after you deleted it is to cancel or Abandon and Close your changes without saving the file. Then open it again and continue.

> **Note**
>
> Note that deleting a *parent menu* (the top menu) automatically deletes its child menus.

Creating Pushbuttons

A pushbutton is a control that institutes an action when the user clicks it or presses Enter while the button is active. The act of choosing the button triggers the button's event, causing the code to execute. Examples of a pushbutton's actions are opening, closing, or displaying something, or beginning a process.

Pushbuttons usually, but not always, appear in dialog boxes. SpeedBar buttons, which are variations of pushbuttons, can also appear in a SpeedBar on a form.

A dialog box always has at least one pushbutton that closes the dialog box, but many have several buttons that perform different actions. Two types of pushbuttons are normally used in a form: a standard type that has as its basis generic buttons; and dBASE custom pushbuttons, which are predesigned with graphics and code. Such custom buttons include the OK, Cancel, Modify, and Help buttons—common in Windows interface boxes. You also can customize pushbuttons to save time and standardize your efforts.

Adding a Standard Pushbutton

Click the PushButton control on the Standard tab of the Controls Palette and move the pointer to where you want to place the button. Then click, or press and drag, the button to the required size.

Figure 7.5 shows a standard pushbutton placed on a form.

You may change the button label by entering a descriptive name from the Text property. Once you are satisfied with the position of the button label, click View, Object Properties. Here you may make changes to as many different items as you wish. The available options are the Access, Edit, Font, Identification, Position, and Visual properties. Clicking a main title with a plus sign in this dialog box expands the box. Type the new text under the title you are interested in changing and close the Properties box. The change takes effect when the dialog box closes.

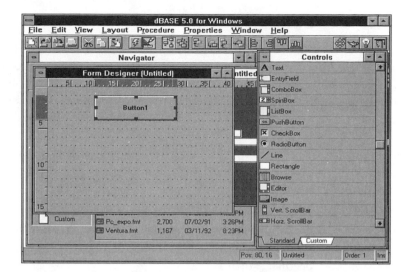

Fig. 7.5
A standard
pushbutton.

Adding a Custom Button

Click the button control on the Custom tab of the Controls Palette. Move the pointer to where you want the button. Figure 7.6 shows several customized button controls, including the ubiquitous OK and Cancel buttons, on a Design menu.

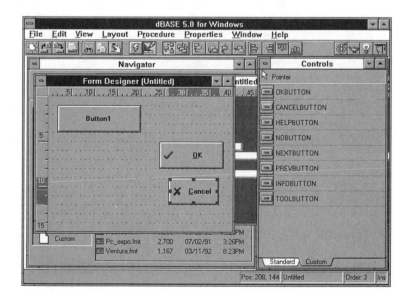

Fig. 7.6
Custom buttons
added to a design
menu.

Creating SpeedBars

A SpeedBar consists of more than one pushbutton. A SpeedBar usually groups its buttons in a horizontal or vertical row as graphical icons. These buttons differ from the other button classes because they appear in an application window whereas pushbuttons most often appear in dialog boxes; they do not become active when the user presses a keyboard combination. SpeedBar buttons usually have graphical labels, not text labels. Unlike pushbuttons, SpeedBar buttons do not become activated when the user presses the Tab or Shift+Tab key combinations. The only way that a SpeedBar can be activated is when the user clicks it with the mouse.

To add a new button to a SpeedBar, click the PushButton control on the Standard tab of the Controls Palette. Move the pointer to where you want the button. Then click, or press and drag, the button to the required size. You then must set the SpeedBar property to True.

To remove a button label, delete the text in the Text property. Chapter 6 describes how to add graphics to your SpeedBars.

Figure 7.7 illustrates an additional button added to a design menu.

Fig. 7.7
An additional button.

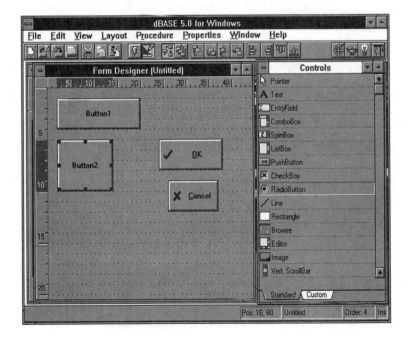

The Default Button

A default button may be specified that is immediately active when the dialog box is opened. A default button is the most obvious choice on a dialog box; the user simply presses the Enter key to choose it.

If a dialog box prompts the user for a confirmation before deleting data, the default button is usually the No or Cancel selections.

The default button is the first button that you should add to your form. If you want to change the default button, display Access properties, and then set the Default property to True. All other buttons on the form should be set to False.

Adding a Graphic to a Pushbutton

Graphics are used with buttons to reinforce visual information about what a pusbutton does. As you are perhaps already starting to see, in a typical Windows application, a Yes or Cancel confirmation button in a dialog box has either the word *Yes* or *Cancel* and a corresponding checkmark, or an *X* sign within the same box. A No button has a semi-stop sign as its graphical counterpart.

dBASE for Windows has its own palette of standard graphical icons that you can use with these applications. Alternatively, you can use your own bitmap image, but you may have to scan and edit it first.

To add a graphic to a pushbutton, complete the following:

1. Select the pushbutton that you want to use.

2. Display the Bitmap Properties from the Object Inspector. This is accomplished by selecting **V**iew, **O**bject Properties from the main menu. Find and open the Bitmap Properties box. (With this dialog box open, clicking a main title with a plus sign next to it expands the dialog box.)

3. Enter the name of the bitmap that you want to use. To see additional choices, select the Tool button at the end of the Focus, Disable, UpBitmap, or DownBitmap lines. Choosing the location and the Bitmap picture provides an additional listing of pictures.

4. Several choices are available in the Bitmap Properties dialog box. *Focus Bitmap* is the graphic that appears when the pusbutton is activated; *Disable Bitmap* is the graphic that appears when the pushbutton is

disabled; *UpBitmap* is the graphic that appears when the pushbutton is lowered; *DownBitmap* is the graphic that appears when the pushbutton is raised.

The change takes effect upon closing the dialog box.

Saving Changes

Save the design to keep the changes that you made to the menu. You choose File, Save **A**s to create a different name for your file, or choose File, **S**ave to save a preexisting file. Make sure that you save the file with a .MNU extension, and not as a .WFM (Form) file.

Figure 7.8 illustrates the dialog box that appears when you choose Save **A**s from the **F**ile menu.

Fig. 7.8
Saving your design with an .MNU extension.

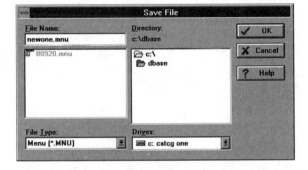

> **Note**
>
> Abandoning changes to a design is a matter of canceling the changes that you made. Choose File, Abandon to execute this action. Alternatively, you can use the key combination Ctrl+Q.

Summary

This short chapter showed you how to use the Form and Menu Designers' capabilities to create and use your own menus with your applications. New menu objects were discussed, and you learned how to create and design cascading or drop-down menus, how to create and place pushbuttons on a form, and how to create SpeedBars.

Chapter 8

Using the Expression Builder

An Expression Builder, as the name implies, allows you to build a series of dBASE elements (called *expressions*), such as constants, functions, and operators that, when executed, evaluate to a single value. dBASE for Windows helps to assemble expressions from easy ones to those considered more complex. You can display any resulting value as a character, date, logical, or numeric value, or as something more specialized, such as an object, a *codeblock* (a short series of commands enclosed in braces ({})), or a function pointer.

Expressions enjoy a constant value; examples are a fieldname (LASTNAME), or a character string ("CO"). A constant, as the name implies, doesn't change: LASTNAME is always a person's last name. In the case of a variable, you take a constant and *do* something with it. In the case of a variable such as PRICE, you can multiply it by a factor (PRICE*0.35); perhaps you want to mark up the PRICE, but you still want to know how much you paid for the item. This equation yields a different value for each examined record. Expressions are typically used with values for such things as creating subsets of data or windows.

In dBASE terms, an *expression* represents a value and does not contain a command. On the other hand, a *command* is a verb. A complete language statement consists of both a command and one or more expressions.

Once you are finished writing an expression, you can insert it into the current window or dialog box without further modification, where it is ready for execution. But you don't have to use the Expression Builder to achieve success. In fact, many programmers are confident enough of their skills that they can type correct syntax into a Command window and have it execute flawlessly the first time. However, because everyone needs a little help now and again, the Expression Builder provides guidance.

dBASE also provides a so-called *safety net* for users unfamiliar with the dBASE command syntax. Although it lies silently in wait for you to make a syntactical mistake before springing into action, it can be very helpful when it comes time to bail users out of trouble. The safety net is covered in detail in the section entitled "Using the Safety Net," later in this chapter.

Opening the Expression Builder

Before you begin, make sure that you open at least one table and it is on your desktop. Then click the Command window to activate it. At that point, an icon appears on both the SpeedBars of the Command window and the Text Editor that represents the Expression Builder. This icon is shown in the left margin.

You can open Expression Builder with one of the following actions:

- Clicking the Expression Builder button on the SpeedBar.

- Choosing **E**dit, **B**uild Expression (or Ctrl+E).

- Activating the Command window and typing `GETEXPR()`.

Figure 8.1 demonstrates the opening view of the Build Expression dialog box.

Fig. 8.1

The Build Expression dialog box is the opening screen.

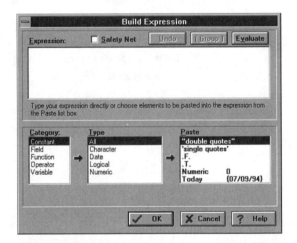

> **Note**
>
> The Build Expression dialog box (**E**xpression box) is shaded white when the safety net feature is off. The dialog box is shaded gray when this feature is on.

The **E**xpression box is the workspace that garners the most attention in the Build Expression dialog box. Below the **E**xpression box are three element lists that help you to select each element of your expression:

- The **C**ategory listbox contains all the main items used in an expression. These items include Constants, Fields, Functions, Operators, and Variables. You make the selection from the category box, and then complete the boxes to the right. These listboxes change as you make the Category determinations.

- The **T**ype listbox provides you with choices for the category (shown in the dynamic Category list). When Field is selected in the **C**ategory list, the second listbox is labeled "Table" rather than "Type," and shows open tables. If you choose a type, the elements of that type appear in the third listbox, the **P**aste listbox.

- The **P**aste listbox shows the actual building blocks and their types within each Category.

The expression is built, assembled, and evaluated in the **E**xpression box, based on these three choices (Category, Table, and Paste). As each element is added, prompts appear that assist you in completing an error-free expression the first time!

Using the Safety Net

Before commencing any expression-building activities, decide whether you want to have the safety net on. With the safety net active, you are limited to selecting elements from the list located in the **P**aste listbox, instead of being able to type elements directly into the Expression box. Colored placeholders represent elements that you need to replace. You can position the insertion point between elements only in the Expression box. If you are not familiar with command syntax, or suspect you may have trouble with it, you should probably turn the safety net on. However, if you desire maximum flexibility to type in parts of an expression, or cut and paste others, leave the safety net off. Then you can type information directly into the Expression box. From there, you can cut, copy, and paste your way through the expressions with the Clipboard commands.

To turn the safety net from one state to the other, click the **S**afety Net checkbox, located near the top of the Build Expression dialog box (review fig. 8.1).

Starting an Expression

Begin to build the expression by selecting one or more elements and inserting them into the **E**xpression box. You can do this by clicking the desired text and dragging it to its location within the **E**xpression box. If you make a mistake (heavens!) either click the **U**ndo button to revert to the last entered operation, or manually delete the text. You can use the Backspace or Delete keys to remove several errors.

You can group items in parentheses by selecting the items in the **E**xpression box and clicking the **G**roup button. When a function or variable is clicked in the **P**aste listbox, a description of the function and its syntax appears in the information panel below the **P**aste listbox. If you click a fieldname, the information includes details of field size and type.

Some functions accept several sets of arguments. Each variation appears in the **P**aste listbox, followed by one or more periods. Using these types of commands, you'll find it more helpful to use the safety net feature, at least until you get used to the command format.

In the example shown in figure 8.2, a table named AIIM is open. From the **C**ategory Field, the table name appears in the **T**able listbox, and the fieldnames for that table are inside the **P**aste listbox. The code in the figure asks for all CITY within the AIIM table that equal "NEW YORK". When the E**v**aluate button box is checked, the result (.F. meaning none) appears below the main expression box. Below the **C**ategory listbox, dBASE shows you that the AIIM->CITY fieldname is a 17-character field.

Fig. 8.2
dBASE evaluates
the results of an
expression.

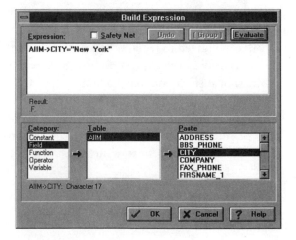

Working with Placeholders

After you paste expression elements (such as AIIM->ADDRESS, RMHT->LASTNAME, and so on) into the syntax, you will want to replace your placeholders with live data.

If the safety net is off, click each placeholder individually and replace it with the appropriate information.

If the safety net is on, dBASE highlights characters that you need to replace with values. Whenever the characters *Op* appear in white, for example, you need to specify an operator there. Operands, or argument placeholders, that appear in yellow represent fieldnames or values. *expC*, for example, can be any constant that evaluates to a character, such as the name of a character field, a function that returns characters, or a literal string of characters embedded between quotation marks.

In the following example, the Expression Builder creates a sample command. The safety net is on.

1. First, identify a table by single clicking it from the Navigator window. Once you have done this, you can access the Expression Builder. Load the Expression Builder by accessing **E**dit, **B**uild Expression. Alternatively, press Ctrl+E from the keyboard.

2. Turn on the Safety Net by clicking in the appropriate box at the top of the Expression Builder.

3. Fill in the expression by clicking on the Category, Type and Paste boxes. In the Category, choose FUNCTION. In the Type, scroll down with the scroll bar until *String Data* comes into view. Select it by clicking it. Finally, access the Paste box, and scroll down until you find the SUBSTR command. When you double-click this last portion of the expression, the entire phrase is pasted into the Expression box. Note that the main portion of the command is colored in black, and that the various pieces that you have just selected are highlighted in yellow.

> **Note**
>
> If you want to fly by the seat of your pants, click the Safety Net off. This activity allows you to type the command in from the keyboard into a white Expression Box. With the Safety Net on, the Expression Box is grayed out, and your information appears in black and yellow.

Tip

If you don't want
to type directly,
right-click the
mouse button and
type the phrase
into the box that
appears at that
point.

Tip

If you don't want
to type, center the
cursor over the
highlighted choice
and hold down
the mouse button.
Drag the informa-
tion to the correct
location in the
variable phrase.
Alternatively, you
may press the
Spacebar and
watch the text
being placed into
the expression.

4. Position the cursor near the first yellow string. Rechoose the Constant category and the character type. Then double-click the double-quotes Paste option to insert those double quotes into the expression. The double-quotes appear in the expression. Click near the the double-quotation marks and begin typing. When you have the phrase inserted, press Enter.

5. Next, replace the start ExpN variable by positioning the cursor near that part of the phrase. Select the Numeric type in the Constant category. Select the 0 by double-clicking it and dragging it to the Expression box.

As you enter the elements and values of an expression, with the Safety Net turned on, the Expression Builder continually evaluates your expression. At any stage in the process, you may click the Evaluate box at the top of the Expression Builder at the top of the screen, and watch as the results appear in the Results pane.

When you finish with the expression, click OK and watch as the expression is pasted into the Command window. You also can click the dialog box from where you started the Expression Builder.

Note

Click the Evaluate button before completing your final paste of the expression into dBASE. If you find that you made a mistake, you may select the entire expression and drag through it with the mouse. With the expression still highlighted, reopen the Expression Builder. The selected text should appear in the Expression box. You may reevaluate it, making changes to it until you have an accurate, logical statement.

In figure 8.3, the safety net box is checked. This action causes activation of the **E**xpression box, which is now shaded. The **U**ndo button bar is active as well.

In figure 8.3, the AIIM.DBF table and the ZIPCODE fieldname are selected for exercise. With the Safety Net turned on, the Category is set to Operator, the Type is All, and the greater than sign (>) has been pasted into the equation. Once the value is completed (VALUE is grayed out in the example because it is yellow), dBASE looks in the ZIPCODE fieldname in the AIIM table for a ZIPCODE number greater than the number you typed into the Expression Builder.

If you enter two elements, such as a fieldname and a placeholder to a string, the Expression Builder inserts the Op placeholder between them. When you replace it, choose the Operator category. Then select Type and the specific operator you want to paste.

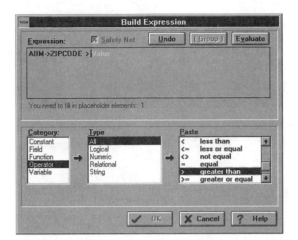

Fig. 8.3
Replacing a character place-holder with a constant.

Figure 8.4 replaces the *Op* placeholder with an equal sign. In this example, the user is asking to display the company fieldname *3M Company*.

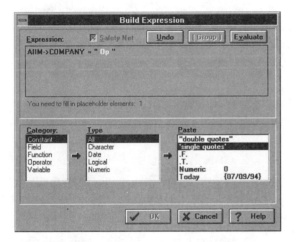

Fig. 8.4
Creating the Op placeholder.

Note

Placeholders are little more than temporary holders for substitute data. In the previous examples, the abstruse phrase expC/Memo field was used for an operator. The English equivalent is *character expression or Memo field*. All you are doing is telling the computer that you will substitute your own characters for those supplied by the machine.

Figure 8.5 shows the resulting command after the *Op* placeholder is replaced with the text.

Fig. 8.5
Replacing the Op
placeholder.

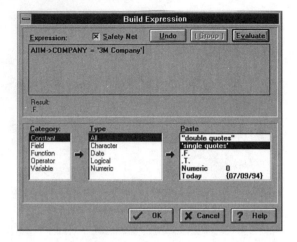

Finishing an Expression

After you have finished writing and editing an expression, choose OK to
paste it into the window or dialog box. You should lend some thought
to clicking the E**v**aluate button before pasting the expression into dBASE
to make sure that everything is as it should be. If the context requires a specific result type, the Expression Builder checks the expression's type before
pasting it into the environment.

If the safety net is turned on, the Expression Builder doesn't evaluate the
expression properly. With the safety net off, the evaluation is attempted and
stops when the incorrect syntax is encountered, which is pretty quickly after
it is submitted.

If an expression requires editing, highlight it and then open the Expression
Builder. Watch the selected text appear in the upper **E**xpression box. You
may then edit the offending characters until they are correct.

Figure 8.6 shows an expression taken from the Command window and placed
into the Expression Builder.

Adding Your Own User-Defined Functions

You may have custom functions that you want to add to the Expression
Builder. In dBASE parlance, these custom functions are called *user-defined
functions* (UDFs).

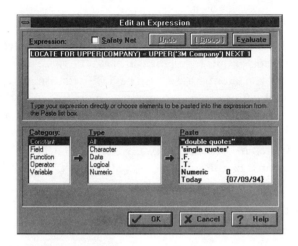

Fig. 8.6
An expression is
removed from the
Command
window for
editing.

You can add your own UDFs into a file named DBASEWIN.FNF. This file
is part of the initial dBASE file inventory, and is located in the default
C:\DBASEWIN\BIN directory. Once these functions are added to the
DBASEWIN.FNF file, those definitions appear in the information boxes
and listboxes.

Use a line editor to make any changes to the DBASEWIN.FNF file.

Table 8.1 shows the listing of editable fields in the UDF file DBASEWIN.FNF.

Table 8.1 Editable Fields in DBASE.FNF	
Fieldname	**Description**
Name	The function's name.
Name_ext	One or more periods to indicate that alternative versions of this function exist. In most cases, this field should be left blank.
Purpose	The function's purpose.
Arguments	A comma-delimited list of arguments for the function named in the Name field.
Categories	A comma-delimited list of language types displayed in the Type listbox.

Note: All fields are character type. The field length can be changed.

When a function is selected in the Paste listbox, information is displayed
from the DBASEWIN.FNF table in the information panel. The first line is
constructed from the name in the Name field, an open parenthesis, the
arguments listed in the ARGUMENTS field, and a closed parenthesis.

Tip
You might create a
backup copy of
this file in case you
make an error that
corrupts the file
when you run
dBASE. That way,
you have some
method of recov-
ery is something
goes awry.

Tip
You can use the PgUp or PgDn keys to go from record to record within the DBASEWIN.FNF file. The phrase `GOTO RECORD` *n*, when typed at the Command window, positions the pointer at the defined *nth* record. You can then edit that record.

To add your user-defined functions (UDFs), open the DBASEWIN.FNF file from the Command window by typing `USE DBASEWIN.FNF`. This file *cannot* be opened from the Navigator because it isn't a .DBF database. Add the information required for the function. It can appear in more than one category if you separate each category name with commas. You can also create a new category by entering its name in the Category field, although you can't change the fieldnames listed in the table. Also, any additional fields that you add are accepted, but ignored by the Expression Builder.

You can easily edit the DBASEWIN.FNF file in dBASE for Windows by typing the following commands in the Command window. Note that although this file is *not* a dBASE table, it behaves similarly to one in its opening, editing, and append commands.

From the Command window, type the following information:

```
USE C:\DBASEWIN\BIN\DBASEWIN.FNF
```

When the computer returns to the cursor, type the word `EDIT` in the Command window to edit the first record. Alternatively, should you wish to add a record at the end of the file, use the `APPEND` command.

Figure 8.7 shows the DBASEWIN.FNF file open with the Name, Name_ext, Purpose, Arguments, and Categories fieldnames for the name ABS (Absolute) positioned in the box.

Fig. 8.7
The DBASEWIN.FNF file.

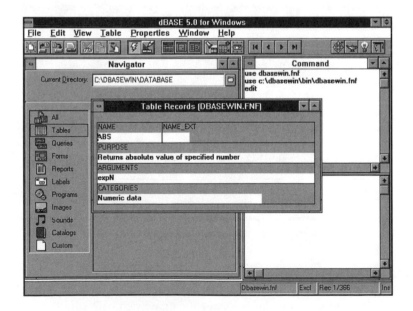

Summary

This chapter showed you how to build complete syntax expressions by filling in the necessary blanks in the Expression Builder. You also learned about the safety net feature, learned how to use placeholders in the Expression Builder, and how to add user-defined functions to your expressions. Finally, the concept of user-defined functions and the use of the exclusive file that holds this information were explained.

Chapter 9

Reporting and Printing

Screen-based data that has spent its life on your hard disk, only to be manipulated and viewed on a computer screen, enjoys a limited capability. The obvious extension is to create reports suitable for printing with a variety of printing devices.

Reports in dBASE for Windows allow you to perform calculations, including cross-tabulations on your data; work with data from more than one table; create true WYSIWYG (*What-You-See-Is-What-You-Get*) reports; and create labels suitable for mass mailings with a report generator.

The greatest advantage to graphics output devices is that page layouts, typefaces, line and box drawing, and imported images may all be used by dBASE for Windows to take full advantage of this developing technology.

Printing Data

It's no secret that the availability of printers on the open market has exploded in recent history. Almost every hardware vendor, it seems, has the latest and greatest in printing technology: if you want high-end graphics that print at upwards of 2400 DPI (or higher) or a color printer, you can get them, although at a price. The middle-of-the road inkjet printers are finding favor with those markets that demand high-end graphics at a pauper's price. And dot-matrix printers still maintain their popularity for those who want to print reports, labels, and invoices, but don't want to go to the expense of printing something that has a limited value.

dBASE for Windows uses current device drivers to configure your existing printers during the initial installation. This is performed with the Windows setup files, and with the printer drivers that come with dBASE. You should have little trouble in getting your existing printers installed and working in a single-user environment. However, users of networks, and those with esoteric printers that use PostScript emulations, may find that their initial setup configuration isn't to their liking, and that they are obliged to tweak the as-installed configurations before getting down to the business at hand.

Printing Outside the Main dBASE for Windows Program

Generally speaking, dBASE for Windows uses existing Windows printer software drivers and software to print your material. If you need to change the printer or printer settings, choose File, Printer Setup while you have a file open. The resulting output is printed with both a header and a footer. By default, header information includes the window name or the name of the current file, whereas the footer prints the page number.

You can use the Windows Printer Setup utility file in Windows to configure your printer. Alternatively, from the Command window inside dBASE for Windows, type the **CHOOSEPRINTER()** command. This command launches the Windows Printer Setup utility, from where you configure additional printers.

You can print a table directly from a series of editing views, including the Browse, Form, Columnar, and Query Results whenever you need a rough outline of the information without the benefit of formatting.

In an editing mode, choose File, Print; or click the Print button in the SpeedBar. If you don't have a table open, the Open Table Required dialog box appears, requesting you to open either a table or a query, as shown in figure 9.1.

Fig. 9.1
The Open Table Required dialog box.

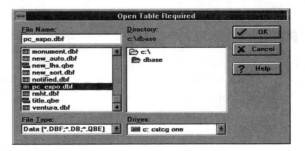

Figure 9.2 shows the configuration possibilities for printing. Note that before you see this dialog box, you must have a table or query open. If you do not have one of these open, you are prompted to open one before the Print Records dialog box appears.

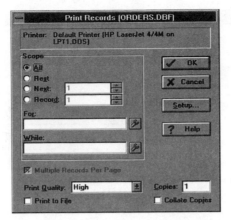

Fig. 9.2
The Print Records
dialog box.

The options in the bottom of this dialog box allow you to control the printed output to the extent that it applies to print quality (still mostly controlled by the print engine), and the number of copies you want to print.

The Scope section permits you to choose from the following options:

■ **All.** Prints all records.

■ **Rest.** Prints all remaining records starting with the current record.

■ **Next.** Prints the next *n* number of records specified, starting with the current record.

■ **Record.** Prints a specified record number.

■ **For.** Prints all records specified by the For expression (as in: `"Print all for ZIPcode="80132"`). This command prints all your records that have 80132 as the ZIP code.

■ **While.** Prints all records selected by the **W**hile expression (as in: `"Print all while city .ne. "Colorado Springs"`). This command prints only those records that do not include the city, Colorado Springs.

Figure 9.3 shows the Print Setup dialog box. Before you see this dialog box, you must have a table or query open. If you do not have one of these open, you are prompted to open one before the Print Records dialog box appears for you to use.

A more complete discussion about printing outside applications programs such as dBASE is available in your Windows User manual.

Fig. 9.3
The Print Setup
dialog box.

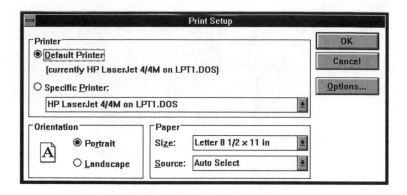

Printing the Table Structure Layouts

In a Table Records window, derived output reflects the on-screen layout. From the Browse window, a printout is generated in which all records appear as columns and rows. Form and Columnar layouts are similarly produced.

You will probably find that Form and Columnar layouts provide the best results for quick data printing because the data in each record fits on a single page in landscape mode. Printing in portrait mode sometimes causes extra opportunities because word wrap beyond the 66th character position on a page does not necessarily conclude the length of a line, which sometimes goes out to character position 132. Most modern laser printers allow users to choose a landscape or portrait mode (with portrait being the default) within the Printer and Setup mode.

Word wrap beyond the 66th character position on a page does not necessarily conclude the length of a line, and you may find that information is lopped off from the 66th character onward. You may also find that the lines in your document are formatted for a length longer than the print codes have formatted them. This causes the line feed to wrap, which causes a ripple effect all the way down the page.

Note

You will probably be obliged to experiment with a new printer, or with a printer that was installed correctly but still refuses to cooperate.

In the Table Design mode, dBASE prints the table's structure on demand. (You type the command **LIST STRUCTURE** in the Command window, and the table's structure is printed in the Results pane. Alternatively, you can type **LIST STRUCTURE TO PRINT**, and the results are sent to the printer.)The output provides a fieldname, its type, width, number of decimal places, and the type of index.

Figure 9.4 shows the Table Structure/Design Mode, and its printable options. Choose **F**ile, **P**rint to print the table structure.

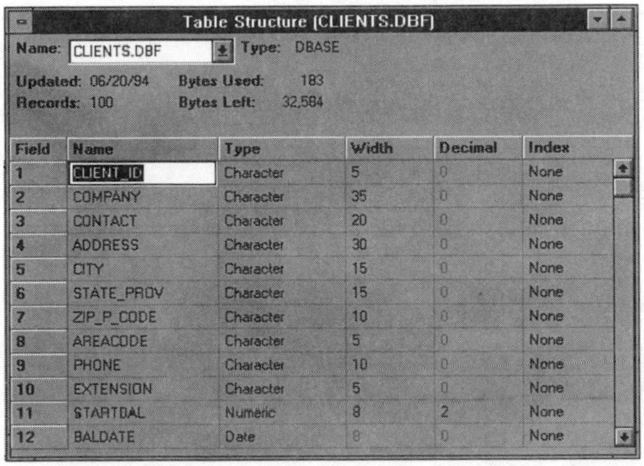

Fig. 9.4
The Table Structure information screen.

Printing Query Results

dBASE prints any query while you are in the Query Designer. You must open a table before going into the Query Designer, or dBASE prompts you to open a table before you can proceed.

You can print any QBE (Query by Example) file that shows the file contents.

Figure 9.5 shows the Query Results print window. This window is similar to that shown in figure 9.4.

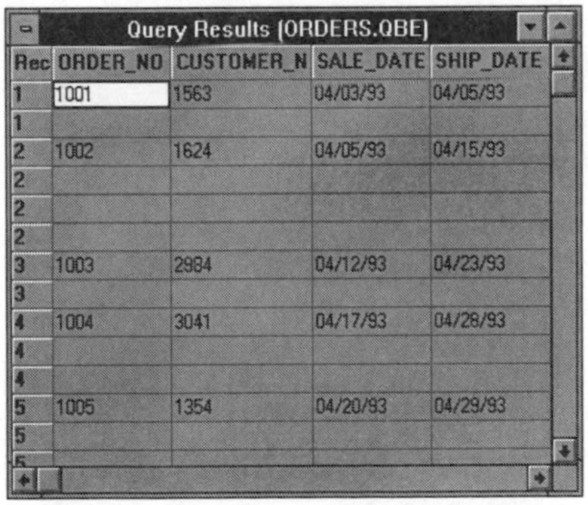

Fig. 9.5
The Query Results information screen.

Choose **F**ile, **P**rint to print the query results to the printer.

Printing a Form Design

When the Form Designer is open, you can print the information in your form. A printed form includes the objects and their contents. Bitmapped files, such as the .PCX and .BMP files, print as they appear. Scroll bars and other housekeeping data are not printed.

Figure 9.6 shows a Customer—View Mode Form Design. A signature has been digitized and entered into this form, as you can see in the bottom-right corner. The Notes section allows users to take notes about a particular customer so that a record is composed of calls and error reporting.

Fig. 9.6
The Form
Designer.

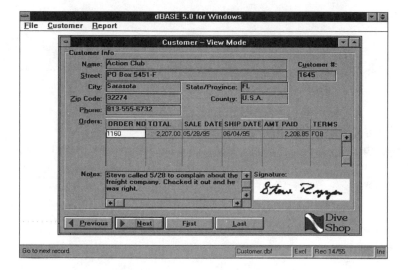

Printing from the Text Editor

The dBASE for Windows Text Editor also allows printing from within its purview. The Print dialog box in the text editor allows you to specify the page range and other controls. This text editor is suitable for creating text files such as .PRG (program) files, queries with a .QBE extension, forms with a .WFM extension, or any ASCII-based text file.

Figure 9.7 shows the Notepad editor. The user typed the MODIFY command in the Command window, and dBASE opened the Text Editor with the file POOH.PRG ready for you to populate.

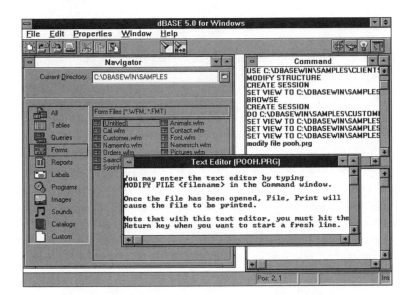

Fig. 9.7
The Notepad
editor.

Printing from the Crystal Reports Report Writer

dBASE for Windows includes an integrated Report Writer designed for those who require complete control over the printed word. To launch this report writer, choose Reports or Labels from the Navigator and then double-click the Untitled icon. Alternatively, choose File, New, Report.

The Report Writer works by linking your proposed report to a table or query, and then placing fields in the Report Designer as you want to see them printed. When the report is generated and then printed, the information appears in the correct X,Y coordinates.

For more information, see the section entitled "Using the Crystal Reports Report Writer."

Sending Output to a File

You can send output to a temporary file on a disk somewhere within your system before sending it to the printer. After the output is sent to the printer and printed, the output file is erased.

Caution

If you use the commands SET PRINTER TO FILE *<filename>* or SET DEVICE TO FILE *<filename>*, nothing happens to your output because the file contains printer control codes and it may not be readable as a standard text file.

A @SAY command sends nonstreaming text output to your printer using a system called *absolute addressing*. In this system, as text is sent to the printer, dBASE positions each character on the page according to something called a *coordinate plane*. In this coordinate plane, characters are mapped into a two-dimensional grid using a normal X,Y coordinate scheme. One normally accepts that in this system, address 0,0 is at the top-left corner of the page, or at the top-left corner of the area reserved for printing.

The width of the character cells depends on the value of _ppitch in the printer's control codes, which are different for each printer, except that the height of each character cell is always one-sixth of an inch: some are the equivalent of pica or elite in the dot matrix printer world, whereas laser printers use a page description language (PDL) to place characters on a page. If the point size of the current font exceeds the preset height, each line of output occupies more than one row of character cells.

The following piece of code sends output to a specified line and column location on the printer, and then prints the data contained between the quotation marks:

```
SET DEVICE TO PRINTER
@ 2, 1 SAY "This line will print at row 2, column 1"
@ 3, 10 SAY "This line prints at row 3, column 10"
CLOSE PRINTER
SET DEVICE TO SCREEN
```

You also can print information to relative positions on the printer's paper. Two commands, PROW() (for printer row number) and PCOL() (for printer column number) allow you to position output on the page relative to the printer location. If you know the printhead's location on the page, you can calculate the coordinates of the material you want to print. The following piece of code allows you to print a character string 10 rows below and five columns to the right of the printer's current head position:

```
SET DEVICE TO PRINTER
@ PROW() + 10, PCOL() + 5 SAY "Print the text here..."
SET DEVICE TO SCREEN
CLOSE PRINTER
```

You can set the page length to the number of lines per page (which is 66 for a normal sheet of paper) by using the _plength variable.

At the same time, you can set portrait or landscape mode by using the _porientation variable. For example, if _porientation="portrait" you have to change _plength from 55 or 60 lines for an 11-inch page to 51 lines for a full page.

Margins and indentations are controlled by several system variables that direct width, columns, margin, and indentation.

Table 9.1 illustrates printing variables and their contribution to the printing process.

Table 9.1 Variables Used for Printing	
Variable	**Purpose**
_ploffset	Determines the distance from the left edge of the paper to the left margin of the print area.
_lmargin	Sets the left margin of the printed output from the beginning of the print area.
_rmargin	Sets the right margin of printed output from the end of the print area.
_pcolno	Determines the column in which the first line of text begins printing.
_indent	Determines an additional indentation for the first line of a paragraph.
pcopies	Determines how many times the output is printed when a print job executes.
_peject	Determines if and when the printer should eject a sheet of paper.
_plineno	Determines the current line number of the printed output.
_ptabs	Determines the current setting for tabulations.
_padvance	Determines where on the page the page advances.
_pageno	Prints the current page number.
_prow	Determines the current row position of the print head on a page.
_pcol	Determines the current column position of the print head on a page.
_plength	Determines the length of the paper.
_pspacing	Determines the spacing on the page. The number 2 is double spacing; 3, triple spacing, and so on.

(continues)

Table 9.1 Continued	
Variable	**Purpose**
_porientation	Determines the orientation of the page. _porientation is set to portrait with the command _porientation="portrait", and _porientation="Landscape" prints in landscape mode.
_ppitch	Determines the printed pitch. A value of _ppitch="Elite" prints in an Elite mode, whereas _ppitch="Pica" prints in pica.

Line spacing and tab stops are determined and controlled through the use of the _pspacing and _tabs variables. If _pspacing equals 2, the subsequent output is double-spaced; set to 3, it is triple-spaced, and so on. Tabulations control the length of tab stops as in tabs="5,10,15,20". If tabs have *not* been specified, the dBASE default is every 8 spaces.

Formfeeds and pagination are controlled with the use of a _padvance command. This variable allows you to determine whether the printer advances the paper with a formfeed (ff), or a linefeed (lf). If the default formfeed is specified, the paper advances one page at a time, moving to the top of each new page according to the printer page length you set. Linefeeds are usually set for dot-matrix printers. You may want to print checks, in which case, short pages are the order of the day. For a setup of this type, set _plength to 20, and _padvance to "linefeeds".

You can generate page numbers with the _pageno, _pbpage, and _pepage variables. _pageno holds the current page number; _pbpage specifies the first page to be printed; _pepage specifies the last page to be printed. Those pages that are less than the _pbpage value or greater than the _pepage value do not print, because they are outside the specified range.

Using the Crystal Reports Report Writer

dBASE for Windows includes an integrated Report Writer designed for those who want complete control over the printed word.

To launch the Report Writer, choose Reports or Labels from the Navigator and then double-click the Untitled icon. Alternatively, choose File, New, Report.

Note

The Report Writer and Report Designer are basically the same things; although, it is important to understand that you use the Report Designer to design the look of the report. The Report Writer works by linking your proposed report to a table or query, then placing fields in the Report Designer as you want them printed.

Figure 9.8 shows the Crystal Reports Report Writer, with an [Untitled] report. The default Page Header, Details, and Page Footer are shown, along with the PC_EXPO.DBF fieldnames, ready for inclusion inside the form's Details section.

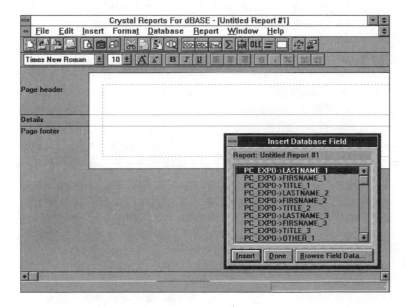

Fig. 9.8
The Crystal Reports screen.

The Report Writer works by linking your proposed report to a table or query, and then placing fields in the Report Designer as you want them printed. When the report is generated and printed, the information is displayed in the correct X,Y coordinates.

Note

The Report Writer does *not* write data back onto your original data files. The original files remain unchanged, no matter how much data manipulation is performed.

The Report Writer window displays typical Windows design features: Minimize and Maximize buttons appear in the upper-right corner of the window; the title bar appears horizontally at the top, with a menu bar located just below it. The SpeedBar is just below the menu bar, and a format bar appears just below the SpeedBar.

> **Note**
>
> As noted elsewhere in this chapter, use the Navigator to click an existing report's icon. A SpeedMenu appears. Select **R**un Report from the menu. dBASE runs the report selected and displays it in the Print Window.

Modifying an Existing Report

Choose **F**ile, **O**pen, **R**eport. Click the Reports icon, and select the Navigator, New Report.

The Report Designer appears complete with Page Header, Details, and Page Footer sections displayed on the report template. The Page Header is usually reserved for information appearing at the top of each page. Entries usually include a report title, field headings, and other information such as a date or time that the report was printed. At the opposite end of the report page is a Page Footer. Here, items such as a page number appear. You can have the date and time-printed field appear here, instead of at the top of the page. Footer information might also include a client name or a project number.

> **Note**
>
> If you are generating many reports, you might like to include a notation on the report for its location on your hard disk. With hundreds of reports floating around and people throwing old copies at you with requests to make changes for next month, or quarter, you need some system to find their reports. You might decide to store everything in a subdirectory like C:\REPORTS\ calling the report JUNE_94.RPT, so that you can find it easily the next time you print it. Information for the main body of the report appears in the space between the page header and page footer. This is the *Details Section;* the place where information appears for the body of the report.

Figure 9.9 shows the Insert Database Field dialog box. Click the database field, and then **I**nsert. The cursor changes to a box. Drag the cursor into the Details section of the form. Place the box where you want it and let go of the mouse button. The box drops where you placed it.

Section markers appear vertically in the right portion of the page. These are used to help you determine where on the form you are currently located. *PH* signifies *P*age *H*eader; *D* stands for *D*etail; *PF* means *P*age *F*ooter.

Fig. 9.9
The Insert Database
Field dialog box.

You may make changes and modifications to this report as you see fit by using the Insert Database Field dialog box to make those selections. As you make the selections, the fields are filled with a series of Xs for a character field (as in "XXXXXXXXX"); "5,555,555.55" for a numeric, or float, field; "DD/ MM/YY" for a date legend; and "YES/NO" if the field is a logical field.

If you want to see the report on-screen to determine its accuracy, use **F**ile, **P**rint, **W**indow, and watch the report being displayed in the print window. You may go back and forth between the window and the report form to perform tweaks to the report until you are satisfied with the way it looks.

You may go up and down within this window by using the arrow buttons located at the screen's bottom, but they are activated only if you have a multiscreen report. If you have a single-page report, they are grayed.

Similarly, a page counter helps you keep track of where you are on your report pages. The legend *Page 1 of 5*, for example, tells you that you are on the first of a five-page report.

A zoom button, similar to a magnifying glass image, allows you to see three separate report magnifications, or sizes. The Enhanced page size blows it up, so you won't need your reading glasses! The Actual page size displays data in a more normal, but full size depiction. The Full Size page size allows you to look at a full page of the report, sized to fit the size of your screen.

Creating a New Report

You can start to create a new report by choosing **F**ile, **N**ew, **R**eport. Click the Reports icon and select the Navigator, New Report.

Click the first SpeedBar icon (the printer icon), and then select Report. Alternatively, you may type **CREATE REPORT** in the Command window.

Similar to the modifying instructions you read earlier, the Report Designer appears with a Page Header, Details, and Page Footer sections, which are blank. You create the report by filling in the correct bits and pieces according to your needs.

Tip
After you finish the report, select **S**ave to overwrite the existing filename, or Save **A**s to create another file with a different name.

The Insert Database Field dialog box appears on-screen along with the Report Designer. A list of fields belonging to that table field appears—select the fields that you want to appear on the report. When you have a field selected, drag the field into the body of the report, and release the mouse button when it is placed correctly. After you finish the fieldname placement, you can add a report title and additional data.

You can insert a report title into the report form by selecting **I**nsert, Te**x**t Field. Type the information that you want to have in the report header. At your option, you may also insert database fields or special fields from the **I**nsert menu.

In some instances, you may not be comfortable with the way the report looks, or how the fieldnames are placed on the page. If this is the case, click the offending box and watch the black handles appear. You may then change the placement of that field by dragging the box to its new location.

Tip

You can group multiple fields by using a Shift+Click combination on the fields that you want to move in a single operation.

Figure 9.10 shows the effects of clicking the right mouse button with a database table field in focus. In this example, the word ADDRESS is selected. You want to change it to "Main Address." Highlight ADDRESS, delete it, and type **Main Address**. Click **A**ccept to continue. These new words should be placed in the Details section.

Fig. 9.10

The Edit Text Field dialog box.

Adding Individual Text to the Report

After you enter and position the data fields using the **I**nsert and **D**atabase Field, the program displays the Insert Database Field dialog box. You already made the selections and placed each field onto the report. However, the name of the field, along with the data that the field ultimately carries, appears in the Detail field.

These names can be somewhat cryptic to the uninitiated. For example, although LASTNAME is fairly easy to decipher, ACCT_REP may not be. In this example, you might want to change the legend to something like Client Name and Account Representative. You can type the new text at the cursor, and then move it into place.

Figure 9.11 shows the Format String dialog box. Click the right mouse button while a field is in focus on the Details section. You can align this text, hide it when printing data, or suppress it if the name is duplicated.

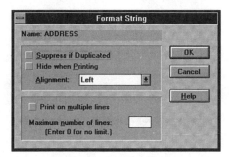

Fig. 9.11
The Format String dialog box.

Figure 9.12 shows a completed report. You have added a Page Number (click Insert, Special Field, and Page Number), and a Date (click Insert, Special Field, Date) in the Header section. A report title is created and centered (Main Contacts List, August, 1994). In the Details section, change the reporting words from the boring LASTNAME, FIRSTNAME, TITLE, and so on to something everyone recognizes.

Adding Value to the Report

You can alter textual data to support different fonts and sizes. You can have dBASE perform calculations on your report as it is being generated. You also can add graphics and spreadsheet data to your report to enhance the report's value.

Changing Fonts and Font Sizes. You may change any textual element on the report page at your convenience. There are generally two classes of information that you can change: the title information and the data.

Changing Title Information Font Size. If you want to change the title information, identify the text that you wish to change, and click and drag that text to highlight it. Then go to the top of the Report Writer Reports and find the current text type: the default is Times New Roman in a 12-point size. Click the down arrow next to the currently selected text style, and select the new style using the standard Windows method.

Fig. 9.12

A finished report.

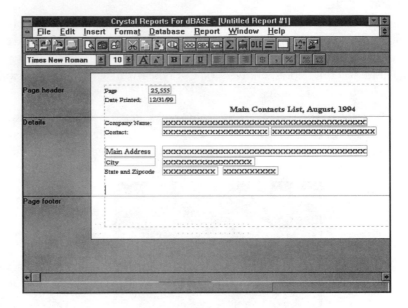

Next, decide what size you want that text to be by dropping the down arrow next to the 12-point default size. You may optionally select the large "A" or small "A" boxes to the right of the text size box. Each time you click the other box, the text size increments or decrements by one point size.

If you want to bold, italicize, or underline the text, choose those options from each of the three boxes next to the size boxes. If bolding and underlining are required, check both of the boxes. When you choose them, each box indents slightly to show that it is checked. To the right are the boxes that control left- center- and right-spacing. You may click these at your option according to the position required.

Changing Data Font Size. This option works in much the same fashion as the text declarations discussed in the preceding paragraph. The only real difference is that you must make sure that you highlight the box containing the data. You will know that the textbox is highlighted because black handles appear at each edge of the border. Once the box is enabled, you can make your changes.

> **Note**
>
> As you make changes to the size of the text within the box (represented by XXXXXs), the box increases or decreases slightly to accommodate those size changes. If there is insufficient room on the form, you see the Detail section of your report decrease incrementally to accommodate your new selection.

Inserting Calculations and Creating Formulas. To insert a calculation into the field, such as a column subtotal, select the Insert Subtotal function, and approve the Insert Subtotal dialog box.

To select the Insert Subtotal function, you must have a column of numeric data that can be summed. Obviously, a character field does not qualify. Position the cursor in the Details section of the report where you want the subtotal to appear. Then access **I**nsert, **S**ummary Field, and click Summary. Note that unless you have numeric fields in your report, this choice is grayed out. The Insert Subtotal dialog box holds your subtotal data, which appears when the report is run. This dialog box allows you to trigger a new subtotal whenever the particular report runs. Ascending (1-9) and descending (9-1) orders are available.

You can insert a grand total by choosing the **I**nsert, and then Grand Total box. Position the cursor in the Details section of the report where you would like the grand total to appear. Then access Insert, Summary Field from the main menu, and click Grand Total. Unless you have numeric fields, this choice is grayed out. When enabled, a data box is added to hold your grand subtotal data, which then appears when the report is run. A new section is created to hold the grand total.

If you want to add a formula, select the **F**ormula Field from the **I**nsert menu. You have to enter a name for the formula through the Insert Formula dialog box, and then enter the formula using the Expression Builder. The Expression Builder, which appears when you make the cursor selection, allows you to build formulas using fields, functions, and operators. When you finish building the formula, choose OK, and place the formula on the report as you do with a database/table field.

> **Tip**
> You can include an entire spreadsheet by selecting **I**nsert, **O**bject from the main menu.

Adding Graphics. You can add a variety of graphics elements (lines and circles), color elements, and bitmapped objects to your report. Choose **I**nsert, Grap**h**ic. This calls a dialog box that allows you to select, and then place, these graphical elements on your report.

Printing the Final Copy

When you finish manipulating the report, you can print it. Choose from a number of options to print—you can print directly to the printer (the most common way); print to a disk file (for printing on a different printer located on a different file / print server); or print to send as an e-mail message to another address.

To print a report, choose **F**ile, **P**rint, **P**rinter.

Summary

This chapter showed you the many options available for printing a report containing required table information. Reports were laid out using the Queries, Reports, and Text Editors. Two methods of printing, first to a file, and then to another filename, were discussed. Finally, this section showed you how to change textual attributes to both header and title information, and to data that appears on the hard report.

Chapter 10

Using the dBASE Editors

dBASE for Windows includes its own Program Editor that you can use for creating and editing program files, as well as a Text Editor for creating and editing text files, such as memos and other correspondence.

If you prefer, you can use your favorite line editor instead to create, edit, and save these individual text files and memos. A typical line editor is the Notepad editor that came with Windows. You may be equally comfortable with Microsoft Word or WordPerfect. In a pinch, of course, you can even use the MS-DOS editor.

In any instance, you can specify your external Text Editor by using the menus or the Command window. An *external editor* is a separate program that runs within its own window on your desktop. You can use the standard MS-DOS Editor as the replacement for Miscrosoft's EDLIN line editor of yesterday's operating systems. Presumably you don't want to use EDLIN, however. This cryptic program used a command such as *1,10L* to list the first 10 lines of file!

When a text editor is used in the dBASE environment, the dBASE application temporarily *shells out* into a background mode while you run the editor. You may run as many of the editor sessions as you wish, cutting and pasting text between the applications a la typical Windows mode.

Selecting Your Initial Editors

To set the default Program Editor, follow these steps:

1. Choose **P**roperties, **D**esktop. The Desktop Properties dialog box appears.

2. Click the Files tab to access the Files property settings. This page contains the Editors listbox, from which you can set the default Program Editor and Memo Editor.

3. To enter an editor in the Program Editor, type the complete path name (if you know it) in the space provided. If you don't know the path

name, click the Tool icon to open the Choose Program Editor dialog box.

Tip
Make sure you type these phrases correctly. A mistake causes a prompt to appear, and you have to recreate the phrase before the program runs.

4. Manipulate the directory and file structure to the location of your editor's executable image (.EXE) and click OK. For example, if WordPerfect is your choice, the filename is WP.EXE. The MS-DOS Editor is normally located in the C:\DOS subdirectory EDIT.COM. Your choice is entered in the Program Editor dialog box.

When you click OK to exit the Desktop Properties dialog box, the editor selections are saved to the DBASEWIN.INI file.

You can follow the same steps for the Memo Editor selection. Figure 10.1 shows the results of selecting the NOTEPAD.EXE editor for use with program files, and the MS-DOS EDITOR.COM editor for editing memos.

Fig. 10.1
Selecting Text Editors from the Desktop Properties dialog box.

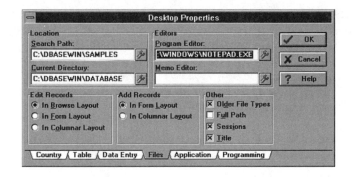

Figure 10.2 shows the Choose Program Editor dialog box. Note that the filename is set to accept a .EXE executable file. The File Type cannot be modified to accept another type of file.

Specifying a specific program or text file in the Command window is equally as easy: activate the Command window and type **SET EDITOR TO** followed by the path and filename. For example, if you wanted to use the MS-DOS Editor, type:

```
SET EDITOR TO C:\DOS\EDITOR.COM
```

Alternatively, to set the Windows NOTEPAD.EXE program as your Text Editor, type:

```
SET EDITOR TO C:\WINDOWS\NOTEPAD.EXE.
```

You can set a memo field editor by activating the Command window and typing:

```
SET WP TO
```

followed by the path and filename. For example, to set the Windows
NOTEPAD program as your Text Editor, type:

```
SET WP TO C:\WINDOWS\NOTEPAD.EXE
```

Both commands are executed by pressing Enter at the end of the command
line in the Command window.

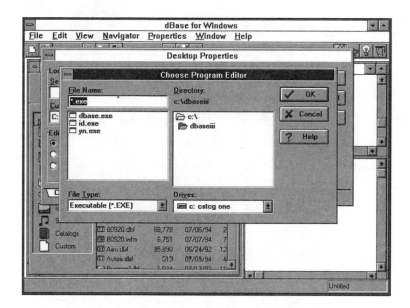

Fig. 10.2
Selecting a
Program Text
Editor.

Setting the Editor's Default Properties

The Editor Properties dialog box allows you to change the Program Editor
properties. To display the Editor Properties dialog box, choose either the Program or Memo Editor from the **P**roperties menu.

Within the Desktop choice, clicking the tool icon at the end of the Program
Editor selection box produces the Choose Program Editor dialog box (shown
in fig. 10.3). From here, you can search the contents of the hard disk until
you see the subdirectory you need. Then change the File Name window to
show the file type you are looking for. Normally this can be accomplished
through the File Type dialog box. However, in this window, the only choice
is an Executable (*.EXE) filename.

Fig. 10.3

The Choose
Program Editor
dialog box.

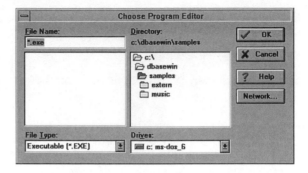

The default properties for this editor are as follows:

- Word Wrap is OFF.

- The right margin position can be indented or outdented.

- The automatic tab indent is OFF.

- The automatic tab indent spacing is available only when the automatic tab indent is set to ON.

- Auto Colors is OFF.

- The on-screen font can be decreased or increased in point size.

The dialog box is the same for both editors; the two editors, however, differ from each other by their default properties and the way they start. Properties of each are not mutually exclusive, although you can change them to reflect any preferences you have.

Using the Program Editor

The dBASE Program Editor offers several advantages that other editors do not. First, it is a part of the overall dBASE program, so switching between dBASE and its Program Editor is not a problem. Second, you can run programs from inside the Program Editor; this feature allows you to test and then debug your code as you write it. Finally, the Program Editor provides easy access to the Expression Builder—you can construct and insert dBASE expressions into your text very easily.

To start the Program Editor, click the Untitled program file icon, or use the **F**ile, **N**ew, **P**rogram command from the main menu. Alternatively, you can go directly to the Command window and type **CREATE COMMAND** or **MODIFY COMMAND** (without a filename). If you use a filename that doesn't yet exist, your Program Editor opens without a specified filename.

Four SpeedBar buttons appear when the Program Editor is active. They are the Expression Builder, the Navigator, the current program, and the Debugger. The Program Editor has the following default properties:

- Word Wrap is OFF.

- Auto Indent is on, with the spacing set to 3.

- Auto Colors is ON.

- The font is Terminal, which is a monospace typeface.

To access the Program Editor that comes with dBASE for Windows, use the File, Properties, and Program Editor. In figure 10.4, text has been typed into an untitled Program Editor file.

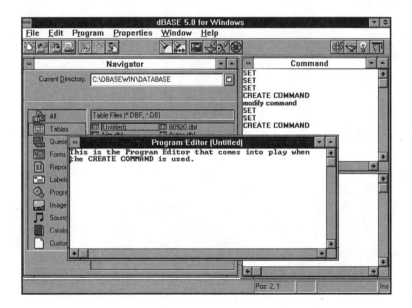

Fig. 10.4
The Program Editor.

If you want to make changes to the way the text and this file is displayed on-screen, while the Program Editor is activated, choose **P**roperties, Program Editor to display the Program Editor Properties dialog box. This box has only one tab to it; it controls the overall atrributes of the text. Figure 10.5 shows the Program Editor Properties dialog box.

Within this dialog box you can change the font and the word wrap. If you turn this option on, it causes the text to wrap according to the size of the right edge of the box position. Otherwise, you get a single line that goes on and on and on, no matter what the size of the box.

Fig. 10.5

The Choose Program Editor Properties dialog box.

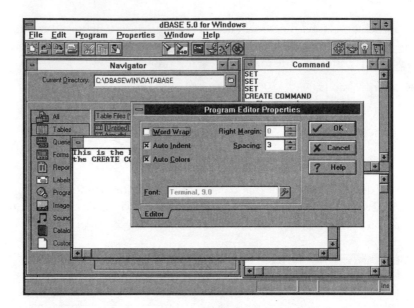

Using the Memo Text Editor

You can create a text file only from the Command window. Type **MODIFY FILE** with no filename in the Command window, and press Enter.

To edit an existing file, type **MODIFY FILE <filename>** in the same window. If the file is not located in the current directory, you have to type the entire filename, or first type the command **SET DEFAULT TO** and then the directory path.

The window title bar now reads Text Editor, followed by the [untitled] legend. This editor has the following defaults:

- **W**ord Wrap is OFF.

- Auto **I**ndent is ON.

- By pressing the Tab key, a true character tab is inserted.

- Auto **C**olors is OFF.

Your file is saved in an ASCII file format. The Save As dialog box does not automatically supply a file extension when it comes time to save the file; an excellent choice is the .TXT extension because it is universally recognized.

Figure 10.6 shows a Text Editor that builds textual material in the MEMO field.

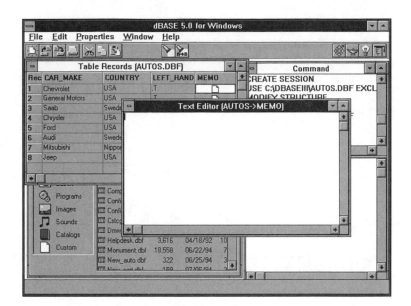

Fig. 10.6
The selected memo
Text Editor,
EDITOR.COM.

Using the Text Editor
To Edit Memo Fields

When you double-click a memo field within a table, it automatically opens a
Text Editor window. From previous discussions, you know that you can type
in a memo field forever—or at least until you exhaust your hard disk space.

This editor has the following defaults:

- Word Wrap is ON.

- The Right Margin is zero (0), which means that the memo field text
  automatically wraps to the current width of the Text Editor window.
  Sizing the window means that you get more or less text on a line, and
  that the memo field wraps to that width.

- Indent is OFF.

- Auto Colors is OFF.

Figure 10.7 shows the results of using the Windows NOTEPAD.EXE editor for
editing text fields.

Fig. 10.7
The text field in
the Text Editor.

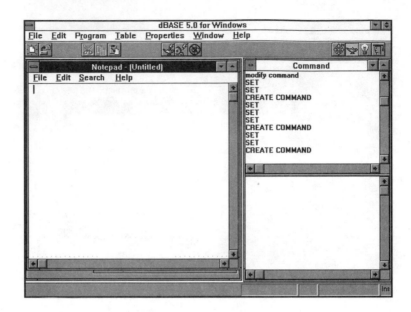

Saving Your Files

You can use the normal Save **A**s and **S**ave commands to save individual text files. The suggested extension for saving files is .PRG, although you can use any three-character alphanumeric set that you want. Alternatively, you may use no file extension. Thus, a file containing a letter can easily be called by any of these names; LETTER, LETTER.TXT, or LETTER.TX, LETTER.A1, and so on.

Caution

Even though you can use any three-character alphanumeric set that you want for your extension, *do not* use one that ends in the letter *O*. When dBASE compiles your code, it creates an object file with the same name and extension as your program file, except that the last letter of the extension is *O*. (PROGRAM.PRG compiles to PROGRAM.PRO.) Therefore, if your program's file extension ends in an *O*, the compilation process overwrites your program file!

Summary

This chapter showed you some methods you can use to select your favorite Text Editor—such as WordPerfect, MS-Word, the MS-DOS Editor, EDLIN, or the Notepad—before entering or modifying text in either a text or program mode. Any editor may be used as long as it doesn't embed control characters into the text as it saves the file. If embedded control characters are used, they interfere with the files' execution in dBASE for Windows.

Chapter 11

Working with the Command Window

The dBASE Command window allows you to type commands directly into the dBASE interface without having to open and close a series of windows.

The Command window consists of two user-interface windows. The upper quadrant is known as the *Input window (or Input pane)*. Here is where you key in the commands and execute them with the Enter key.

The lower quadrant provides the command sequence results, and is known as the *Results window (or Results pane)*. Results of all commands entered into the input windows are displayed here—including your errors. All dBASE DOS commands execute in this window unless you are using special programs that open their own windows. The Command window is the equivalent of the old "dot prompt" command line of older versions of dBASE.

You can size either window to suit your purposes by positioning the cursor at the horizontal line separating the upper and lower quadrants, clicking the mouse button, and dragging up or down. To restore them to their default sizes, double-click the horizontal divider.

You can close the Command window by double-clicking the Control menu box in the window's upper-left corner. To Open the Command window, choose **W**indow, **C**ommand Window ; or click the Command window's SpeedBar button.

The Command window may be modified to suit your needs by choosing **P**roperties, **C**ommand Window to display the dialog box. You also can select fonts and orientation options from this dialog box.

Figure 11.1 shows the Command Window Properties dialog box. By default, the input pane position is set to the top of the screen. The Input Pane text is set to a 16-point system font, and the Results Pane is set to a 12-point terminal font. You can customize any of these settings.

Chapter 8 explains the Expression Builder and provides some additional information for use within the Command window.

Fig. 11.1
The Command
Window Proper-
ties dialog box.

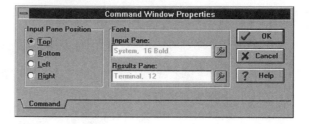

Fig. 11.1
The Command
Window Proper-
ties dialog box.

dBASE keeps a complete history of previously entered commands in the Command window so that you have access to it at any time. To reuse a command, first scroll the Command window to the point where you can see the command you want to reuse (or modify before reusing). Click the command line; then execute the command by pressing Enter or by clicking the Run SpeedBar button.

Figure 11.2 fills the entire screen with the command line. The Input pane resides in the upper portion, whereas the Results pane sits below it. You can resize the screen with normal Windows commands by clicking the Minimize triangle located at the top-right corner of the window.

Fig. 11.2
The Command
window.

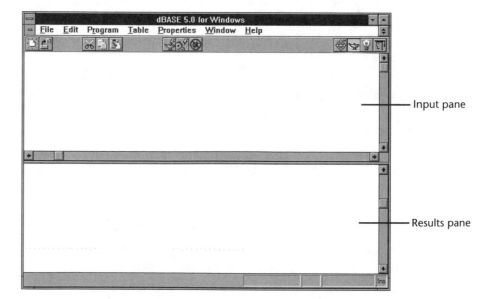

Entering and Executing Commands

To execute a command, type the command in the Input pane (top half) and press Enter. You also can click the Run button on the SpeedBar; or choose **E**dit, E**x**ecute Selection.

Entering Multiple Statements

You can enter multiple statements on a single line by separating each command with a semicolon. For example:

```
CLEAR; FOR I=1 to 20; ? I; NEXT
```

However, because the Enter command executes the line, you must press Ctrl+Enter to enter more than one line into the Command window.

The command line defaults to insert mode. When the insert mode is enabled, a box in the bottom right corner of the main dBASE for Windows exhibits INS. The mode is a toggle switch: press the INS key from the keypad or the control pad to its right to turn the insert function on or off.

The maximum number of characters that you can type in a command line is 32,767! The number of lines that the Results pane holds is limited only by the amount of memory in the computer.

Note

You can minimize the Command window by double-clicking the control menu box; or by choosing **F**ile, **C**lose when the Command window is active. You can open (or reopen) the Command window by choosing **W**indow, Command, or by clicking the Command Window SpeedBar button.

Pasting Syntax from Help

You can copy syntax from the language portion of the electronic on-line Help system. After you paste the syntax and supply an argument, you add a question mark (?) so that the Results pane displays the function's return value. The complete command is

```
? YEAR ({9/2/94})
```

Place the cursor on the command line, press Enter, or choose the Run button on the SpeedBar. The results of this command appear in the Results pane. For the YEAR( ) example, you see "1994", which is a full, four-digit, expression for the supplied date.

Pasting in Syntax from Help

Command syntax can be copied from the Language reference section of the on-line Help system that comes with dBASE for Windows. The feature is added to dBASE to help you use accurate, syntactically correct text without having to search around for the correct command line input. For example, you may not be sure how a command is terminated. Does it have a ( )? How do I fill in and complete the information within the brackets? And...is there information that I need to fill in between the brackets, and if so, what does it consist of?

The following steps copy a YEAR( ) function into the Command window as an example:

1. Open the Command window and make it active on the desktop. Access **H**elp, **L**anguage to open the Language reference section of Help. Scroll down to find the Categorical List and click it. This action brings up the Categorical List of the Language section. Choose Search, and type the YEAR( ) function that you are looking for. Click Show Topics from the selection box to paste the function into the Go To box. Then click Go To. This actions brings up the YEAR( ) function box. Figure 11.3 shows the YEAR( ) function in the Search dialog box.

Fig. 11.3

The YEAR( ) function in the Search dialog box.

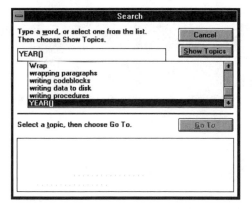

2. Choose **E**dit, **C**opy to open the Copy dialog box. Highlight the Year( ) function and click the Copy button to copy it into the Windows clipboard. Note that the clipboard is a one-time paste buffer. In figure 11.4, the specific YEAR( ) function information box appears. This dialog box displays all information particular to the function in question, including the syntax, a physical description of the function, and its purpose.

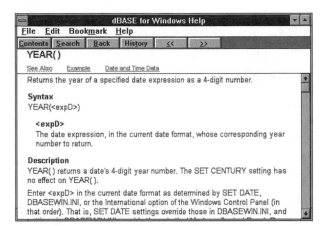

Fig. 11.4
The YEAR ( )
function dialog
box.

Note

Whatever you may currently have in the buffer is replaced by the arrival of a new piece of physical information. Thus, it is a good idea to cut and paste back and forth with important, vital information that cannot easily be duplicated.

In figure 11.5, the Copy dialog box is shown. Here, one selects the information to be copied into the paste buffer by highlighting the choice and choosing Copy.

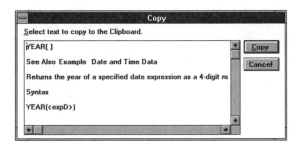

Fig. 11.5
The Copy dialog
box with YEAR ( )
identified for
copying purposes.

3. When the required information has been successfully transferred, choose **F**ile, **E**xit from the Help window to leave the Help system. Alternatively, you may exit with Alt+F4. The information resides in the paste buffer.

4. Reselect the Command window and position the cursor where you want the text to appear. Alternatively, open the Program Editor and position the cursor inside the window where you want the text. In either case, choose **E**dit, **P**aste or Ctrl+V to paste the function in at the

cursor point. The buffer-stored text should appear at the selected point in the Program Editor or the Command window.

Pasting Syntax from Other Files

You also can paste commands from a program file by opening the file, copying the commands, and pasting them into the Command window. You can then test or modify the commands in the Command window until they run correctly. The sample files provided in the dBASE program (C:\DBASEWIN\SAMPLES\) are an excellent source of proven commands.

If the Input pane contains dBASE code that you intend to use again, you can copy and paste it into a new program. Then you can name the new program (perhaps as a .PRG file), and insert it into an existing program file. You can do this not once, but many times over. Code used in this way is known as *boilerplate* code because of its tendency toward multiple usage.

You can also block and edit text and copy it to a file. dBASE displays the Copy to File dialog box. This dialog box always defaults to a .PRG file extension, but you can change it to a selection of your own. If you don't mark text before you make this selection, dBASE selects the entire Command window's contents.

In figure 11.6, lines of text previously highlighted in the Command window are readied for copying into a file by using the **E**dit, **C**opy to File command.

Fig. 11.6
You can copy text into a file and use it again, and again, and again.

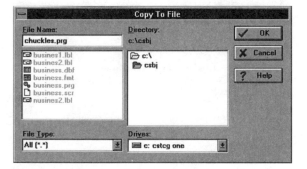

Some Common Commands and Their Descriptions

Table 11.1 offers some of the more common commands, with a description of each.

Table 11.1 Popular Command Window Input Commands

Command	Description
HELP	Opens the Help system. If you type the command alone, you receive the main Help screen. If you specify a command with the HELP command, (as in HELP BROWSE) you see the entry for that command.
DIRECTORY	Displays the names of all the tables located in the current directory. Use DIRECTORY *.* to display all the files in the current directory or DIRECTORY *.ABC for a file specification.
SET PATH	Sets a new search path for your files. The format is SET PATH TO *<path list>* where *<path list>* is one or more path specifications connected with semicolons.
CD	Changes to a specified directory. For example CD ACCOUNTS, or CD C:\ACCOUNTS.
SET DIRECTORY	Sets a new current directory. The format is SET DIRECTORY TO *<pathname>*.
? and/or ??	Evaluates and prints a response of a value or expression in the results pane, a printer, or in a file.
DO	Runs a program. You may quickly run a dBASE program by typing **DO** and the program name. For example: **DO REPORTS**. Note that the .PRG extension is not needed in the command line. If the file is not in the current directory and the path is not set, you have to include an entire pathname, as in DO C:\ACCOUNTS\REPORT.
USE	Opens tables and their indexes. For example, USE COCO opens the table COCO and all its associated index files.
BROWSE	Allows you to view or change the contents of a table. You can modify BROWSE to suppress fieldnames at the expense of others in a table. For example, BROWSE FIELDS LASTNAME, FIRSTNAME.
EDIT	Similar to Browse, but used to alter a single record or multiple records with similar entries. For example, EDIT ALL FOR LASTNAME="Puce", or EDIT RECORD 17330.
DISPLAY MEMORY	Displays the contents of all currently defined user or system memory variables. Not for the faint-hearted, this feature is especially handy when programming. This command shows you how variables are being handled in memory, what they hold, and how many variables are available.

Tip
You can obtain a more complete list from dBASE's electronic Help listing. The commands are not case-sensitive, but it sometimes helps to have the initial and system-level commands in uppercase to help identify incorrect syntax during debugging sessions.

Tip
BROWSE is used primarily for multiple record presentations, whereas EDIT is used for a single record alteration.

(continues)

Table 11.1 Continued	
Command	**Description**
DISPLAY STATUS	Displays the current status of all SET command settings, function key assignments, search paths, database information such as open indexes, index key expressions, and database relations. Also includes such settings as ON ESCAPE, ON ERROR, ON KEY, and SET KEY.
MODIFY COMMAND	This command opens the text editor with the specified program file, as in MODIFY COMMAND *<filename>*. If no filename is provided, the text editor opens with an [untitled] filename.
CLEAR	Clears the Results (lower portion) pane.
QUIT	Elegantly closes dBASE for Windows, shutting down all open files in an orderly manner and removing everything from temporary memory.

Running and Debugging Programs

You can create, save, and run programs as you write them. To run a program, select the .PRG file icon and click the Run button in the SpeedBar.

To debug a program, select the same .PRG file icon and choose Debug from the Navigator menu.

Fixing Program Errors

Inevitably, you will find a program that is still buggy. When you run an un-stable program, dBASE generates an error message and the program dies (or crashes!). The results can be quite spectacular, not to mention devastating to your ego. After you recover from the shock, however, your main interest probably is to investigate the reasons for the error.

Figure 11.7 shows the dialog box that appears when dBASE finds an error in a program file—the Program Alert dialog box. This dialog box appears every time dBASE finds an error in a program, providing you with an opportunity to correct the defect.

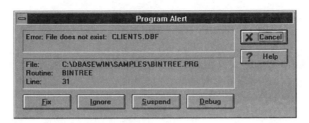

Fig. 11.7
The Program Alert
dialog box.

The Program Alert dialog box includes a series of buttons that allows you to make some choices about your program. These buttons are described in Table 11.2.

Table 11.2	Buttons in the Program Alert Dialog Box
Button	**Description**
Cancel	Stops the execution of the program and returns you to the editor, catalog windows, or the Navigator.
Fix	Opens the program file in the editor, with the insertion point on the line containing the error. Arguably, this is the choice for people who don't yet write error-free code!
Ignore	Ignores the error and continues to execute the program.
Suspend	The program's execution is stopped at a specified endpoint. This only applies to runtime errors. You may continue executing the program by typing **RESUME** in the Command window, or terminate the program with the CANCEL command.
Debug	Opens the debugger and allows you to examine the code further. This only applies to runtime errors.

Summary

In this chapter, you learned how to interact with the Command window—by entering and executing commands. The scenario behind finding, cutting, pasting, and then using text from the help level was described. Some common commands and their descriptions were introduced to provide you with a basis on which to commence programming activities. Chapter 11 should stand you in good stead as you progress toward the remaining chapters in this book, where programming activities are explained and a good number of examples is presented.

Chapter 12

Using SQL Data

Structured Query Language (SQL) is a time-tested standard language developed specifically for microcomputers by D.D. Chamberlin and other researchers at the IBM Research Laboratories. IBM developed SQL (sometimes pronounced "sequel") to be used with a variety of database-management systems. It is *data-independent*, meaning that users don't have to worry about how the data is physically accessed. SQL is also *device-independent*, which means that the same query language is employed to access data located on mainframes, mini-computers and personal computers.

dBASE for Windows allows you to access data built and stored by other relational database management systems (RDBMS) that employ SQL as their main language interface system. To use SQL with dBASE, however, you must have the Borland International Database Engine (BDE) and its programming interface (IDAPI) installed. The connection between the BDE and your database server is provided by a separate product, called Borland SQL Link.

Making the Connection

To access a SQL table, you must use the appropriate version of Borland SQL Link, dependent on the server you are using. The SQL Link drivers that come with the program translate commands from the BDE into the appropriate SQL dialect that your server can then use.

A number of language drivers is provided to convert characters between your desktop machine and the server to which you are connected. To specify the language driver, use the IDAPI configuration utility, which you start by double-clicking its icon in the dBASE for Windows Program Group before dBASE is opened. Figure 12.1 shows the opening menu from the IDAPI configuration icon in the dBASE for Windows Program Group. The driver name is selected as a PARADOX version, and the corresponding default parameters appear to the right.

The following code shows SQL code. This example code executes an SQL SELECT statement on a file server.

```
table Company
SET DBTYPE TO DBASE
OPEN DATABASE CAClients
SET DATABASE TO CAClients
errorCode = SQLEXEC("SELECT Company, City FROM ;
Company WHERE State_Prov='CA'", "StateCA.DBF")
IF errorCode = 0
SET DATABASE TO
USE StateCa
LIST
ENDIF
RETURN
```

Table 12.1 shows some common SQL commands and their meanings. This table is by no means exhaustive. There are many professional and technical books available that deal exclusively in SQL databases and related topics.

Table 12.1 Common SQL Commands	
Function Name	**Description**
ERROR( )	Returns the *number* of the most recent dBASE for Windows error.
DBERROR( )	Returns the *number* of the last IDAPI error.
DBMESSAGE( )	Returns the *error message* of the last IDAPI error.
MESSAGE( )	Returns the *error message* of the most recent dBASE for Windows error.
OPEN DATABASE	Establishes a connection to a database server or a database defined for a specific directory location.
SET DATABASE	Sets the default database from which your tables may be accessed.
SET DBTYPE	Sets the default table type to one of either dBASE or Paradox.
SET PATH	Specifies the directory search route that dBASE is set to follow in order to find those files that are not in the current directory.
SQLERROR( )	Returns the *number* of the last file server error.
SQLEXEC( )	Executes an SQL statement in the current database, or on specific dBASE for Windows or Paradox database tables.
SQLMESSAGE( )	Returns the most recent file server *message*.

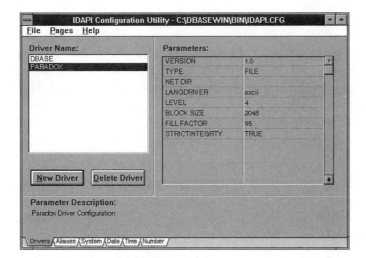

Fig. 12.1
The IDAPI configu-
ration utility.

Next, go to the System tab and select the LANGDRIVER option. You must create at least one database alias to your server. To browse or edit a table, click the Table from the Database button located in the All or Tables window of the Navigator. Specify the database alias and table, as shown in figure 12.1.

> **Note**
>
> These buttons appear only if one or more database aliases are defined using the IDAPI configuration utility.

Working with SQL Data

If you begin by opening something other than a table (for instance, you are running a query, form, or report built on SQL data), the Open Database dialog box appears. Enter your name and password.

After you have access to a remote SQL database, you can perform almost exactly the same tasks with that data that you can with "regular" dBASE information.

Some SQL events act differently than those within the dBASE environment, because SQL uses the concept of *transaction processing*. Such a concept involves a series of steps that either succeed or fail as one entire unit. Transactions are considered vital to ensuring data integrity in situations where large tables are accessed by a several users simultaneously.

When a dBASE table is in use, you expect that as each activity is completed, the computer will update the commands one at a time. In transaction processing, however, the computer waits until all the transactions are completed before processing the changes. Then they are performed at the same time as a long string of events. If dBASE detects an anomaly, the entire process aborts, the results are rolled back to the beginning of the session, and nothing is committed to the hard disk.

dBASE places a lock on each record as it is accessed by the user. This record-locking mechanism ensures that no one else can access the same record until you finish using it. This activity prevents multiple saves, all of which cancel each other out, except for the last person who leaves that record.

When SQL data is used in a Table Records window, however, all of the examined records are changed as each user finishes using the table. This way, all changes are committed at one time in a single transaction. If someone else tries to change a locked dBASE record, dBASE produces an error message.

dBASE for Windows allows the following activities to occur with its SQL tables.

- **Tables:** You can create tables, and read, edit, add, modify, and delete records, although you cannot modify a table's structure.

- **Queries:** You can create queries, join tables, filter data, and select certain fields for the view, which are fully editable in most cases, except for those of a read-only nature. The results of a query can be mapped to a local file/table (one on your own hard drive).

- **Forms:** You can create a form and set its view to an SQL table. You can query on SQL data.

- **Reports:** You can use the data from an SQL table or query as the basis for a report.

Before considering forms and reports, give some thought to what you are allowed to do in your local area network (LAN) and the privileges granted you by the System Administrator (SYSADMIN). You might have to ask for additional privileges.

Indexing on SQL

SQL Link requires an index that uniquely identifies each record in the table for updating or deleting record exercises. If this index is absent, your view of the table is read-only.

You can add an index to an SQL table by opening the table and using the **T**able, **T**able Utilities, **M**anage Index command. Click the Create button to create a unique table.

Figure 12.2 displays the Create Index window for the selected database. Note that all dBASE tables or databases have a .DBF extension, whereas those of the Paradox flavor have a .DB filename. See Chapter 6 for more on indexing and sorting.

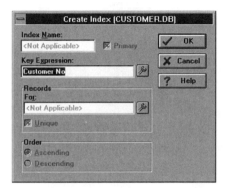

Fig. 12.2
Creating a Paradox table index.

Bear in mind the following caveats as you go about indexing your SQL data:

- Index names must be unique throughout each database.

- You can create an index for multiple fields.

- You cannot index SQL tables on an expression.

- You cannot create a *conditional index* (an index based on a condition).

- You cannot index on binary fields.

Summary

This section touched on some of the issues surrounding Structured Query Languages (SQL) data and their potential relationship with dBASE for Windows data.

This book's scope does not permit more than a cursory glance of the SQL subject. For a more complete discussion of using SQL with dBASE for Windows, refer to Que's *Using dBASE 5 for Windows*, Special Edition; or to Que's *Killer dBASE for Windows*.

Chapter 13

Programming in dBASE for Windows

Most old-style programmers punched their code in character-by-character, line-by-line, cursing and debugging it as it crashed. This latest version of dBASE for Windows allows you to use a newer concept—visual programming—to determine the correct coordinates and then place them on an electronic form. These coordinates are even easier to use because they are event-driven.

Three types of interfaces are available to you for programming tasks:

- *Command-line interface*, where you type commands at the Command window.

- *Menu-driven interface*, where you select choices from a variety of options.

- *Event-driven interface*, which is dependent on what activities are taking place either with the keyboard or with the mouse.

dBASE for Windows has a built-in C-style preprocessor that allows you to include source files, define constants, and predefine expressions. The preprocessor software allows you greater control of the compilation process, improved performance, and greater productivity when developing software code.

In addition, the following system capabilities have improved from earlier versions:

- Enhanced arrays

- Enhanced parameter passing

- Random data-generation for testing purposes

- Full-featured debugger that displays program code and its derivatives in multiple windows

A user-friendly interface permits *modeless program execution* (a system that allows events to trigger code that doesn't run until that event occurs) that allows you to run programs along side interactive desktop components. A full set of graphical interface elements and Windows controls—including menus, pushbuttons, checkboxes and radio buttons, SpeedBars, listboxes, combination boxes, and editors—is available.

Graphical-user-interface commands adhering to the UI standard follow dBASE syntax. Full support for DLLs and Windows API calls is available to you—either interactively or through a program function call. You can incorporate multimedia sound and graphics into any presentation or application; either playing them back or displaying them using Windows multimedia formats.

Getting Started

A dBASE program is a text file that contains syntactically correct dBASE statements. Such statements in a program file (.PRG) are generically called *program code* (or in programmer parlance, *code*).

Documenting Your Code

Experienced programmers document their code as they write it. If you don't, chances are you won't remember what your code means or does six months from now. Header lines at the top of each file combined with comment lines throughout the program serve you well when you make modifications to existing code. They are also very helpful when other programmers need to modify your code.

dBASE recognizes several comment markers that, when placed in the code, are ignored by dBASE as it inspects and executes each line:

- Double ampersands (&&)

- An asterisk (*) as the first character on a line

- The word NOTE in upper- or lowercase at the beginning of a line

Creating the Program File

You can use any standard ASCII text editor to create your code. If you use the dBASE editor, use the CREATE or MODIFY commands (for example, MODIFY FILE CONTACTS.PRG) to open an editor window where you can insert new code or modify existing lines. Note that here you need the full filename, including the extension. The code for the CONTACTS program opens as a text file in a window.

In figure 13.1, the MODIFY command opens a nonexistent file. Here, the Notepad executable that came with the original Windows environment, NOTEPAD.EXE, is the editor of choice.

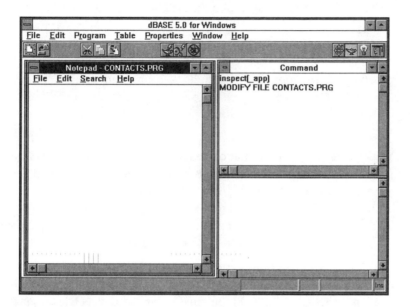

Fig. 13.1
A new .PRG file is opening in the Notepad editor.

After you write your program, you must compile it into machine language to create an executable object code file. Table 13.1 shows default extensions for files in the dBASE purview.

Table 13.1 Default dBASE File Extensions		
File Description	**Source Code File Extensions**	**Compiled File Extensions**
Program File	.PRG	.PRO
Generated Form File	.WFM	.WFO
Generated Query File	.QBE	.QBO
Generated Menu File	.MNU	.MNO

> **Note**
>
> Compiled file extensions match source code file extensions, except that they have an O at the end.

You can choose between these commands to run your programs:

- DO compiles a program and then runs it if no errors are found.

- SET PROCEDURE TO *<filename>* searches for a compiled program file. If a .PRO file is not found, a .PRG file is used.

You do better over the long run to compile your program directly, because compiling neither executes or opens the specified files. Secondly, dBASE accepts filename wildcards, compiling related or unrelated files.

After the program compiles, dBASE detects any syntax errors in each line of code. Depending on the severity of the error, one of four error buttons appears on-screen—a Cancel button, which cancels compilation completely; an Ignore button, which also cancels your code but continues to examine other lines in the file if you used a wildcard file filter; a Fix button, which opens the source code in an editing window and positions the cursor on the offending character; and a Help button used to provide context-sensitive help.

Figure 13.2 shows the Program Alert dialog box that appears when a program finds an error. You can choose to **F**ix or to **I**gnore the problem encountered on line 41 of the DBCLOCK.PRG program, or you can **C**ancel the program outright.

Fig. 13.2
dBASE finds a
syntax error.

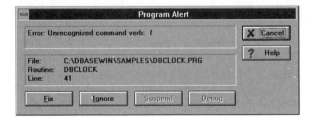

Figure 13.3 shows the results of the same program after fixing the error on line 41. Note the data that appears in the Results pane, allowing you to monitor a program's execution.

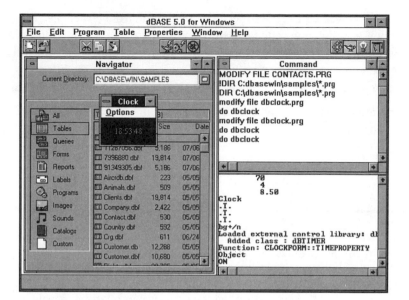

Fig. 13.3
An executed
program that
displays the
Windows clock
on-screen.

Creating, Compiling, and Testing Programs

After you write and debug a program, you might want to test it to make sure that it contains adequate error-handling. In many instances, you should run some test data on the tables. It also is useful to see how much of the data actually executes when the program runs.

Two commands test your programs: GENERATE and SET COVERAGE.

With one exception, the GENERATE command allows you to fill table fieldnames with random characters and numbers. The exception is that if a table already contains records, GENERATE leaves the records intact and appends the number of records you specify to the table. You can clear the old data using the ZAP command, which erases all information and leaves the structure intact.

Caution

Take great care when using the ZAP command to erase data from records. You cannot retrieve data from ZAPped records. After you confirm the operation, everything except the table's structure goes to the bit bucket. This data cannot be generated in memo, binary, or OLE fields.

If you want to generate random records at any time from either the Navigator or Catalog window, open the table to which you want to add random records. Choose **T**able, **T**able Utilities, **G**enerate Records. Enter the number of records you want to add in the Generate Records dialog box. As the records are generated, a small, colored box at the bottom of the screen shows your progress.

To generate those random records from the Command window, use the following commands:

USE *<tablename>*	*<tablename>* is the table for which you want to generate the records.
GENERATE *<expN>*	*<expN>* is the number of records to add to that table.

The SET COVERAGE command allows you to set coverage for all your programs. The results of the coverage analysis allow you to see which programs executed and which did not. Without coverage analysis on, you might never know that one (or more) of your programs didn't open, and thus you think your program runs correctly, but it in fact does not.

When you have SET COVERAGE on and compile and run your program, dBASE analyzes the program during runtime, storing the results in a binary file called a *coverpage file* (with a .CVO extension).

To start the coverpage analysis, type **SET COVERAGE ON**, followed by **COMPILE** or **DO** **<program name>** in the Command window. Alternatively, choose **P**roperties, **D**esktop; or issue the SET command from the Command window.

For example, typing and running the following program automatically turns coverage analysis on, and compiles the main program and its subroutine file. Coverpage files for three program files are generated:

```
* Pooh's Program File
#include 'version.h'
#ifdef DEBUG
SET COVERAGE ON
#endif
Compile MAIN
Compile sub1
Compile sub2
Compile sub3
```

Note that you can turn on the coverpage analysis in a program by using the preprocessor directive #pragma COVERAGE(ON). A program should not contain two similar directives, because the second cancels out the first.

Before dBASE creates a coverage file for a program, you must compile the program when SET PROGRAM is on. If a program is compiled while SET COVERAGE is off, the program does not produce a coverage file.

When you finish using coverpage analysis, turn it off and recompile the program. To SET COVERAGE to off, issue the SET COVERAGE OFF from the Command window; or uncheck the Coverage checkbox in the dialog box. Then recompile the program. Alternatively, you can edit the previous program and either turn the #pragma command off (#pragma COVERAGE (OFF)), or comment it out.

> ### Note
>
> A #pragma command is a directive embedded at the user's choice at the top of a file. With the command inserted, the computer is told whether or not to create a coverage file when the file is compiled. When the coverpage file is created, it contains, in binary format, each instance of how many times dBASE for Windows entered and exited the file in an attempt to run the file's contents.

Use DISPLAY COVERAGE from the Command window to see the information one screen at a time in the Command window. The command LIST COVERAGE sends the information to a disk file or to a printer.

Using Procedural Calls and Codeblocks

Programming software that allows you to write modularized code makes your life more simple, because it allows you to create small, self-contained units (called *modules*), which are supposedly easy to maintain, debug, and reuse. Such programs can be *procedures* (a short program that contains one or more program statements and usually returns a value), *functions* (a short program similar to a procedure, but always returns a value), or *codeblocks* (groups of logically related expressions that always return a value). These programs interact with each other in performing your tasks. Codeblocks hide routines that are used to perform specific tasks from the rest of the code. Procedures or codeblocks can be assigned to memory variables or to an object property. See Chapter 14 for more information on object properties.

To declare a procedure in a program, you must first write and compile it to determine that it runs correctly. Then you should copy it to the end of that program. The first line of a procedure is a declaratory statement (PROCEDURES <name of procedure>). The name can be up to 32 characters, and can include underscores to increase readability (as in *<name_of_procedure>*). Next, write the statements that perform the task. The last line of the procedure file is RETURN and the name of the expression you want dBASE to return or the name of the program module to return to.

Copy the procedure file to the end of the program file in which the procedure is to be called. This is a good place to group procedures if you are not using a procedure file. Table 13.2 contains a summary of dBASE procedures, functions, and codeblock usages.

Note

Using RETURN without adding the name causes the program to run until a breakpoint is reached at the first RETURN command that dBASE for Windows finds in the program. A PROCEDURE always occurs before the rest of the information required by the procedure is defined. So you call the PROCEDURE by name, and then call any required parameters. A procedure ends when it has processed all the specified input and program execution continues with the next line of code in the program.

Table 13.2   A Summary of Procedures, Functions, and Codeblock Usages

Type of Call	Usage	Example
Procedures and Functions	To create a named, usable group of program statements that perform a task, with or without returning a value.	An OnClick event handler that calculates a value.
Statement or Command Codeblock	To create a subroutine that consists of at least one command that may be assigned to a memory variable or an object property.	An OnClick event handler that skips forward to the next record.
Expression Codeblock	To create a subroutine that consists of at least one expression that displays a dynamically evaluated value when the subroutine is executed.	A VALID event handler.

The following example skips though a table one record at a time. First, you name the procedure and tell it to skip through the table one record at a time until it gets to the end of the table. When the procedure reaches the end of the table (as signified by the IF EOF() line), the pointer is repositioned at the top of the table and the procedure concludes:

```
PROCEDURE skip_records
     SKIP                      ( Go to the next record
     If EOF()                  ( if at the end-of-file
          GO TOP               ( go to the top of the table
     endif
RETURN
```

Declaring Parameters

Parameters are one or more memory variables named in a procedure declaration. The idea is that values are passed to the procedure using the memory variables by modifying a procedure's behavior with other program modules. Parameters also alter the behavior of a procedure by making the procedure work with many different values.

You can pass parameters to the procedure named with the call operator. When the call operator is used, the declared parameters are local to the procedure. Two parameters are supported by dBASE for Windows: *local* and *private*. Local memory variables cannot be modified by variables that have the same name in other parts of the program. Private variables can be unintentionally overwritten by other procedures that use the same variable name.

The following example uses parameters to accept a variable from the number of records to skip and moves the record pointer by that number:

```
PROCEDURE skip_records ("Numrecs")
                                   ( Procedure declaration with
                                     a variable
IF TYPE ("Numrecs") = "N"
                                   ( Type check the variable to
                                     see that it is a numeric
                                     field
Skip Numrecs
                                   ( Skip by the number in
                                     Numrecs
IF EOF()                           ( If at the end-of-file
     GO TOP                        ( Go to the first record in
                                     ENDIF
                                   ( the table
ENDIF
RETURN
```

If a procedure does not return a value, you can omit the RETURN command at the end of the file. A procedure is finished when it processes all the specified input and proceeds to the next line of code in the program.

You can use a total of 193 procedures in each program file; although you can open many more files, each containing 193 procedures, and one additional library file.

Understanding the Library File

The dBASE for Windows program fully supports library files in addition to procedures. When you run a file, the computer searches through the open library file for a procedure if the procedure being called doesn't contain all the information that the procedure requires to run properly.

Tip
Although a subdirectory called LIBRARY doesn't exist in the dBASE for Windows structure, you can create one to keep all your library files there.

To open a library file, use the SET LIBRARY TO <*filename*> command. After you finish with the library, close the file with the SET LIBRARY TO command without naming the filename. dBASE for Windows closes a currently open library even if it is not named with this command. Obviously, with a named filename, the library is closed.

Creating Codeblocks

A codeblock is a series of commands or an expression enclosed in braces. Codeblocks are usually shorter than procedures and contain statements or expressions. If the codeblocks include statements, they are known as *statement* codeblocks or *command* codeblocks. If the codeblocks include statements, they are called *expression codeblocks*.

You can use codeblocks to attach a method to an object event property. In the following example, it is easy to look at the code and determine what actions are assigned to a particular property. Here, an expression is embedded between two statements:

```
Onclick = {;close form MAIN}                    (     Statement
Valid = {.not. EOF()}                           (     Expression
mFirst.OnClick = {;saveit() ;GO TOP ;paintbox}(       Statement
```

You can call a codeblock by using the *function pointer* assigned to the codeblock. The codeblock is thus reusable, because many function pointers can be called more than once in a program. Function pointers are more convenient for coding long, repeated tasks, whereas codeblocks are better suited when coding one-time events.

> **Note**
>
> A function pointer is a method whereby one can call a codeblock's memory variable (to which the codeblock has been assigned). The codeblock may be considered reusable at this point, because a function pointer can be addressed more than once in a program.

Working with Memory Variables

A *memory variable* is a declared memory location used temporarily to store a single unit of data. An *array* is a set of memory variables structured into rows and columns. Arrays are typically used to perform calculations, control program executions, and store constant values.

You can use any naming convention that you want to name variables, but try to make the name describe the variable's contents or function, such as cost or total_cost. You must preface the variable's name with a letter that indicates its data type and scope, as in the following individual examples.

In the next example, three different character variables are displayed.

```
cName = "totalcost"
nWeight = 185
LOCAL nCounter
```

If the variable corresponds to a field in a table, it should have a similar name, such as mCity for a city field. Mixed capitalization is allowed. Variable names are not case-sensitive; and in some cases mixed capitalization makes it easier to read the code.

You can use four commands to declare memory variables: PUBLIC, PRIVATE, STATIC, and LOCAL. When you use PUBLIC or STATIC, dBASE creates the variable and initializes it with a false value (.f.). If PRIVATE or LOCAL is used, dBASE doesn't automatically create or initialize the variable.

Variables are not necessarily connected to a dBASE for Windows session. A variable declared to be public or private in one session can be accessed by another subroutine that happens to be running in another session. Recall from an earlier discussion that the user can open multiple sessions to run programs, and that each defined session doesn't necessarily impact another session.

Using the Public Variable

Public, or global, variables are the most used, available in any subroutine. They are not released until the RELEASE or CLEAR ALL commands are issued. They are most useful in settings that apply to an entire application, such as login names, or default paths that point to data. Their greatest shortcoming is that protection isn't provided for variable overwriting.

Tip
Although it is permissible to begin variable names with an underscore (as in _ppitch), doing so may cause you more problems than it's worth. dBASE for Windows uses this naming convention to name its own system variables.

Using the Private Variable

Private variables are available in the subroutine that created them and in any lower-level subroutines.

Using the Local Variable

A local variable, as suggested by its name, is available only to the procedure or function in which it is declared. Because a local name restricts the variable's availability to use in a single subroutine, any type of temporary variable should be stored in a local variable.

When a parameter is declared for a user-defined function by the placement of parameters in parentheses after the function name, the parameters are automatically local to the function.

Using the Static Variable

A static variable can continue to exist even when the subroutine that declared it finishes executing. However, in order to use it again, you must reinitialize it for a second use. A static variable is only available in its originating subroutine, although it retains its value each time its creating subroutine calls it into use. Static variables are most useful for storing incremental values.

In Table 13.3, the scope, lifespan and availability of each of the four variables are defined.

Table 13.3	Memory Variable Lifespans	
Name	**Length of Use**	**Where Available**
PUBLIC	Released only when explicitly released by using either the RELEASE or CLEAR ALL commands.	Available in all subroutines whether they are high-level or low-level.
PRIVATE	Released when the routine that created it finishes its execution.	Available in the subroutine that created it as well as any lower-level subroutines.
LOCAL	Released when the routine that created it finishes its execution.	Available only in the subroutine that created it.
STATIC	Released only when explicitly released by using the RELEASE or CLEAR ALL commands.	Available only in the subroutine that created it.

Caution

If a specific name isn't declared, any variables created in the Command window are automatically relegated to the PUBLIC length of use. Those variables created in a program file are automatically relegated to the PRIVATE length of use.

Note

If you use these names within a small or short program, you probably will find that the default name is sufficient. Declaration (PUBLIC, PRIVATE, LOCAL, and STATIC) statements may be skipped as long as each variable is declared individually in the subroutine in which you intend to use it. However, when higher level programs are written, modularity and reusability is improved if each name is declared on an as-needed basis.

The following example demonstrates variable declarations and initializations:

```
Public mName            (    Declares mName as public.
? mName                 (       Returns .F.
mName = SPACE(30)       (    Give mName a specified value
PRIVATE nCost           (       No value for nCost
? nCost                 (Returns an error, since nCost
                        (    doesn't have a value
nCost = 500             (    That's better!
PUBLIC mCode, mDesc     (Declares more than one value
LOCAL cName             (    cName doesn't have a value
STATIC lFinished        (    Initialized as .F.
STATIC nTotal = 100     (Static variables alone are declared
                        (and initialized to a specific
                        (value in a single statement.
```

You can save memory variables to files and use them later. Such files, with .MEM extensions, are used to store data that would otherwise fit in a single table record, such as program configuration or printer settings.

You can use two main commands to manipulate these .MEM files: Save and Restore. Save holds all or some memory variables in a memory field, but it doesn't save function pointers, object references, or system memory variables. Restore, on the other hand, restores all the variables from a memory file into memory. All existing memory variables are released before those in the file are restored. If you want to retain existing memory variables, use the ADDITIVE command.

The following code demonstrates the use of Save and Restore in a program file:

The ADDITIVE() command allows you to retain the variables that have been temporarily stored in RAM for use in or with more current variables.

```
*       Pooh's Save vs. Restore Program
If File("savedar.mem")              (  Does the memory
                                    (  file exist?
RESTORE FROM savedar                (  If so, restore it
                                    (  into memory
ELSE                                                (
dFirstRUN = Date()                  (  Store the first time
                                    (  this program was run
SAVE TO savedar                                     (
ENDIF                                                (
IF DATE() - dFirstRun >= 30         (  Was this program run
                                    (  fewer than thirty
                                    (  days ago?

ENDIF
```

You create a memory variable by assigning a value to a name using either the STORE or the equals (=) commands. You can retrieve the value for that command by using the variable name in an expression:

```
? 5 * 3         (       Expression using no variables
STORE 5 to X    (       Creates a variable containing the value 5
Y=3             (       Creates a variable Y, containing 3
? X * Y         (       Same expression using variables
X=6             (       Variable X now containing the value 6
? X * Y         (       Returns the value 18
```

Figure 13.4 shows the commands from the previous section, including the CLEAR command, after the exercise is over.

A variable remains in memory until you release it. You might consider RELEASEing it to conserve your memory resources once an object is no longer needed. It can be explicitly released with a RELEASE command or the CLEAR ALL command.

Note

Note that the command CLEAR ALL releases all variables, effectively flushing your buffers, whereas RELEASE releases only specified variables.

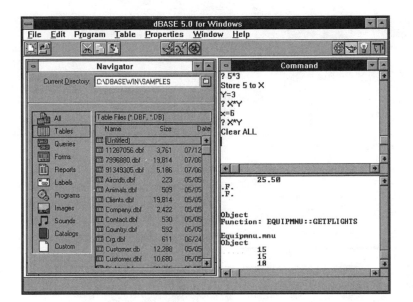

Fig. 13.4
You can store memory variables by using a variety of methods.

In the following line of code, when the form being used is closed, the variable that was used in conjunction with it is released.

```
this.OnClose={;Form.Release()}
```

Working with Data Types

A data type is a classification for data types that use memory variables and fields to provide funtions for manipulating and formatting data of each type. Each type has rules that dictate how you must work with the data, and what each field can contain. Although it sounds obvious, numeric fields can contain only numbers, whereas character data can contain letters, numbers, or punctuation marks. As you see, you cannot perform calculations on the actual numbers. You can perform calculations only on declared variables.

In the dBASE arena, data is any information that you can act on. You can assign a codeblock to a property, pass it on as a parameter, or execute it. Data might also be a person's printed name or a pushbutton object that the user clicks.

Table 13.4 illustrates the supported dBASE for Windows data types.

Table 13.4   dBASE for Windows Data Types

Data Name	Data Type	Symbol
Variables or fields	Character	C
	Date	D
	Floating Point	F
	Boolean Logical	L
	Numeric	N
Variables only	Bookmark	BM
	Codeblock	CB
	Function Pointer	FP
	Object	O
Fields in dBASE Tables	Binary	B
	Memo	M
	General OLE	G

Note

No built-in defaults exist for date, time, currency, or number formatting. These defaults are located in the WIN.INI Windows file, which you can modify from the Control Panel. Avoid changing the WIN.INI file; however, because you can override these defaults by editing the DBASEWIN.INI file in the C:\WINDOWS subdirectory.

Character data, perhaps the most common of all data, is treated as a string of symbols. For that reason, they are sometimes referred to as *strings*. You can manipulate such strings in dBASE by using delimiting character strings within expressions. Delimited characters can be single quotes, double quotes, or square brackets. You must use the same delimiter character at both ends of the statement.

Table 13.5 provides some ways that you can manipulate character data within a program. Note that each function is enclosed in parentheses.

Table 13.5   Manipulating Data with Functions

Task	Function	Example
Measure string length	LEN()	LEN(PART_NAME)
Find the position of a substring within a larger string	AT()	AT("Tue","Monday, Tuesday")
Extract a substring	SUBSTR()	SUBSTR(Part_ID,7,4)

Task	Function	Example
Extract from the LEFT	LEFT()	Left(Part_name,9)
Extract from the RIGHT	RIGHT()	Right(mPart_id,4)
Insert from one string into another	STUFF()	STUFF(mTERMS,8,2,mDays)
Repeat Characters	REPLICATE() SPACE()	REPLICATE "?",16) mName=SPACE(30)
Concatenate Strings	+ operator - operator	mFirstname + mLastname mFirstname-mLastname

Concatenating Strings

When you concatenate something, you add the first piece of data to a second piece of data. For example, you have two fieldnames, one called FIRSTNAME and the other called LASTNAME. Inside these fields, you name the characters ROBERT and GREEN. You can *concatenate* them to create ROBERT GREEN by telling the computer to add the field FIRSTNAME to the field LASTNAME with the command FIRSTNAME+LASTNAME.

Taking it one step further, if you use the TRIM command, you can lop the end off of each fieldname that contains any extra spaces. Thus, if you were displaying "ROBERT   GREEN" and wanted to eliminate the extra spaces, using the command FIRSTNAME+(TRIM)LASTNAME provides the desired result.

On occasion, you might need to alter the displayed characters that appear inside a character string. You can use several functions to change from lowercase to uppercase:

UPPER()   Converts a string to UPPERCASE. ISUPPER() returns as true if the case is already uppercase.

LOWER()   Converts a string to lowercase. ISLOWER() returns as true if the case is already lowercase.

PROPER()   Converts a string to proper noun format.

The following commands allow you to replace the contents of a two-character field in a table called *Customer*.

```
USE CUSTOMER

REPLACE ALL STATE WITH UPPER(STATE)
```

(continues)

(continued)

Or, you can modify the NAME field of the CUSTOMER table to capitalize only the fist letter of the country. The remaining letters remain lowercase. Be careful that all open parentheses are matched with closed parentheses at the statement's conclusion.

```
USE CUSTOMER

REPLACE NAME WITH
UPPER(LEFT(Name,1))+LOWER(SUBST(NAME,2,9));

        FOR ISUPPER(SUBSTR(NAME,2,1)
```

This example changes the name of a country such as *Great Britain* to *Great britain*. A better way of converting names of this nature is with the command PROPER(). The following example accomplishes this goal—converting the country *great britain* to *Great Britain*.

```
USE CUSTOMER

REPLACE ALL NAME WITH PROPER(NAME)
```

You use the TRIM() command to remove extra spaces at the end of a string. TRIM() and RTRIM() are identical functions designed to remove spaces from the right end of a string, whereas LTRIM() removes characters from the left end of a string. These commands are important because the fields in a table have fixed lengths to accommodate the longest data string. You don't always use all that space, so unless you trim the superfluous spaces, your display (form, printed labels, and so on) doesn't look as professional.

The following command strips extra space from the end of a line:

```
    ? TRIM(CITY)+", "+STATE+",  "+ZIP
```

It produces the following line:

```
Colorado Springs, Colorado, 80920
```

You can have dBASE generate repeated characters for you automatically by using the repeating characters commands. For example, the command SPACE() repeats a space character *n* number of times; REPLI-CATE() repeats any specified character *n* number of times. The following examples illustrate these commands:

```
    mName = Space(30)        ( Initializes a variable
                             ( with 30 spaces
```

```
mWork = Space(50)          ( Initializes a variable
                           ( with 50 spaces



mStars = REPLICATE("*",45) ( Creates a row of 45
                           ( asterisks

? mStars                   ( Displays
                           ( *********************
```

Numeric data, either *fixed point* or *floating point,* is treated in much the same fashion as the alphanumeric information described in the previous section. If you assign a numeric constant to the variable, the type is N; if you assign it the contents of a field, the type matches the field type. If you assign it the return value of a function, the type depends on the function. Some mathematical functions, such as PI() (pi, or 3.142) and SIN() (sine), return floating values, whereas other functions, such as LEN() and AT(), return numeric values.

Both numeric and float values can be based in an expression without converting to a single data type. You can combine these variables, but doing so automatically converts the numeric values to floating, and the resulting value is of type *F.*

In the following example, the local RBOC (Regional Bell Operating Company) needs to know the length of a piece of cable required to support a tower. The cable needs to be anchored at a distance of 600 feet from the base of the tower, and rise at an angle of 50 degrees. This admittedly simple code divides the distance to the tower by the cosine of the angle expressed in radians.

```
Distance = 500                          ( Radius is type N
CableLength = Distance / COS(DTOR(50))  ( Should be type F
? CableLength                           ( Should be 777.86
? TYPE ("Cablelength")                  ( Returns F
```

Figure 13.5 illustrates the commands from this example. Commands are typed into the Command windows and the results appear below in the Results pane.

Table 13.6 illustrates dBASE's general numeric functions.

Fig. 13.5
Command
window and
results pane.

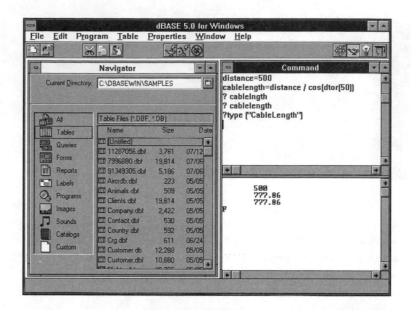

Table 13.6   Numeric Functions

Function	Returns
ABS()	The absolute value of a number.
EXP()	The base *e* raised to a specific power.
LOG()	The natural log to the base *e* of a number.
LOG10()	The common logarithm of a number (base 10).
MAX()	The maximum of two numbers.
MIN()	The minimum of two numbers.
MOD()	The modules remainder after one number is divided by another.
PI()	The number of pi or the ratio of a circle's circumference to its diameter.
RANDOM()	A random number.
SIGN()	The number's sign (not sine). As in positive or negative.
SQRT()	A number's square root.

When using financial data, you should take additional care in formatting numbers used in a total or subtotal field. The functions don't change the value of any numbers displayed. Rather, they affect the numbers' appearances on-screen or on paper.

Table 13.7 displays settings for such numbers.

Table 13.7 Display Settings for Numbers	
SET Command	**Display Setting**
SET CURRENCY	Specifies if a currency symbol ($) is displayed at the left or right of the number. The command SET CURRENCY LEFT places the currency symbol at the left of the number, as in $453.21. The command SET CURRENCY RIGHT places the currency symbol a the right of the number, as in 453.21$.
SET CURRENCY TO	Specifies the character to use for the currency symbol.
SET DECIMALS	Sets the number of decimal places to be displayed.
SET POINT	Specifies the character that should separate the decimal digits from integer digits.
SET PRECISION	Specifies the number of digits used internally in mathematical operations using numeric values.
SET SEPARATOR	Specifies the character that separates each group of three digits in a value greater than 999.

You can display numbers on a control, such as an entry field, text box, or spin box, as long as a numeric field or variable is associated with that control. A *function property* specifies formatting and/or input restrictions for the entire variable or field. A *picture property* specifies how the formatting and/or input restrictions are handled for a portion of the variable or field.

For example, assume you are interested in converting from United States dollars into French francs:

```
Money = 738915.6285          ( A charitable conversion rate!
SET CURRENCY LEFT
SET CURRENCY TO "Fr"
SET DECIMALS TO 2
SET POINT TO ","
SET SEPARATOR TO "."
? MONEY
     ? MONEY PICTURE "999,999.99"
? MONEY PICTURE "@999,999.99"
? MONEY FUNCTION "$"
```

Figure 13.6 shows the results of this transaction.

Fig. 13.6
The results of the
financial calcula-
tions converting
money functions.

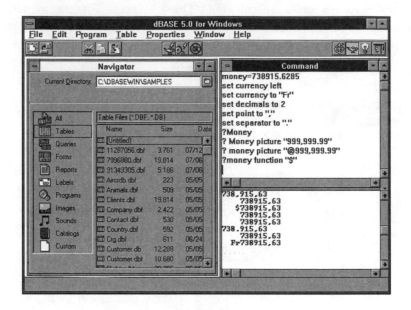

Table 13.8 shows examples of how you can format numeric data in the
Picture and Functions properties.

Table 13.8 Formatting Numeric Data	
Format Setting	**Property**
A number displayed exponentially	Function "^"
Display limited to *digits*, *signs*, and *blanks*	Picture "999", or Picture "####'
Display zero values as a blank string	Function "Z"
Leading zeroes shown as zeros, dollar signs, or asterisks	Function "L"
Display a number in standard currency	Function "$"
Display a CR for credit after a positive number, or DB for debit after a negative number	Function "C" Function "X"
Display negative number in parentheses	Function "("
Center, right-align, or left-align a number	Function "I" Function "J" Function "B"

The following example defines an entry field to display a person's name. The PICTURE property setting restricts data entry to that of characters only. The FUNCTION property trims both leading and trailing blanks.

```
DEFINE ENTRYFIELD Weight of This PROPERTY;
WIDTH 3
Top 11
Left 21
Height 1
ColorNormal = "bg+/b"
FontHeight 11, Border .F., Picture "XXXXXXXXXXXXXX", Function "T";
DATALINK "DIAGNOSIS"
```

Note

The PICTURE function uses Xs as placeholders. If you want a picture field that is 0 characters wide, type 10 Xs between the quotation marks. If you end up not using them all, or you require additional space, perform the appropriate adjustment at that point in the file.

Performing Financial Calculations

You can perform financial calculations by using three separate commands involving interest, investments, and loans.

- ■ FV() calculates the future value of a loan, or investment given equal periodic payments at a fixed interest rate.

- ■ PAYMENT() calculates a periodic payment amount required to pay a loan or investment based on a given principal, term, and interest rate.

- ■ PV() calculates the present value of a loan, or investment given equal periodic payments at a fixed interest rate.

An investment of $500 per month with an annual interest rate of seven percent compounded monthly over a 10 year period, for example, is computed with the following future value:

```
mAmount = FV(500, 0.9/12,12*10)
? mAmount Function "$"
```

In this example, the amount return by the program is $96,757.14. The total amount of deposits and interest generated after 10 years is written as:

```
? mAmount - (500*120)
```

The amount is $36,757.14, because 30,000 dollars was paid over the life of the loan. The last example determines the maximum mortgage amount an individual should assume with a desired payment level and prevailing interest rates. You use the PV() variable. The consumer wants to pay $894 per month with a 30 year, fixed mortgage at 6.75 percent interest. Note that this computation does not provide for taxes and insurance (the *TI* portion of the *PITI* [Principal, Interest, Taxes, and Insurance] equation).

```
mLoan = PV(894,0.0675/12,12*30)
? Loan Function "$"
```

The answer in this example is $137,835.74. Finally, you can use the PAYMENT() command when you know the principle and you want to determine the periodic payment amount. Using the figures from the previous example, you want to know the monthly house payment on your new $150,000 place in the sticks. The interest rate is 6.75 for 30 years:

```
mPayment = PAYMENT(150000,0.0675/12,12*30)
```

The answer is $972.90.

Figure 13.7 shows the results of the previous three paragraph examples.

Fig. 13.7

Results of financial examples.

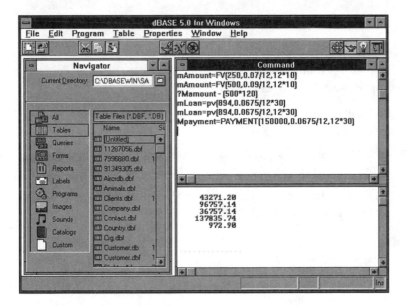

Computing Engineering and Scientific Formulas

You often need engineering and scientific computations to provide complex answers to equally complex questions. Table 13.9 lists the trigonometric functions that dBASE uses. These functions always return float values as part of their answers.

Table 13.9	Trigonometric Functions
Function	**Response**
ACOS()	The arc cosine of a number.
ASIN()	The arc sine of a number.
ATAN()	The arctangent of a number.
ATN2()	The arctangent of a given point.
COS()	The cosine of an angle.
DTOR()	The radian value of an angle measured in degrees.
RTOD()	The degree value of an angle measured in radians.
SIN()	The sine of an angle.
TAN()	The tangent of an angle.

For example, assume that you want to find the length of a steel beam for a 40-foot room with an angle of 40 degrees and an overhand of 24 inches.

```
mBeam = (40/2)/COS(DTOR(40)) + 2.0
? mBeam
```

The answer is 28.11.

Numeric expressions like the previous one often deliver responses that include decimal values. You can round those numbers (for example, from 24.59 to 25.00), or truncate them (for example from 24.59 to 25). The following commands perform these actions for you:

- CEILING() returns the nearest integer that is greater than or equal to the specified number.

- FLOOR() returns the nearest integer that is less than or equal to a specified number.

- INT() returns the integer portion of a specified number, but truncates the decimals.

- ROUND() rounds a specified number to a certain number of decimal places. The command SET DECIMALS rounds decimal values, too, but to the extent that they are greater than the number of specified decimal points.

In the example of the steel beam, assume now that you want to change the display—not the value—of the numbers:

```
? CEILING (mBeam)          (      Returns 29.00
? FLOOR (mBeam)            (      Returns 28.00
? ROUND (mBeam,1)          (      Returns 28.10
? INT(mBeam)               (      Returns 24.00
? mBeam - INT(mBeam)       (      Returns on the decimal
                           (        portion of 00.11
SET DECIMAL TO 8           (      Default is 2 decimal places
? mBeam                    (      Returns 28.10814579
? Round(mBeam,2)           (      Returns 24.11000000
SET DECIMAL TO 2           (      Default is 2 decimal places
? Round (mBeam,2)          (      Returns 28.11
```

To convert the decimal remainder of the steel beam to inches, use the following code:

```
mInches = 12*(mBeam - INT(mBeam))
mEighths = 8*(mInches - INT(mInches))
mBeamlen=LTRIM(STR(INT(mBeam)))+" Ft.
➥"+LTRIM(STR(INT(mInches)))+;
" "+LTRIM(STR(mEighths))+"/8 Inches"
?mBeamlen
```

The answer is 28 feet, 1 2/8 inches. The fraction normally rounds to a quarter-inch, but this example didn't make allowances for quarter inches.

Figure 13.8 illustrates the code.

Fig. 13.8

When you type the example data into the Command window, the results appear in the Results Pane.

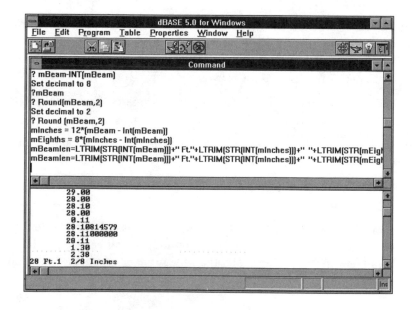

Working with Date Data

Date data present special opportunities, even when it is easy to pronounce the phrase without tripping. Although date values have some of the characteristics of numbers, they also require that you enter the data exactly as written, with the obligatory front slash mark (/) included. The following statement determines a date 30 days from today's date, as determined by the system clock in the computer.

```
mDue = {10/14/94}
mDue30 = mDue-30
?mDue30
```

The answer should be 09/14/94. Figure 13.9 illustrates the command-line syntax.

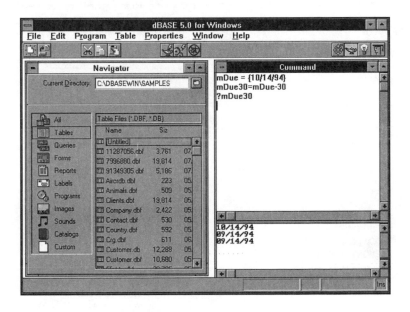

Fig. 13.9

The command-line syntax for your date data.

You can display dates in several formats, but the default is the date set in the WIN.INI file through the International option of the Windows Control panel.

Table 13.10 lists the commands and functions required to format and display dates correctly.

Table 13.10 Formatting and Displaying Dates	
Command/Function	**Description**
CDOW(), DOW()	Displays the day of the week as a word (CDOW( )) or as a number (DOW( )). *Sunday* is considered to be the first day of the week.
CMONTH(), MONTH()	Displays the month (CMONTH( )) as a word or a number (MONTH( )).
DAY()	Displays the day of the month as a number.
DMY(), MDY()	Displays the date formatted as DDMMYY, or as MMDDYY.
SET CENTURY	Displays the number of digits, either two or four, in the year portion of the date.
SET DATE	Displays the general formatting of dates, as in MM/DD/YY, DD-MM-YY, according to the specific country conversions.
SET MARK	Displays the characters used as separators in the day, month, and year.
YEAR()	Displays the years of a date as a four-digit number.

Formatting is demonstrated by the following lines of code:

```
mDate = {01/07/91}

SET CENTURY OFF
? CDOW(mDate)                           (        Returns Monday
? DOW(mDate)                    (       Returns 2
? CMONTH(mDate)                 (       Returns January
? MONTH(mDate)                          (        Returns 1
? DAY(mDate)                    (       Returns 7
? DMY(mDate)                    (       Returns 7 January 91
? MDY(mDate)                    (       Returns January 07, 91
SET CENTURY ON
? mDate                                 (       Returns 01/07/1991

SET DATE JAPAN
? mDate                                 (       Returns 1991/01/07
SET MARK TO "*"
? mDate                                 (       Returns 1991*01*07
SET CENTURY OFF
? YEAR(mDate)                           (       Returns 1991
```

Figure 13.10 illustrates these examples.

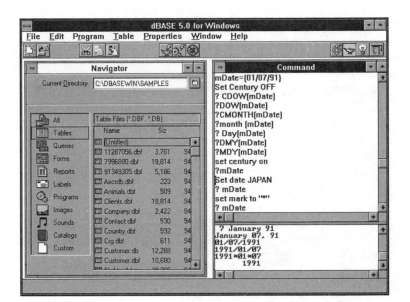

Fig. 13.10
The date examples illustrated in the Command window.

You can store time data as a character string and manipulate it as such. The TIME() function returns the current system time as a character string. You can store the current time in a memory value by typing **mTIME = TIME()**.

Table 13.11 lists the commands and functions that interact with the TIME() variable.

Table 13.11	Formatting and Displaying Times
Command/Function	**Description**
ELAPSED()	Displays the amount of elapsed time between two specific time periods.
SECONDS()	Displays the number of elapsed seconds since 12:00 am (midnight).
SET HOURS TO	Allows either a 12- or 24-hour format.
TIME()	Displays the system time.

For example, you can use the TIME() function to determine how long it takes to execute a subroutine:

```
mStart = TIME()
DO dbclock
mEnd = TIME()
mDURATION = ELAPSED(mEnd,mStart) / 3600
? mDuration
```

Figure 13.11 shows the results of running a program named DBCLOCK.PRG. You start the timer, run the program, stop the timer, and ask the computer to tell you how long it took for the program to execute (0.05 seconds).

Fig. 13.11
The results of running a timer program.

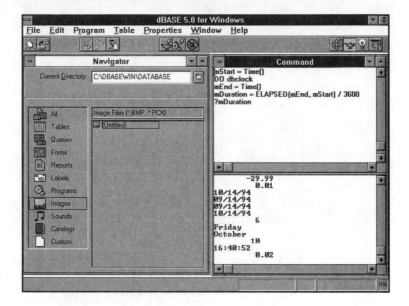

Working with Logical Data

dBASE allows you to work with *Boolean* data, which is data in the form of one of two values: *true* or *false*. Such fields typically store data that can have only one answer, such as Yes/No, Paid/Unpaid, Exempt/Non-Exempt, and so on.

When creating logical expressions to display this data, you can prepare two logical fields. dBASE accepts true (.T.) or false (.F.) data for this field—the response must be *positive* or *negative*.

Converting Data Types

You can convert data from one type to another. You can display data that is a character string, combined with a date or number. Calculations require that all data be converted into one type.

Table 13.12 shows how you can convert functions.

Table 13.12 Using Functions To Convert Data	
From/To Conversions	**Function**
Characters to numbers	VAL()
Numbers to Characters	STR()
Float to Numbers	FIXED()
Numbers to Float	FLOAT()
Characters to Date	CTOD()
Date to Characters	DTOC()
Indexing Date to Characters	DTOS()
Numbers, Logical	TRANSFORM()
Date to Characters	TRANSFORM()

Note: *The* TRANSFORM() *command returns a string of data in a specified format. For example,* TRANSFORM *should be used to format data in a report whenever* DISPLAY *or* LIST *is used to format that output. The formatting includes the alignment of text and the display of numbers in scientific notation.*

In the following example, TRANSFORM() is used to print BEGINBAL with commas and a BAL_DATE displayed in the DD/MM/YY format.

```
USE CLIENTS.DBF
INDEX ON COMPANY, BEGINBAL, BAL_DATE
SET FIELDS TO COMPANY, BEGINBAL, BAL_DATE
SCAN
? COMPANY, TRANSFORM(BEGINBAL,"999,999.99"),;
TRANSFORM(BAL_DATE,"@E");
ENDSCAN
```

The following example illustrates a method of indexing by date and amount. It then converts both the date and number fields to character strings:

```
INDEX ON DTOS(DATE_ORDER)+STR(AMOUNT,8,2) TO DATE_AMT
```

This second example extracts two characters each for the month and year fields from a MM/DD/YY date format. The data is then concatenated (joined) with a customer identification number to generate a unique invoice number:

```
mThis_year = RIGHT(DTOC(DATE()),2)
mThis_month = LEFT(DTOC(DATE()),2)
mInvoice_no = mCust_id + mThis_year + mThis_month
```

Using Preprocessor Directives

Preprocessor directives, as the name suggests, are statements that instruct dBASE to execute before compiling your code. You might want to perform some cut-and-paste routines or specify some other conditions.

This section describes how you can use the preprocessor directives to your benefit. When you compile a program, dBASE for Windows scans the code for any embedded preprocessor code. If it finds this code, it evaluates the code, generally creating a temporary file. Chapter 15 covers preprocessor directives in more detail.

Table 13.13 illustrates some preprocessor directives.

Table 13.13 Preprocessor Directives	
Directive	**Description**
#define	Defines an identifier.
#if/#endif	Compiles a section of code if an identifier has a certain value.
#ifdef/#endif	Compiles a certain section of code if an identifier is defined.
#ifndef/#endif	Compiles a certain section of code if an identified is undefined.
#include	Inserts a source code file at the current position.
#pragma	Specifies a compiler option.
#undef	Undefines an identifier.

> **Note**
>
> A preprocessor directive must start with a number sign; in fact, any line with a leading number sign is suspect as a preprocessor directive.

Defining Constants

One way of improving a program's performance is to represent constants with something called an *identifier*. This is a descriptive name applied to program text using the *#define* directive.

The simplest and most direct method of using constants is with a literal command. In the following example, a literal value of 2500 is used to represent the maximum number of customers: `DO While nCURRENT_CUST < 2500`.

You also can use memory variables to represent constant values. These variables are intended to make code easier to understand. However, using one slows the performance of the computer because the program has to revisit the variable constantly to decide whether it is still valid. Additionally, each defined variable uses a small amount of memory. Thus, defining many constants uses up memory resources.

The best way to represent constants is with the #define variable. The following line of code modifies the DO While nCURRENT_CUST < 2500 command shown previously:

```
#define nMax_Cust 2500
Do While nCurrentcust < nMaxCust
.
.
.
nCurrentCust = nCurrentCust + 1
Enddo
```

Every occurrence of the nMaxCust code is replaced with 2500 at compilation. This command is especially helpful when calling DLL functions that use integers and hexadecimal code.

Including Header Files

A program file inserted into another piece of code (typically at the top, but not always) is called a *header file*. During the preprocessing pass, dBASE substitutes all those lines it finds beginning with the #include statement with the contents of the filenames in the #include statement (as in #include stdio.h). If any of the header file information needs to be updated, it must be changed in the header file. Any statement that includes the STDIO.H file, for instance, uses the new definition.

Table 13.14 demonstrates some examples of data that fit well into header files.

Table 13.14 Examples of Data for Header Files	
Header File Information	**Example**
Identifiers that represent RGB values	#define COLOR 56,62,155
Identifiers that represent values displayed by INKEY(), READKEY(), LASTKEY(), and NEXTKEY()	#define CTRL-W 23
Application-specific constants	#define MASITEMS 10000

(continues)

Table 13.14 Continued	
Header File Information	**Example**
Function prototypes declared with the EXTERN command	EXTERN CWORD Funct() LIB.DLL
Constants used in Windows APIs	#define MB_ICONHAND HTOI("0010")
Custom class definitions	CLASS MyPushbutton of PUSHBUTTON

Debugging Your Programs

dBASE utilizes a full-featured debugger that you can run from within the program; or you can run it as an independent operation. Standard debugger operations allow you to control program execution through the Command window; watch and inspect the values of your variables, fields, arrays, objects and expressions; view and observe subroutine modules; and temporarily suspend or halt continued program execution at predefined points in the program. See the section on the debugger later in this chapter for additional information on how to use it to debug your programs.

You find three types of bugs in dBASE code:

■ *Compilation errors,* where syntactical errors are made. Examples of this error are when the number of open brackets does not equal closed parentheses and when the program is expecting a comma where you typed a period.

■ *Runtime errors,* where the program is trying to do something impossible, such as trying to open a nonexistent file in an equally nonexistent directory.

■ *Logical errors,* where things might look OK to you and the program might execute normally. However, when you come to inspect the results, you find that some error in your logic created an output file filled with trash. Although this is the most dangerous of the errors, it is the easiest to find with the debugger.

You can start the debugger within dBASE or start it as a stand-alone program from the Windows Program Manager. In dBASE, use the Navigator window to select Programs. Then right-click the program you want to debug and choose Debug from the SpeedMenu. You can also use the Command window to issue the command DEBUG. Once the Command window is on, click the DeBugger SpeedBar button.

Figure 13.13 illustrates the Debugger window. Either use the Navigator window to select the option, or click the red bug icon. Clicking the bug icon opens the Execute Program dialog box, shown in figure 13.12. Select the filename to run, and click OK to execute it.

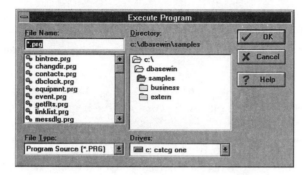

Fig. 13.12
The Execute
Program dialog box.

To load a program file when the debugger is open, select the Programs option from the Navigator window. Then choose Debug from the SpeedMenu. When the program is loaded, the program file opens in the Module window.

Figure 13.13 shows the Debugger window that opens when you call a program to run it.

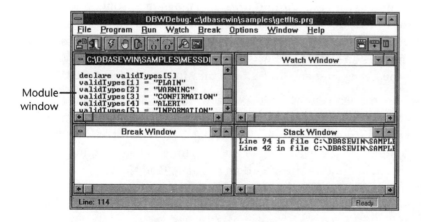

Fig. 13.13
The Debugger
window.

Four main windows constitute the debugger. The *module* window contains the source code of the program to be debugged. The *watch* window contains the watchpoints of any variables, fields, arrays, objects, and expressions that you set. The b*reak* window contains breakpoints that you set. Finally, the *stack* window keeps a count of all program calls to other modules, procedures, and UDFs. You can use the standard Windows commands to expand, contract, or close these windows.

After you load a program in the debugger, you can then load its subroutines (if any exist). If you load a main program that calls other program files, the debugger loads all files. However, you can also load a subroutine program file in the debugger before executing the calling command that would automatically load it. If you want to perform this option, choose File, Load Module from the Debugger menu. If you are in the module window, right-click the module window to bring up the module window SpeedMenu. Then choose Load Module. In the Select Module dialog box, specify the program file to be loaded.

You can go to any line number within this file by using the Program, Go To Line option. The program places the cursor at the beginning of the line you chose.

To find a text string in the current file, choose Program, Find from the Debugger menu. Type the text string that you are looking for, and then click OK. This text string command is case-sensitive: you must type the exact string that you are looking for, substituting a question mark for unknown text. In case of multiple entries, a Find Next command is available for you to find the next occurring text string quickly.

Using the Debugger's Text Editor

You can return to the text editor to work on a program at your option. Perhaps a line of code doesn't look right, or you want to add some material. You can return to the Text Editor from the Module window by moving the cursor to the offending line where you wish to begin editing. Then choose Program, Fix from the Debugger menu, or Fix from the Module window SpeedMenu.

You may use the text editor to find a current string or line of text in a file. To do this, choose Program, Find from the Debugger menu. Then specify the text that you are looking for in the Find dialog box. When the text is found, the cursor moves to the beginning of the text string. If you want to find the second occurrence of that string, choose Program, Find Next from the Debugger menu.

Caution

The search will begin from the cursor's current position and move forward through the file. It is also case-sensitive, so if you are looking for something very specific, you have to narrow your search accordingly. You may consider moving the cursor to the top of the file before you begin searching for text that you only suspect may be included in the file currently under consideration.

Controlling Program Execution with the Debugger

dBASE for Windows allows you to control a program's execution by employing several methods:

- *Animating* allows the debugger to continuously execute the program, but it pauses at each program line, updating all the information in the windows.

- *Tracing* allows you to run a program in the debugger and stop at whichever line you want.

- *Stepping* through a program is identical to tracing except that stepping steps over any command that calls a subroutine. Although the call to the subroutine still occurs, you don't see it being made.

- *Breakpoints* determines when to stop program execution. You can stop at a certain point to evaluate progress through the program or to check the value of variables, fields, arrays, and so on.

- *Stopping* allows you to terminate a program at full speed or under animation.

After a program is running, it generally ignores these execution considerations until it reaches the line of code in the module window where you placed the cursor prior to executing the program. If you want to run a program until it encounters a RETURN command, choose **R**un, **U**ntil Return from the **R**un menu.

Using Program Animation

In program animation, the debugger continues to execute the program, but it pauses at each line and updates all information in the other boxes at that point.

If you want to perform program animation, choose **R**un, **A**nimate from the Debugger main menu. The speed of the program may also be controlled separately by choosing **O**ptions, **A**nimation Speed. Then specify the speed in the Set Animation Speed dialog box by moving the scroll box in that scroll bar. Moving the scroll box to the left increases the animation speed; moving it in the opposite direction decreases the speed.

Using Program Tracing

This feature of the Debugger allows a program to be executed line by line throughout the program. Although this might seem a tedious job, it is sometimes a helpful option when all else has failed to find those pesky last minute errors. Don't confuse tracing with stepping (described next), however. Although tracing and stepping both execute line-by-line, tracing continues to execute and pause at each line in subroutines that the program calls. Stepping steps over all calls to subroutines, concentrating on the main program.

To trace through a program, click the Trace Into icon located on the Speedbar. Then choose **R**un, **T**race Into.

Using Program Stepping

Using program stepping is similar to using program tracing, except for the way that the method deals with subroutines. If you are not interested in stopping program execution within a subroutine, simply *step over* the command line that calls that subroutine. Although the call to the subroutine still occurs, you do have to watch the line-by-line execution of that piece of code.

> **Note**
>
> The debugger still stops at the first command line after the enountered subroutine.

To step through the program and over the command lines that call your subroutines, click the Step Over icon on the Speedbar. Then choose **R**un, **S**tep Over.

Using Program Breakpoints

Program breakpoints tell the program when to stop executing, allowing you to evaluate the results of your code as the program executes. You may want to perform ad hoc checks on such items as the value of variables, arrays, objects, and expressions.

One of the better aspects of performing breakpoints on your code, however, is that if you suspect that a particular piece of code is buggy, you can then set a breakpoint at that suspicious point in the program. When the program is executed, it runs as normal up to the point where you placed the breakpoint. Then the program halts temporarily while you check that what is produced is correct.

To set a breakpoint in your code, move the cursor into the Module window. Click when the cursor becomes a hand. Alternatively, you may move the cursor to the line of code where the breakpoint is to be applied, and choose **B**reak, **T**oggle from the Debugger menu. These two mechanisms provide a way for breakpoints to be added to your code.

After you identify the problem area, you obviously don't want to keep the breakpoint resident in your code, because to do so always causes the program to halt at that point. The clearest move is to remove it.

To take the breakpoint out of the code, move the cursor to the command line that contains the breakpoint. Then choose **B**reak, **T**oggle from the Debugger menu.

If you desire to remove all breakpoints within the code, choose **B**reak, **R**emove All from the Break window.

You may also choose to edit a breakpoint by selecting the breakpoint that needs work, and choosing **B**reak, **E**dit from the Debugger menu. You can then edit the breakpoint's description in the Edit Breakpoint dialog box.

Using Program Stopping

In addition to performing the previously described program execution activites, you can stop any program at any point in its progression by choosing **R**un, **S**top from the Debugger menu, or by clicking the Stop speedbar.

Note that stopping the program is the equivalent to pausing it: the program stops at the current line, which is highlighted, and the computer awaits your further instructions. Because the program is still running, that word appears at the right end of the status bar.

You may choose to reset the program currently running. If you choose to perform this action, be aware that the debugger first stops the program's current execution, clears the program from memory, and then reloads the program afresh from the hard disk. This activity is performed in order to guarantee that all memory registers are cleared of variables that might otherwise contribute to the corruption of your program when the program runs again.

> **Note**
>
> In order to terminate a program and clear it from memory completely, choose **R**un, **T**erminate, or **R**un, **S**top from the main menu. The debugger remains open, allowing you to load and run another program.

To terminate program execution, you simply click the Stop SpeedBar button. Alternatively, you can choose **R**un, **S**top from the Debugger menu.

Note that stopping a program merely halts it. Buffers are not cleared and the program is not closed. The program stops at a certain line, which remains highlighted in the Module window. If you want to terminate the program completely, select **R**un, Ter**m**inate; or **R**un from the SpeedMenu. Then choose **S**top.

Loading Subroutines

After a program has been loaded within the Debugger, you may be interested in loading any, or all of the subroutines that your program calls in order to view the sources code. Although the Debugger automatically loads all files, including those that call other program files when you run a main program, you can load a subroutine into the Debugger before executing the calling command that loads it automatically.

If you want to load the subroutines, perform the following commands from the Debugger menu:

1. Choose File, Load Module. The Select Module dialog box appears. Type in the subroutine program file that you want to load. This file is in addition to the current or main program file.

2. Then, from the Module window, right-click the Module window to bring up the SpeedMenu. Choose Load Module, and specify the program file that you want to load into the Debugger from the choices available.

Navigating around in the Module Window

In conjunction with the text editor, you may elect to cruise around your program's source code independent of program execution in the debugger.

For example, if you want to go to a specific line number, choose Program, and Go To Line from the Debugger menu. Alternatively, you may specify the number in the Go to Line dialog box.

> **Note**
>
> When you go to a line number, the cursor is placed at the beginning of the line selected. Program execution isn't affected.

The Debugger retains a history of all the line numbers that you accessed during the course of your programming session. If you later wish to revisit any line number, choose Program, Go to Line from the Debugger menu. Then click the down arrow to the right of the line numbering selection in the Go to Line dialog box. You may also choose an earlier-accessed line number from the pull-down menu.

To return to the previous line from the Debugger menu, choose Program, Previous Line from the Debugger menu.

Evaluating Watchpoints

The term *watchpoints* is really a fancy term for watching what's going on with your code as it executes. You may decide that you want to keep an eye on the values of your expressions using value placeholders. The debugger provides this type of assistance within the Watch window; you may also set up a watchpoint for an expression before any other variable, field, array, or object it contains is initialized by your program.

With a watchpoint in place, dBASE for Windows evaluates them and displays their current values embedded between parentheses located to the right of them in the Watch window. The watchpoint value is always displayed as your program executes; you may determine whether an incorrect value has been assigned to a variable as the program runs.

To add a watchpoint into your code, highlight an expression, such as a variable. Then move the cursor to the expression that is located in the Module window. Choose Watch, Add from the debugger, and watch the selected expression appear in the dialog box.

After a watchpoint has been added, you may elect to edit it by choosing Watch, Edit from the Debugger window. Once the Edit Watchpoint dialog box appears, you may edit the description.

Inspecting Your Expressions

Performing an inspection on an expression is not the same thing as watching as one executes. Although you are free to create a watchpoint for an expression at any time, you can establish an inspection process for one only after the variables and other expressions are initialized. This is so the expression has some value in the current program.

If you want to inspect an expression, highlight the expression, and click the Inspect Speedbar button from the Module window. Then choose Program, Inspect and watch the selected inspection appear in the Inspect dialog box. Each window contains its own inspect window which you can open by right-clicking the mouse within the window. When the Inspect Window Speedmenu is clicked, you can perform an upper or lower range, change the value of the selected item, or descend to establish an inspection for the selected item in the current inspect window.

Configuring the Debugger

You can set environment options in the Debugger menu by selecting the **O**ptions menu from the Debugger menu. You can append these changes to a .CFG file or restore them to the current session by loading an existing .CFG file. You can create more than one .CFG file, each containing different configuration settings.

You can create an initial configuration file from the Options dialog box and then choose Defaults. You can set the following parameters: *Desktop*, where the particular arrangement of the four debugger windows and the location of the SpeedBar are changed; *Application*, where the particular application to debug is named; *Breakpoints*, where currently set parameters are listed; and *Watchpoints*, where currently set parameters are listed.

In figure 13.14, the Defaults dialog box is displayed. Along with the aforementioned configuration options, you can display the SpeedBar in four ways (including off).

Fig. 13.14
The Defaults
dialog box.

When you finish making these selections, choose **O**ptions, Save **O**ptions. If you do not name a file at this point, a DEFAULT.CFG file is created containing your new selections. Until you have a .CFG file, the computer uses the defaults in Windows configurations.

Figure 13.15 shows the Save Configuration dialog box. The file is saved as a DEFAULT.CFG file unless you name it as something else. You can, for example, have several configuration files, each of which contains data specific to each of your projects.

To specify the configuration options that you want to save into a new .CFG file, choose Options, Defaults from the Debugger window.

The Options dialog box allows you to make changes to the way the screen appears. From the options box, you can alter the way the desktop is arranged with respect to the four debugger windows and the placement of the SpeedBar, select which default application is debugged, determine which breakpoints are currently set in the Breakpoint window, and determine which watchpoint sets are currently set.

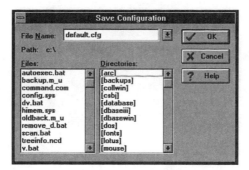

Fig. 13.15
The Save Configuration dialog box.

You can turn off the debugger SpeedBar, or reposition it on-screen by clicking the following buttons: Off, Popup, Horizontal, Vertical. The Horizontal setting is the default.

When you choose Options, Save Options from the main menu, the settings are saved to a .CFG file of your specification.

> **Note**
>
> Unless you create and restore a .CFG file, the Debugger employs the Windows system font, the current working directory, and the fastest animation speed as its defaults. All windows are showing when the Debugger opens, and the SpeedBar is located in the area immediately beneath the main menu. There are no default breakpoints, watchpoints, or applications set to run for you; all these options you must set yourself.

Running Multiple Instances of the Debugger

You might, at some point, decide to run multiple instances of both dBASE and the debugger. If the debugger is started from dBASE, it automatically attaches to the running copy of dBASE. If multiple copies of the software are running, you can execute different applications in each window. You can then decide which version you want to attach the debugger to. To run multiple instances of the debugger, choose **F**ile, **A**ttach. In the Attach to Active Application dialog box, specify to which application you want to make the attachment.

Figure 13.16 shows the Attach to Active Application dialog box. You can minimize the window on your desktop after you make the attachment. Your application runs in the background, notifying you when problems arise.

Fig. 13.16
The Attach to
Active Application
dialog box.

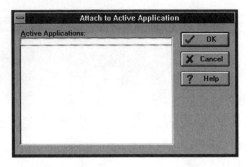

Summary

This chapter showed you a large number of programming options commands for use in dBASE for Windows. You learned a lot about syntax and functionality for implementing your applications. The use of the dBASE for Windows Debugger was also discussed. Effective, accurate programming still takes time to develop, but the days when you must laboriously type every command into the computer have been replaced by graphical user interfaces that quickly identify errors in your code.

Chapter 14

Performing Object-Oriented Programming

The dBASE for Windows environment is based on a relatively new concept in programming known as *object-oriented programming*. dBASE programming employs objects and classes, which enable you to reuse program code. You can create objects from built-in classes or from classes declared by users. You can query a property, and in most cases, alter its value. You can add new properties to an object; dBASE makes the changes immediately so that you can see them as you continue.

Using Objects

In the dBASE for Windows world, *objects* are a collection of memory values that store and use memory variables. These memory variables can hold data or they can reference subroutines that the computer references during program execution. An object-oriented program thus uses a combination of data and subroutines that is *self-reliant*—outside sources are not required for the program to execute. The object becomes a part of a larger program as part of a containerized effect. Each small program builds on the capability of another. Again, with respect to dBASE, forms are probably the most common examples of how an object becomes contained. The main form object is the container, also known as a parent. The elements of a form, notably entry fields, listboxes, pushbutton, and so on, which are also a part of the user interface, are known as the *child,* because they are subordinate to the parent object.

Using Classes

A *class* is a specification that allows for the multiple creation of a particular object. In the absence of a class, each time you wanted to use a piece of code, you would have to rewrite it, debug it, and run it to make sure it is what you required. Classes have become metamorphosed into manufacturing facilities that crank out finished products consisting of identical classes. If you consider the entry fields and other elements of the form just described, you can see that having to reproduce a new element each time the same form is utilized is a chore. Using a search class to define the element and then create as many instances of that element as you need is much simpler.

Classes also allow the declaration of custom classes by using a native set of classes or by creating and using your own data.

There are three subsections to this chapter:

- Understanding the concepts behind object-oriented programming.

- Using objects, which as you just saw, are collections of memory values used to store and use memory variables.

- Using classes that allow you to create multiple copies of the same object.

Property Programming Activities

With the object-oriented capabilities provided with dBASE for Windows, it is now possible to develop code with assign statements. In the so-called property-programming environment, which allows you to change the properties objects through code enhancements, you make those changes directly to the object that you want to change; the computer does the rest for you, making its modifications as you work along.

For example, if you want to open a simple form named TEST1 within the dBASE for Windows environment. Either type the following two lines of code into the Command window of dBASE, or create and execute a program file containing them:

```
DEFINE FORM Test1
TEST1.OPEN()
```

The results of these two commands are shown in figure 14.1. This is an example of an instant form class, which in this case, is called TEST1.

You can now add to these lines and start to customize the form a little.

You must either add the following code to the lines previously typed or begin
with a new series of information. You may also create a .PRG (program file)
containing these lines and run the program. However, doing so does not
allow you to examine these lines without adding a series of WAIT statements
in the code.

```
TEST1.TOP = 10
TEST1.TOP = TEST1.TOP + 5
TEST1.ColorNormal = "b+/GB"
TEST1.WindowState = 1
TEST1.WindowState = 0
```

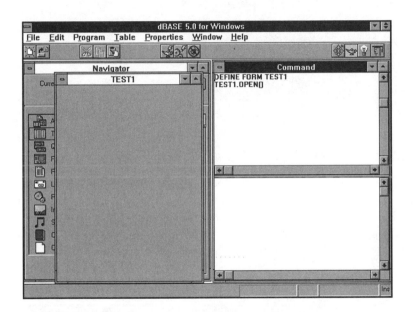

Fig. 14.1
Defining two lines
of code to open a
form.

In figure 14.2, the lines added to the Command window first move the form
to row 10 and then down five additional rows. The color of the form's interior is then changed to a blue/green color. The color has changed, although
the results printed in this book are in black and white and do not reflect your
actual (color monitor) results. The next line, where the WindowState is set to 1,
minimizes the form. You can click the form to return it to its original size.
Finally, the second WindowState command restores the form to its original
position.

Fig. 14.2

The New TEST1 form with additional properties.

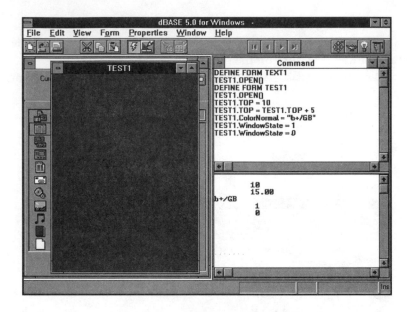

Using the Object Inspector

The Object Inspector allows you to edit all of an object's properties interactively—on the fly. To look at the previous examples, launch the Object Inspector by typing **INSPECT(TEST1)** in the Command window. This command opens the Object Inspector with the TEST1 properties exposed. Figure 14.3 shows the Object Inspector for the TEST1 form.

Fig. 14.3

The Object Inspector open to the TEST1 form.

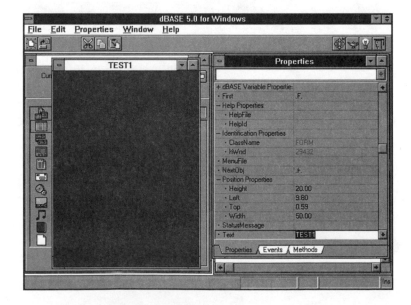

To ensure that you see all the Object Inspector has to offer at this point, make sure that the Properties tab is selected. With the name of the form (TEST1) in the Properties and Form boxes, you know you have the correct form and the allied Object Inspector box on-screen. Note that in figure 14.3, each plus (+) sign next to a major heading means that there are additional subheadings below that main title. The legend .F. means that a particular value is false. At the title level, Position Properties, you can see the current location of the TEST1 box. If you want to change these values, click the TEST1 box and move the height, left, top, and width attributes. As you move them, the attributes in the Object Inspector move interactively.

Finally, you may change the title of the box from TEST1 to something of your own creation by eliminating the legend TEST1 from the text box at the bottom of the Object Inspector Properties tab.

> **Note**
>
> You can change the vertical sizing of the Object Inspector according to your wishes. Move the cursor into the vertical dotted line. Wait for the icon to change to a double-headed arrow, and then move to make the title box larger, or the data box smaller.

When you finish manipulating the Object Inspector and the TEST1 form, you can close them independently by clicking the box in the upper-left corner of each box.

Understanding Object Containership

Objects, as you may suspect, can contain other objects. When such an arrangement is made, the relationship is known as a parent/child association. The parent is the main object, whereas each subordinate is a child. Qualifying child objects include items such as dialog boxes, entry fields, pushbuttons, and so on.

In the following example, a form object (the parent) is created with a text object (Text) and an entry field object (Entry). You can type the lines of code into dBASE's Command window:

```
DEFINE FORM TEST2 PROPERTY TOP 5, LEFT 3
DEFINE TEXT TEXT of TEST2 PROPERTY Top 2, Left 2, Text "Name"
DEFINE ENTRYFIELD ENTRY of TEST2 PROPERTY Top 2, Left 9, Value
"Perron"
OPEN FORM TEST2
```

In figure 14.4, the results of these four lines of code appear. First, the form name (TEST2) is defined. The text entry field that fits inside the TEST2 box is then defined; finally the entryfield—the information that fits inside the ENTRYFIELD box—and its location is defined. Finally, the computer is told to open the as-defined TEST2 form.

Fig. 14.4
The TEST2 dialog box.

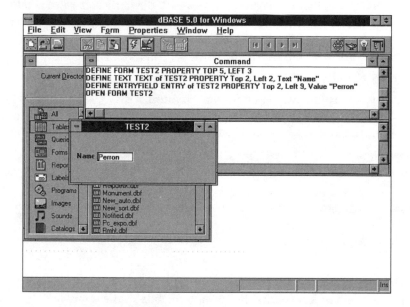

> **Note**
>
> The Command window and the resulting box in figure 14.4 were moved from their original locations to provide a full line of code and a full box display on-screen. Your initial results do not show this screen.

Creating Objects

As you saw from the introduction, when you create a memory variable, you simply declare it as a name. It can be anything you want to call it, but you must declare the number and the number of rows and columns that you intend for it to occupy. In the following example, an array is declared that is 5 rows by 2 columns.

```
DECLARE ARRAY[5,2]
ARRAY[1,1] = "First Item"
```

You can create objects in dBASE for Windows in one of two ways. Either use the DEFINE command to create an object and set the initial values that it will contain with one command, or use the NEW operator in a memory variable assignment statement. The NEW operator creates an object but, unlike the DEFINE command, doesn't specify any values for its properties. You must declare additional assignment statements in order to assign property values.

The NEW command is usually used to create an object when its properties do not have to be changed.

Tip
Always remember that the first number declared in a statement of this nature is a row, and the second number, separated from a row by a comma, is the column.

Referencing Object Members

You create a reference variable by using the name of the variable in an expression. In the following example, a memory variable is declared and a value is assigned to it. In the first declarative statement, a 10-by-10 array is created and a value is assigned to the element. The final line prints a string of text on-screen, with the expression declared at its conclusion.

```
LOCAL FIRSTNAME
Firstname = "Pooh"
Replace FIRSTNAME with FIRSTNAME
DECLARE ARRAY1[10,10]
ARRAY1[1,1] = "Hunnee"
?  "Sorry, we are fresh out of ",ARRAY1[1,1]
```

Understanding the Dot Operator

The periods that appear midway through the second and third line in the following example allow you to reference members by a specific name. This *dot operator* is the most common method used to name object properties or methods.

Caution

Don't confuse the dot operator with the old *dot prompt*. They are not the same thing.

The dot operator's syntax is usually known as *dot notation* and takes the following syntax:

```
DEFINE FORM FORM1
FORM1.LEFT = 200
FORM1.TEXT = "Hi There!"
```

In the previous example, the three lines of code define a form called FORM1. This form is opened with a left property of 200 and prints the phrase "Hi There" in the Results pane.

A dot operator can also define an object reference, referring to a child object. References may be made to child objects by building a path of object references that lead to the referenced property. In the example code that follows, the two lines should be added to the three listed previously. The first definition defines a pushbutton called FORM1. The second line sets the top property of FORM1 that will be located in FORM.

```
DEFINE PUSHBUTTON FORM1
FORM,BUTTON=2
```

> **Note**
>
> You are not obliged to type text in as either uppercase or lowercase. In examples where text is mixed case, it is sometimes easier to identify errors in your code.

Using the Index Operator

Next in line is the *index operator,* which is separated by a pair of square brackets []. Index operators make reference to a member by number instead of by name. The index operator is normally used to reference array objects, because it is from arrays that the index operator derives its name. Brackets thus enclose the index location of an element within an array. The index operator takes the following syntax:

```
OBJECT = NEW Object()
OBJECT[1] = "Our Street Number is 1"
OBJECT[2] = "The Physical Street is 2"
? OBJECT[1]
? OBJECT[2]
```

Using Custom Properties and Methods

Custom properties, as the name suggests, allow you to add sole-use properties to members of an object. All methods begin life as a subroutine of some type. They become methods when they are associated with a class. You associate a subroutine by assigning it to a function pointer or code block variable that is a member of a class.

Three methods exist to associate a method with a class:

- You can declare a function or procedure in the class definition, which means that any subroutine declared inside the class automatically causes dBASE to create a function pointer variable of the same name within the class.

■ You can declare a function outside the class definition and assign a property within the class to the subroutine name.

■ You can assign a codeblock to a variable within a class definition. This last choice is the safest if you are creating code that is a only a few lines long.

Custom properties are added with either one of the following commands:

■ Use the DEFINE command with the CUSTOM option. The CUSTOM option marks the beginning of a custom property declaration list just as the PROPERTY option begins a list of built-in properties.

■ Use the NEW operator only to type the new property or method name after the dot operator.

The following commands use the CUSTOM option of DEFINE to add a custom member of an object, whereas the second offers a NEW operator example.

```
* First Example : A Custom Operator
DEFINE FORM CUSTOM1
PROPERTY
TOP 5
LEFT 10
CUSTOM
GREETING " Hi There!"
LOTTO 21

* Second Example: a New Option Operator
CUSTOM1 = NEW FORM()
CUSTOM1.TOP =5
CUSTOM1.LEFT = 10
CUSTOM1.GREETING = "Hi There!"
CUSTOM1.LOTTO = 21
```

Caution

Make extra sure that when using the dot operator to set your properties, you do not misspell any aspect of the assignment statement. If you do so, dBASE for Windows assumes that you want to add a new custom member with the misspelled name. When it does that, no additional errors are provided, and it is possible that you won't notice that a new variable has sneaked into your code until a good bit further down the road.

You can create objects also within other objects by using the aforementioned DEFINE or NEW operators. Then, once you make the reference, you can use these operators together.

The following piece of code demonstrates the use of DEFINE with the parent reference option. There is a single reference to the child:

```
DEFINE FORM FORM3
DEFINE PUSHBUTTON FORM3 of FORM2
```

With the NEW operator, a reference is passed to the parent object as a parameter.

```
FORM3 = NEW FORM()
FORM3.BUTTON1 = PUSHBUTTON(FORM3)
```

Unlike the DEFINE operator, NEW can create two references to the child. In the following lines of code, two references are made to the child. The first is a member of the parent, and an additional reference is specified in an assignment statement. PUSH1 and PUSH2 are created with one reference, whereas PUSH3 is created with two references:

```
DEFINE FORM FORM3
DEFINE PUSHBUTTON PUSH1 of FORM3
FORM3.PUSH2 = NEW PUSHBUTTON(FORM3)
PUSH3 = NEW PUSHBUTTON(FORM3,"Third")
```

Thus created, both PUSH1 and PUSH2 may be accessed with a command similar to FORM3.PUSH1.<member name> or by using FORM3.THIRDPUSH1.<member name>, or finally with the command PUSH3.<member name>.

Using Object Reference Variables

Traditional memory variables *always* contain values of some type. A numerical variable contains a number; a character string always contains letters. If you assign a memory variable to another variable, the contents of the first variable are always copied to the contents of the second variable. Any changes that are made to the first have little affect on the contents of the second variable.

In the following example, two variables are named, FIRSTNAME and SECONDNAME. The first name contains the string "Rabbit", whereas the second string contains the string "Pooh". When you question the computer the first time, you find that these variables are true. Then you switch the names and, upon asking the computer for the variable names again, you find that they have changed.

```
FIRSTNAME="Rabbit"
SECONDNAME= FIRSTNAME
FIRSTNAME="Pooh"
? FIRSTNAME
? SECONDNAME
```

Type these lines into the Command window and watch the Results pane in the bottom half of the Command window display the results of the lines of code.

An *object reference variable*, however, contains *a reference* to an object, not the actual object. If one object reference is assigned to another variable, the object isn't duplicated; it merely contains a second reference to the same object.

In the following lines of code, a form is created with a reference to the original form. The form is opened, and the text and top properties are changed. Then a second object reference variable is opened and variables alter the form object.

```
FORM1 = NEW Form()
Open Form FORM1
? Type("Form")
FORM1.TEXT = "My Form"
FORM1.TOP = 10
```

Type these lines into the Command window and watch the Results pane display the results of the second set of code.

This next series of code creates a second object reference variable. These lines may be entered into the Command window and the results observed in the form's behavior. Watch the Results pane.

```
FORM2 = FORM1
? FORM2.Text
FORM2.Text = "This is a Good Form"
? FORM2.TEXT
? FORM1.TEXT
```

These two lines of code have now been tied together in that they both refer to the same object.

Using Arrays as Objects

In previous paragraphs, you read about arrays being objects within the dBASE arena. When an array is created, it is really an object that is based on the built array class. However, by using objects as arrays within dBASE for Windows, you may work with them in different manners.

You can create an array with the DECLARE command or with the NEW operator. When you use DECLARE, you must specify the array's dimensions, whereas the NEW operator allows you to pass the dimensions as parameters.

The following lines of code show two ways to declare arrays; the first uses the DECLARE command and the second uses the NEW array variable.

```
DECLARE ARRAY1[6,3]
ARRAY1.DIR()
```

In the first example, a six-by-three array is declared and then filled with a current directory listing. In the second example (following), the array is declared with the NEW operator to be a six-by-four array.

```
ARRAY1 = NEW ARRAY(6,4)
ARRAY1.FILL(0)
? ARRAY1[2,2]
```

Table 14.1 summarizes some of the more important array class methods.

Table 14.1	Array Class Methods
Method	**Description**
ADD( )	Adds an element to the array.
COPY( )	Copies an element to another array.
DELETE( )	Deletes an element, column, or row.
DIR( )	Fills the array with a current directory listing.
ELEMENT( )	Displays the element number of a specified element subscript.
FIELDS( )	Fills the array with the structure of the current table.
FILL( )	Inserts a specified value into one or more elements.
GROW( )	Adds an element, column, or row.
INSERT( )	Inserts a false value (.F.) into a specified element.
RESIZE( )	Increases or decreases the size of the array.
SCAN( )	Searches a declared array for a specified expression.
SORT( )	Sorts the elements into a one- or two-dimensional array.
SUBSCRIPT( )	Displays the subscript for a specified element number.

Working with Classes

As you saw at the beginning of this chapter, a class is a specification that allows you to create multiple copies of a particular object. In previous examples, if you wanted to reuse a piece of code, you had to rewrite it. In this section, you learn about classes, hierarchies, and creating and using classes that are based on other classes.

Declaring Classes

Classes are declared by using a CLASS/ENDCLASS command. A class consists of a method declaration and constructor code, which executes when an object of that class is created. A method declaration statement contains code that executes at the same time after the object is created.

In the following piece of code, a simple class declaration is built that names the class and uses constructor code to initialize properties.

```
CLASS ITEM1
This.Item = "Things"
This.Size = 15
This.Cost = 12.49
This.Qty = 2
Function CalcCost
Local X
X=This.COST*This.Qty
Return X
ENDCLASS
```

Caution

You may type this code into a .PRG file and then run it from the Command window. The line refuses to execute if you try to type these commands individually into the Command window.

So far, the previous example allowed you to build a degree of self-contained code, where all the variable and parameters are neatly ensconced between the CLASS and ENDCLASS statements. In the next example, you use an outside entity to return a value. The word THIS refers to the object that is created by the class. Any assignment statement that begins with THIS declares a property for those objects declared by the class.

```
CLASS SQUARE
This.Num = 3.142
This.SquareNum = This.Num * This.Num
ENDCLASS
```

Note

You can declare memory variables in constructor code to store temporary values while you create the object. Constructor code allows you to declare local, private, and public variables, but you cannot declare static variables.

Using Methods Associated with Classes

A method normally begins life as a subroutine and metamorphoses into a method once it becomes associated with a class. The association is made by assigning it with a function pointer or codeblock variable that is associated with a class.

Three main techniques are available to make this association. First, to declare a function of procedure within the class definition, declare a function outside the class definition, or assign a codeblock to a variable within a class definition.

In the first example, a function is declared within the class definition. Every time a subroutine is declared inside the class, dBASE for Windows creates a function pointer variable of the same name within the class.

```
CLASS OBJECT1
this.text = "My own object"
this.top = 15
this.left = 7
PROCEDURE Beep
? chr(7)
RETURN .T.

PROCEDURE TTFN
? "See Ya Later"
RELEASE Object this
RETURN .T.
ENDCLASS
```

The second example places a declared function or procedure outside the class definition. You can place the subroutine in a procedure file where it can serve as a method for more than one class.

```
CLASS OBJECT1
this.text = "My own object"
this.top = 15
this.left = 7
this.Beep = Beep
this.TTFN = Tarah
ENDCLASS

PROCEDURE Beep
? chr(7)
RETURN .T.

PROCEDURE Tarah
? "See Ya Later"
RELEASE OBJECT this
RETURN .T.
```

Finally, here is a piece of code that assigns a codeblock to a variable within a class definition. Arguably, this is the simplest way of declaring a method with a few short lines of code.

```
CLASS OBJECT1
this.text = "My own object"
this.top = 15
this.left = 7
this.Beep = {;?chr(7))
this.Tarah = {;? "See Ya Later";
➡RELEASE OBJECT this}
```

> **Note**
>
> If the same name is assigned to both a method and a property, dBASE for Windows assumes the property name in expressions.

Declaring Class Parameters

Class parameters are declared in a declaration passed to the constructor code when an object is created.

You can place the parameters between a set of parentheses at the end of a class name. This is the preferred method because parameters passed in this manner are local to the class. You also can use a PARAMETERS statement as the first line of the constructor code.

In the following two examples of code, the parameter is first declared as a local parameter:

```
* Declaring a local Parameter
CLASS Square()
this.Num = n
this.SquareNum = n*n
ENDCLASS
```

In the second example, a private parameter is declared:

```
* Declaring a private Parameter
CLASS Square()
Parameters n
this.Num = n
this.SquareNum = n*n
ENDCLASS
```

Using Class Hierarchies

Classes based on hierarchies are called *subclasses*. They inherit members of the class on which they are based, allowing you to add or modify subclass members. You can then use existing classes similar in scope to previous entities.

The greatest benefit to subclasses is when a hierarchy of classes is built, with each subclass inheriting most of its functionality from a superclass. A *superclass* is a regular class that has inherited members. Look here at a simple example.

You built a series of forms and reports, each of which has pushbuttons that execute in the *event-driven* style. You want each of the forms and reports to have a consistent look and feel about them, and in order to do this, you decide to develop a style for your pushbuttons. The pushbuttons will look the same each time you use them in your application. This class declaration helps to define the characteristics of your pushbutton design:

```
CLASS BUTTON(Form, Top, Left) OF PUSHBUTTON(Form)
this.Top = Top
this.Left = Left
this.Text = "Button"
this.FontName = "Times Roman"
this.FontBold = .T.
this.FontWidth = 6
this.SetWidth = {;this.width = LEN(this.Text)+2}
ENDCLASS
```

This piece of code defines how the button is positioned on-screen: its font, its width, and its style. In the next code lines, you decide that all button bars should beep when they are clicked. You inherit the piece of code from the previous example and add to it:

```
CLASS BEEP(Form, Top, Left) of BUTTON(Form, Top, Left)
this.Text = "Beep"
this.SetWidth()
PROCEDURE OnClick
? CHR(7)
RETURN
ENDCLASS
```

Finally, you decide that a button should also move when it is clicked. The previous example's code is inherited again; then you modify it to create specifications that move the button over by five spaces:

```
CLASS BEEPMOVE(Form, Top, Left) of BEEPBUTTON(Form, Top, Left)
this.Text = "Beep and Move"
this.SetWidth()
PROCEDURE OnClick
BEEPBUTTON::OnClick(
this.left = this.left+5
RETURN
ENDCLASS
```

In a final example, a beeping button grows by some amount when it is selected. There are few changes from the previous example—the OnClick command is overridden with a codeblock instead of a procedure.

```
CLASS BEEPGROW(Form, Top, Left) of BEEPBUTTON(Form, Top, Left)
    this.Text = "Beep and Grow"
    this.SetWidth()
    this.SetWidth()
    this.OnClick = {;Super::OnClick();this.Width = This.Width + 1}
ENDCLASS
```

Two explanations are required for this last piece of code. First, Super in the penultimate line of code defines a superclass of code instead of a subclass. Following Super is a double colon (::). In this example, the double colon is known as *a scope-resolution operator*. You already know that a single dot associates a member with an object; the scope resolution operator associates a method with the class in which it is declared.

Subclasses work best when they have been built into a hierarchy of classes, such that each subclass inherits its functionality from a superclass. One of the goals of object-oriented programming is the capability to group related tasks into classes and then arrange those classes into hierarchies. If you can do this effectively, the result is a series of modules that is easily maintained with a high degree of reusability.

Using the Scope Resolution Operator

You previously read about the dot notation operator and how it references an object's methods. A reference may also be made directly from the class in which it resides. This technique is most useful for calling methods that are declared in different levels of a class hierarchy.

To use the reference method from a class, you use a scope-resolution operator (::). As stated earlier, this operator associates a method with the class in which it was declared.

In the following piece of code, the OnClick event for the pushbutton is set to the BUTTON1_ONCLICK procedure in the current class:

```
CLASS Beep of FORM1
                this.EscExit = .T.
                this.Text = "My Form Name Goes in Here"
                this.Width =                  65.25
                this.Top =                     8.08
                this.Left =                   25.00
                this.Height =                 34.25
DEFINE PUSHBUTTON BUTTON1 of this;
                PROPERTY;
                OnClick class::Button1_ONCLICK,;
                Text "Button One",;
                Width          21.00,;
                Top            12.00,;
```

```
Left              12.00,;
Height             4.00,;
PROCEDURE BUTTON1_OnClick
? chr(7)
ENDCLASS
```

Tip
With many differ-
ent lines of code
that contain num-
bers, use the Tab
key to align them.
When it comes to
debugging time,
you will find it
easier to find the
error if all the
numbers are
aligned.

You can type this code into a .PRG file and execute it from the Command window.

Designing an Object-Oriented System

An object-oriented system is one that was born to create simplicity out of chaotic and often complex computer software systems. OOPs is the preferred strategy for developing applications that go beyond the simple, everyday types of objects and their properties that may be set without having to think much more about what is happening beyond the subject's immediate scope.

When larger projects are the order of the day, it is easier to build software modules using modeling techniques. A team approach may be successfully used in which more than one programmer is engaged in building code. S/he is able to share modules and code among other members of the group without the other members having to build and rebuild their own modules. Thus, a more cohesive, robust, and shareable series of modules may be built. Finally, with OOPS code in place, a new programming team can come on board and quickly pick up after the development team to support field-based applications.

Once the programming team has been assembled, you should generally approach the problem from a top-down process that identifies the global requirements for the job, breaking down each task into separate operating modules, each with its own distinct requirements, beginning and ending points. The OOPs programming team breaks the problem down into classes and assembles those classes into hierarchies that eventually form the backbone of the finished application.

Having touched upon the global design steps, there are several vital steps that you should take before your programming team warms to its task. First, identify the classes that make up the application. This portion of the package involves consideration of the project's central requirements: what data is needed, how it will be derived and tracked, what output is required, and so on. After you identify this data, you should determine what classes will carry what portion of the overall project.

You then should generate a list for each class that catalogues each piece of information that will be used, and the tasks it is expected to perform. As this data comes together, the common elements among the classes should be identified. By definition, some stand alone, whereas others can be grouped into a hierarchy of some type. Finally, implement the classes into their respective divisions.

It goes without saying that you should document every step of the way, including pictures and diagrams that depict and describe the many relationships each enjoys. Whether you are a manager of a development group, a client who has ordered a particular piece of code, or an entrepreneur who wants to try his or her hand at commercially available software, a technical journal of every aspect of the journey is helpful to everyone after the job is done.

For more information about the software development process, I suggest the following books:

- *Managing the Software Process*, by Watts S. Humphrey, Addison-Wesley Publishing Company, Reading, Massachusetts

- *The Decline and Fall of the American Programmer*, by Edward Yourdon, Prentice Hall, Inc., Englewood Cliffs, New Jersey

Summary

This chapter introduced you to some concepts behind the new industry buzzword surrounding object-oriented programming. Objects, classes, and property programming were defined, and the Object Inspector, which allows you to edit all of an object's properties interactively was demonstrated. I showed you how to create and reference objects and various submembers. Then I described how custom properties and methods are declared and added to properties. Finally, an overview of the steps and methods required for creating useful, maintainable computer code was presented.

Alternatively, you can use the DEFINE command:

```
DEFINE DDELINK LinkObj
```

Table 15.1 summarizes the DDELink class properties.

Table 15.1	DDELink Class Properties
Property	**Description**
Advise( )	Creates a hot link by asking the server to notify the client when an item in the server document has changed.
ClassName	Identifies the DDELink object class.
Execute( )	Sends instructions to the server in a native language.
Initiate( )	Begins a conversation with a DDE server application.
OnNewValue	Executes a subroutine when a hot-linked item in the server application has changed.
Peek( )	Retrieves a data item stored in a server document.
Poke( )	Inserts a data item into a server document.
Reconnect( )	Restores a DDE link terminated with the TERMINATE( ) command.
Release( )	Removes the DDELink object definition from memory.
Server	Holds the name of the DDE server application.
TimeOut	Determines the amount of time that dBASE waits before returning an error.
Topic	Contains the topic's name specified with the INITIATE( ) command.
Unadvise( )	Asks the server to stop notifying the DDELink object when an item in the server document changes.

Establishing and Terminating the Link

The server must be running before you can identify a client, thereby establishing a link. You use the INITIATE() command to open a session and establish a link.

The following code attempts to initiate a server session in Microsoft Excel for Windows, open a spreadsheet file named LOAF.XLS, and establish a data link between dBASE and Excel.

In the following example, the client tries to establish a link with the initiate command INITIATE(). The first portion of the command ("MXW") is the main executable file of the server application. The second position is the name of the data file in the server session to which the client/server relationship will attach.

```
public LinkOBJ
LinkOBJ = new DDELINK()
     if LinkOBJ.Initiate("MXW", C:\MXW\BREAD\LOAF.XLS")
          ? "Connection to Excel Begins"
     else
          ? "Connection has failed..."
     endif
```

In the following example, a line may be terminated by using the TERMINATE() command.

```
Public LinkOBJ
LinkObj = New DDELINK()
LinkObj.Initiate("("MXW", C:\MXW\BREAD\LOAF.XLS")
LinkObj.Terminate()
```

> **Caution**
>
> The TERMINATE() function cancels the relationship between dBASE for Windows and the server application. When you use TERMINATE(), you can restore the link with RECONNECT(). However, if you use RELEASE(), the link cannot be restored and the DDELINK must be reissued.

Exchanging Data Between the Client and the Server

After you establish a connection between the two systems, you can request data from the server document by using the Peek() command. You also can send data to the server document by using the Poke() command.

The following program opens a file named LOAF.XLS and copies the value of cell A:A1 into the memory variable xValue using the Peek() command. It then inserts the character string "17330" into the same cell using the Poke() command.

```
public LinkOBJ
LinkOBJ = new DDELINK()
LinkOBJ.Initiate("MXW", C:\MXW\BREAD\LOAF.XLS")
xValue = LinkOBJ.Peek("A:A1")
LinkOBJ.Poke("A:A1", "17330")
```

Sending Commands to the Server

You can control the server and its applications from the client site by sending the server commands in its native language.

In the following example, the program requests a link with Microsoft Excel by opening a worksheet named BRANCH.XLS. A link is established with a DDE between Excel and the current dBASE session. The program then uses EXECUTE() to create a new text file called DATA.TXT, and sends the contents of cells A1, A2, and A3 to DATA.TXT. The DATA.TXT file is then closed.

```
public LinkOBJ
LinkOBJ = new DDELINK()
LinkOBJ.Initiate("MXW", C:\MXW\TREE\BRANCH.XLS")
LinkOBJ.EXECUTE('{OPEN "C:\DATA.TXT",W}')
LinkOBJ.EXECUTE{"WRITELN +A:A1}")
LinkOBJ.EXECUTE("WRITELN +A:A2}")
LinkOBJ.EXECUTE("WRITELN +A:A3}")
LinkOBJ.EXECUTE{"CLOSE}")
```

Establishing Hot Links

A *hot link* in a client/server environment can notify the client when a specific item in the server document has changed. The hot link is created with the Advise() command by assigning a codeblock, or subroutine, to the OnNewValue property. dBASE can then execute that code whenever it notices that a change has occurred.

The following program illustrates how Advise() is established with the A:A1 cell in the Excel worksheet. On line five that follows, the LinkOBJ.ADVISE("A:A1") line establishes the hot link between dBASE and the server. When this line changes, dBASE (and the user) is notified. Then in line eight, you get a prompt that says whatever is in A:A1 has changed to whatever the new value is.

```
LinkOBJ = new DDELINK()
LinkOBJ.OnNewValue = ValueHandler
LinkOBJ.Initiate("MXW", C:\MXW\TREE\BRANCH.XLS")
LinkOBJ.EXECUTE('{OPEN "C:\DATA.TXT",W}')
LinkOBJ.ADVISE("A:A1")
FUNCTION ValueHandler
PARAMETER ITEM, VALUE
    ? item,"has changed to ",value
    return .T.
```

Once the hot link has outlived its usefulness, you can delete it with the UNADVISE() command, like so:

```
LinkOBJ.UNDAVISE("A:A1")
```

Creating a Server Application with the DDETopic Class

An external client application can use an external application as easily as a DDE server. Such a client application can read and write data to a variety of dBASE documents and send directives to the dBASE session.

If dBASE is performing as a server, you use DDETopic to perform actions as data-exchange demands are made. The DDETopic determines how data is sent, queried, or how it receives other instructions. As you might suspect, dBASE cannot act as a server without the presence of an active DDETopic object.

You use two different commands to create the DDETopic link with the NEW operator. You can enter the following code:

```
public ServerOBJ
ServerOBJ = NEW DDETOPIC("ALLMINE")
DEFINE DDETOPIC
```

Table 15.2 describes some DDETopic properties.

Table 15.2	DDETopic Properties
Property	**Description**
ClassName	Identifies the DDETopic object class.
Notify( )	Notifies a client application that a dBASE item has changed.
OnAdvise	Executes a subroutine when an external application requests a hot link to the dBASE session.
OnExecute	Executes a subroutine when a client application sends a directive to dBASE.
OnPeek	Executes a subroutine when a client application requests to read a value from dBASE.
OnPoke	Executes a subroutine when a client application requests to insert a value into a dBASE data item.
OnUnadvise	Executes a subroutine when a client requests to remove a hot link.
Release( )	Removes the DDETopic from memory.
Topic	Activates the DDELink topic.

Starting dBASE from a Client Application

Before a DDE link is established, a topic object must reside in memory. The client first starts a dBASE session and instructs dBASE to execute the startup program using an *initiation handler*. The client then initiates the DDE link with a dBASE document.

The following example is trying to call Excel for Windows from within dBASE:

```
{EXEC "DBASEWIN TESTING.PRG", 1}
(INITIATE "DBASEWIN", "TOPIC1", CAKES}
```

TESTING.PRG is the name of the dBASE program that contains the initiation-handler code. This parameter tells dBASE to execute the program file immediately upon beginning the dBASE session; TOPIC1 is the topic invoked by Excel. The client can then send anything it wants as the topic, but it often is a table or other file—CAKES is the name assigned to the Excel spreadsheet cell. It contains an automatically generated identification number that addresses the DDE link from other existing links. EXEC launches a dBASE session.

Using the Windows API

One of Windows most endearing features is its capability to share data between applications. It does this with a software device that is known as *dynamic linking*. As the name implies, an electronic link is established between two applications so that a communications channel is opened between them.

> **Note**
>
> Dynamic Linking is a method of linking data that is shared by two programs. As data is altered in one program, the data is changed in the other, because the two are dynamically linked. By using a *hot link,* information may be copied between one document and another. Windows has a Paste/Link command in most of the applications software that supports the Windows environment hot-linking. Not all Windows software performs dynamic linking, but the presence of a Paste/Link, or Paste Special choice in a menu is a good indication that the application conforms to this specification.

The Windows API (**A**pplication **P**rogramming **I**nterface) is a library built into the Windows environment. It contains a large number of useful C programming functions, all stored as DLLs. Such DLLs are a bridge to these programming languages; however, in order to use the library functions correctly, you need to know the name of the function and the name of the DLL file that contains the function. Furthermore, the data types of the parameters and their returned values, if any, must be identified. Although most Windows functions use a Pascal calling convention, it is helpful to know the calling convention that the function uses.

The dBASE DLL support option provides dBASE programmers with access to these Windows APIs. You make Windows API function calls in a similar manner to other DLL functions, with the following differences:

- The DLLs that compose the Windows API are automatically initialized when you use Windows. You never need a command such as LOAD DLL, but you should specify the DLL name that contains the API function when it is prototyped with EXTERN.

- Most API functions, as noted previously, utilize the Pascal calling convention. As such, the CDECL option of EXTERN cannot be used.

dBASE provides a header file named WINAPI.H that contains EXTERN prototypes and constant definitions for common Windows API functions. You can cut and paste from those prototypes and constants and use them in your programs. Alternatively, you can make calls to the WINAPI.H file with the #include preprocessor directive, covered in the next section.

Using Preprocessor Directives

Preprocessor directives are a class of statements inserted into dBASE for Windows code. The instructions tell the compiler to act on the code before actually compiling it. Perhaps you want to perform some search and replace textual replacements, or set up options for the compiler to act on. dBASE for Windows searches for preprocessor directives, evaluating them automatically when the code is compiled.

If the COMPILE command compiles your program code, dBASE performs a one-time pass through the code with a built-in processor. The code is scanned for any preprocessor directives, evaluating them as it goes. The results are a temporary intermediate file that the compiler is then able to compile.

Table 15.3 presents a summary of dBASE for Windows preprocessor directives. Each directive begins with a pound sign (#).

Tip

Any line in a program file that begins with a pound sign (#) is a preprocessor directive. Any line that begins with an asterisk (*) is a remark, and is ignored by the compiler during the compilation process.

Table 15.3 Preprocessor Directives	
Directive	**Description**
#define	Defines an identifier to the compiler.
#if	Begins the section that compiles a section of code if an identifier has a certain value.
#endif	Ends the section that compiles a section of code if an identifier has a certain value.
#ifdef	Compiles a section of code if an identifier is not defined.
#ifndef	Ends the section that compiles a section of code if an identifier has a certain value.
#include	Inserts a source code file at the current position.
#undef	Undefines an identifier.

Tip

A simpler way to improve a program's performance is to represent constants with identifiers. These are descriptive names that can be assigned to program text using a #define directive. The #define directive is useful when calling dBASE for Windows functions from DLL that use obscure integers and hexadecimal numbers, such as the Windows API.

There are three main ways of defining constants in dBASE for Windows: employing a literal value as a constant, employing memory variables as constants, and employing identifiers to represent constants.

Employing Literal Values as Constants

In the following code example, the literal value 2500 represents the maximum number of customers counted. The biggest problem with a design of this nature, as you might suspect, is that there is no way to increase the maximum number of customers without searching through the program to find where the variable containing the number 2500 is stored.

```
DO WHILE nCUR_CUST < 2500
        nCUR_CUST = nCUR_CUST + 1
ENDDO
```

In the next example, the problem is corrected by using a memory variable to represent the constant value. At the very beginning, you set the variable to 2500, and the program segment concludes once that number is reached:

```
nMAX_CUST = 2500
DO WHILE nCUR_CUST < nMAX_CUST
        nCUR_CUST = nCUR_CUST + 1
ENDDO
```

Employing Memory Variables as Constants

Code is somehow easier to understand when memory variables represent constants.

Be warned, however; using a memory variable slows performance in an area that is likely to be already slowed by the compilation process. dBASE for Windows constantly evaluates the variable through the DO WHILE loop. Each variable also has to be stored somewhere, if only on a temporary basis, and the choice is usually in RAM. Finally, dBASE places a limit on the number of variables that can be defined in one program, so defining too many variables in one program can exhaust memory resources.

Employing Identifiers to Represent Constants
Far and away the best method for constant representation is using the #define function. With the exception of an initializing statement, identifiers are used in the same manner as identifying constants for memory variables.

The following example is identical to that in the section describing literal values for constants, except that the #define defines CUR_CUST as a constant:

```
#define CUR_CUST 2500
DO WHILE nCUR_CUST < nMAX_CUST
nCUR_CUST = nCUR_CUST + 1
ENDDO
```

Using the Windows API Functions

dBASE for Windows helps you make calls to Windows API (application programming interface) functions by providing a header file called WINAPI.H.

The following three pieces of code employ Windows API functions. The first example displays the number of bytes of system memory available:

```
EXTERN CLONG GetFreeSpace (CINT) krnl.exe
FreeMem=LTRIM((STR(GetFreeSpace(0)/1024))+"K"
? "Free system memory: "+FreeMem
```

The second piece of code displays the percentage of system resources available:

```
EXTERN CWORD GetFreeSystemResources (CINT) user.exe
FreeRes=LTRIM((STR(GetFreeSystemResources(1)))+"%"
? "Free Resources: "+FreeRes
```

This third example displays the number of tasks currently running in Windows:

```
EXTERN CWORD GetNumTasks() krnl.exe
NumTasks=LTRIM((STR(GetNumTasks())))
? "Tasks Running: "+NumTasks
```

Consider the files USER.EXE and KRNL.EXE, either one of which is called at the conclusion of the first line of each referenced example. These are two files that contain a Windows API function called MessageBox(). The following example displays a dialog box with "Hello World!" in it, the stop sign icon, and two buttons—OK and Cancel. The return value, observable in the Results pane, is 1 if OK is chosen, and 2 if Cancel is chosen.

```
EXTERN CWORD MESSAGEBOX(CHANDLE,CSTRING,CSTRING,CWORD) USER.EXE
nResponse = MessageBox(0, "Hello World!", "From Windows API", 17)
```

Figure 15.1 shows the code as typed into the text editor and saved as MESSAGE.PRG. To run the program, position the cursor in the Command window, and type the line **DO** followed by the program name. For example, to run the MESSAGE.PRG file that was saved in C:\DBASEWIN\DATABASE type **DO C:\DBASEWIN\DATABASE\MESSAGE.PRG**.

Fig. 15.1

The MESSAGE.PRG file showing inputted text.

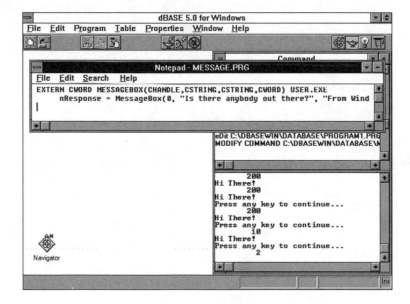

In figure 15.2, the results of running the MESSAGE.PRG file are shown. Note that the Navigator was minimized to an icon to clear the monitor. Because the user pressed Cancel, the number 2 shows in the bottom half of the Results pane.

Several third-party books, as well as the Microsoft Windows Software Development Kit (SDK), describe Windows API function calls in great detail, listing the functions contained in each Windows DLL.

dBASE for Windows provides some limited assistance with these function calls by supplying a WINAPI.H header file with the program. Inside this file are EXTERN prototypes and constant definitions for the more common API functions. You can cut and paste these functions into your applications.

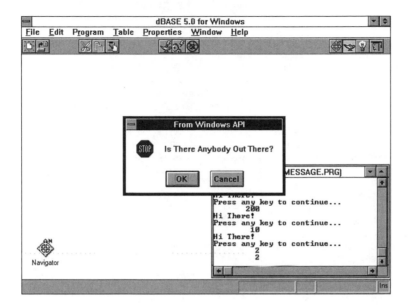

Fig. 15.2
The results of running MESSAGE.PRG.

If you find yourself using a large number of these API functions, you can invoke the #include preprocessor function to include all the elements of the header file in your program. This action is similar to calling the STDIO.H header file in a C routine: You get everything even though you might not use all of it.

In the following example, the first few lines of the WINAPI.H header file are replicated to show you what an all-inclusive file it is. This file may be found in the C:\DBASEWIN\INCLUDE subdirectory.

```
#define NULL      0
#define FALSE     0
#define TRUE      1
#define CBYTE     CWORD
&& because a minimum of a CWORD is read anyway
#define RGB(r,g,b)  (r + g*256 + b*65536)

*** Constants for pixel screen dimensions

          #define PIXELROWS    GetSystemMetrics(1)
&& Screen Rows in pixels
          #define PIXELCOLS    GetSystemMetrics(0)
&& Screen Columns in pixels
```

```
*** External Function Declarations

****************** Drawing and Windowing functions

extern   CLOGICAL   AnyPopup(CVOID) USER.EXE
extern   CLOGICAL   Arc ( CHANDLE,CINT,CINT,CINT,CINT,CINT,CINT,CINT,CINT )  GDI.EXE
extern   CINT       ArrangeIconicWindows(CHANDLE) USER.EXE
extern   CLOGICAL   BitBlt ( CHANDLE,CINT,CINT,CINT,CINT,CHANDLE,CINT,CINT,CLONG
                          ➥)GDI.EXE
extern   CWORD      CascadeChildWindows(CWORD,CWORD) USER.EXE
extern   CLOGICAL   Chord ( CHANDLE,CINT,CINT,CINT,CINT,CINT,CINT,CINT,CINT )  GDI.EXE
extern   CVOID      CloseWindow( CHANDLE ) USER.EXE
extern   CINT       CombineRgn ( CHANDLE,CHANDLE,CHANDLE,CINT )  GDI.EXE
extern   CHANDLE    CopyCursor ( CHANDLE,CHANDLE )  USER.EXE
extern   CHANDLE    CreateCompatibleDC ( CHANDLE ) GDI.EXE
extern   CHANDLE    CreateCursor ( CHANDLE,CINT,CINT,CINT,CINT,CSTRING,CSTRING)
                          ➥USER.EXE
extern   CHANDLE    CreateDc ( CSTRING,CSTRING,CSTRING,CPTR) GDI.EXE
extern   CHANDLE    CreateEllipticRgn ( CINT,CINT,CINT,CINT )  GDI.EXE
extern   CHANDLE    CreateHatchBrush ( CINT,CLONG )  GDI.EXE
extern   CHANDLE    CreatePatternBrush ( CHANDLE )  GDI.EXE
extern   CHANDLE    CreatePen ( CINT,CINT,CLONG)  GDI.EXE
extern   CHANDLE    CreateRectRgn ( CINT,CINT,CINT,CINT )  GDI.EXE
extern   CHANDLE    CreateRoundRectRgn ( CINT,CINT,CINT,CINT,CINT,CINT ) GDI.EXE
extern   CHANDLE    CreateSolidBrush ( CLONG )  GDI.EXE
extern   CHANDLE    CreateWindow( CSTRING,CSTRING,CDOUBLE,CINT,CINT,CINT,CINT,;
                          ➥CHANDLE,CHANDLE,CHANDLE,CLONG ) USER.EXE


        etc..
```

Using the Windows API Constants

The Windows API uses a considerable number of constants to represent common controls that users employ in their daily tasks. These include such things as icons and cursors. Although some constants are defined as integers, others are hexadecimal numbers.

In the following example, the constants SM_CXSCREEN and SM_CYSCREEN define the width and height of the screen:

```
#define SM_CXSCREEN 0
#define SM_CYSCREEN 1
EXTERN CINT GetSystemMetrics(CINT) USER.EXE

? "The Screen Width is" , GetSystemMetric(SM_CXSCREEN)
? "The Screen Height is" , GetSystemMetric(SM_CYSCREEN)
```

When using constants, it is often a requirement that integer values be converted into hexadecimal values. For these conversion needs, dBASE for Windows provides the following conversion functions:

HTOI( )   Converts a hexadecimal number that has been stored as a character string into an integer.

ITOH( )   Converts an integer into a hexadecimal number that has been stored as a character string.

The following example uses the function HTOI() with the MB_ICONQUESTION constant to display a question mark in a message box:

```
#define MB_ICONQUESTION HTOI("0020")
EXTERN CWORD MEssageBox(CHANDLE,CSTRING,CSTRING,CWORD) USER.EXE
MessageBox(0,"We're havin' Fun, Now!", "From Funpark
➥USA",MB_ICONQUESTION)
```

Figure 15.3 shows the code inputted into a file named FUNTIME.PRG.

Fig. 15.3
The
FUNTIME.PRG
program file.

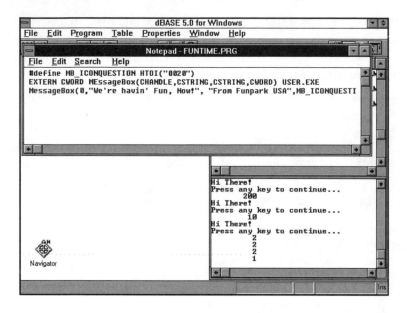

Figure 15.4 shows the results of the FUNTIME.PRG file when it runs.

Fig. 15.4
The FUNPARK
USA message box.

Summary

This chapter showed you how to use dynamic-link libraries in linking applications programs within dBASE. You learned how to create, establish, link, and terminate an application. Data swapping, sending, and receiving commands to and from the server were also covered. You also learned about the Windows Application Program Interface (API), and how to use pre-processor directives.

Working in a Shared Environment

Anyone who has worked with database applications for longer than a few months inevitably comes up against the first nonaccountable rule governing the process of data manipulation: How to handle conflicts when two users simultaneously attempt to update data. In many computer operations, it's a case of the last one out winning the updating game: This person's data is the last and final change made to the database at the expense of earlier updates going to the bit-bucket.

dBASE provides some measure of safeguarding against this type of activity by invoking either an automatic or an explicit record- and table- locking method before data is updated.

In the dBASE file-sharing environment, tables must be stored on a network drive in order to all but guarantee sharable data. In a *single-user environment* (only one person at a time is working with data), there is little worry about file sharing and consequent data corruption. If you have the data and Bob from Accounting wants something, you either provide him with the answer, or use the sneakernet shuffle. With the introduction of more people who desire access to your carefully guarded data, sharing becomes more important.

Instead of one user having all the data resident on her/his local hard disk, information is typically available to every plenary group member. The usual solution is to remove the data from the local drive and install it on a file server computer where access is guaranteed to everyone requiring it. An alternative is to make the local hard disk sharable, but most system administrators opt for the first solution.

Once an application is sharable, it is available for plenary members to use. The next issue to resolve is how to handle electronic conflicts when two people try to access the same table or record. This activity is known as a *collision*; software designed to work in a shared environment must have some electronic mechanism in place to avert such impacts.

These paragraphs depict an open architecture that suggests that anyone may gain access to anything on the network. The next level suggests the implementation of a security methodology so only certain users are allowed system privileges. For example, you wouldn't want everyone fooling around in a table that printed checks to vendors for services rendered, but you might like to make sure that when the system adminstrator takes that well-earned vacation in Laguna Beach, he/she's left the system intact with a responsible party.

Programming for a Shared Environment

You can access shared data on the same computer using any of the following procedures:

- Having multiple instances of dBASE running simultaneously by setting a localshare environment variable to ON in the IDAPI.CFG file.

  A *localshare* environment is one that has the capability to access local data between an active IDAPI and a nonactive IDAPI application. The switch in the IDAPI.CFG file can be turned ON (the default is OFF or FALSE), or set to TRUE if you want to work with the same file(s) through both an IDAPI and non-IDAPI application.

- Issuing a DOS-based SHARE command.

- Opening a table with the USE command. By default, the EXCLUSIVE environment setting must be off; then any open tables are allowed shared access and updating.

Opening a Table for Exclusive Use

If an attempt is made to open a table already in exclusive use by another user, dBASE issues a warning indicating that the table is already in use.

The USE and EXCLUSIVE commands open a table exclusively; once the table is open, no other users can use it until one of the following commands is issued: CLEAR ALL, CLOSE ALL, CLOSE TABLES, USE, or QUIT.

Table 16.1 shows dBASE commands that require some additional attention to ensure that your database tables are opened and closed correctly.

Table 16.1   dBASE Commands for Multiuser Systems

Command	Purpose
CONVERT	Adds an extra field to a table that tracks lock detection for use in a multiuser system. Example: CONVERT [TO <numeric expression>].
COPY INDEX	Converts an individual index file to index tags in a multiple index file. Example: COPY INDEXES <.ndx file> [<TO <.mdx file>]. Syntax: SET INDEX TO INFORMAT COPY INDEXES INFORMAT
COPY TAG	Converts an index tag in a multiple index file to an individual file. Example: COPY TAG <index tag name> [OF <.mdx file>] TO <.ndx file>. Syntax: USE STUFF COPY TAG LASTNAME to LAST

DELETE TAG	Deletes a specified index tag from the multiple index file. The .MDX filename is omitted; the production multiple index file is used. Example: DELETE TAG <index tag name> [OF <.mdx file> / <.ndx file>].
	 Syntax: USE STUFF
	          DELETE TAG LASTNAME
	          DELETE TAG ACCOUNTNO OF ACCOUNTS

INDEX ON... (Tag)	Creates an individual index file in which all records are ordered according to the instructions specified in the key field. Such records may be arranged in alphabetical, chronological, or numeric order. Example: INDEX ON <key field> TO <.ndx file> / TAG <index name> [OF <.mdx file>][UNIQUE][DESCENDING].
	 Syntax: USE STUFF
	          INDEX ON LASTNAME TO LASTNAME
	          DESCENDING
	          INDEX ON LASTNAME+FIRSTNAME TO
	          PERSON

INSERT (BLANK)	Adds a new record to the database at the current record location. Example: INSERT [BEFORE][BLANK].
	 Syntax: USE STUFF
	          GOTO 4
	          INSERT

MODIFY STRUCTURE	Modifies the table's structure. Syntax: USE STUFF MODIFY STRUCTURE
PACK	Removes all records that were marked for deletion with the DELETE command. Once the PACK command is issued, the index tags are rebuilt.

(continues)

Table 16.1 Continued	
Command	**Purpose**

	This command can take some time to finish if the table contains large numbers of records or has a high number of indexes associated with it.
	Syntax: `USE STUFF`
	`    DELETE RECORD 5`
	`    PACK`

REINDEX	Similar to `INDEX`, this command rebuilds the indexes.
	Example: `REINDEX`
	Syntax: `USE STUFF`
	`    SET INDEX TO LASTNAME`
	`    REINDEX`

RESET	Resets a program running in the Debugger. If the program is reset, it stops running and clears from memory. The program is then reloaded back into memory, and loaded into the Debugger, starting with the first line.
ZAP	A *very dangerous command*. Deletes all data records from the current table without deleting that table's structure. You may *not* recover these records except from backed-up copies from other media. Example: `ZAP` Syntax: `USE STUFF` `    ZAP`

Suppose, for example, that you want to modify a table structure in order to add or delete some fieldnames. Issuing the `USE FILENAME EXCLUSIVE` command before the `MODIFY STRUCTURE` command ensures that no one else can access the table while you are updating it.

> **Caution**
>
> ZAP is *very dangerous command*. It deletes all data records from the current table without deleting that table's structure. You may *not* recover these records except from backed-up copies from other media.

Opening a Table for Read-Only (RO) Access

Access to a table that enjoys *RO* (read-only) status means that the user can only view the table, not modify it. This type of access can be changed only through the security function on a network.

Notwithstanding the issues surrounding a system administrator's function, should you want to prevent any updates from being made to a table, the following command provides this function:

```
USE TABLENAME NOUPDATE
```

Locking Data

As previously discussed, when more than one user tries to access the same table or the same record within a table, problems usually don't occur until one of them tries to save and exit the task. dBASE uses two methods to ensure that one (and only one) user is permitted access to a table at a time—*automatic locking* and *explicit locking*.

In *automatic locking,* table records are automatically locked in BROWSE or EDIT commands when a key is pressed that normally changes a record. The exceptions are for those commands used to navigate the table (for example GOTO) or for activities that require making a menu selection.

Explicit locking applies equally to both table and the records within that table. It goes back to the *collision* discussion at the beginning of this chapter. Using explicit locking allows you to define which table, by name, and which record, by number, will be locked from a second person trying to access it. Explicit locking is usually a faster method: If you lock a table, other users are prevented from using it until you finish with it. That might be several hours. On the other hand, if you lock record 34, you may only be in that record number for a couple of minutes.

Table 16.2 describes both the commands and the types of locking effects they have on dBASE tables. Under the *Type of Lock* entry, *Record* means that the record within a table is locked and *Table* means that the entire table is locked. After you complete the update and move to another record or table, dBASE releases that element for others to use.

Table 16.2 dBASE Record and Table Locking Commands	
Command	**Type of Lock**
APPEND	Record
APPEND FROM	Table
AVERAGE	Table
BLANK	Record

(continues)

Table 16.2 Continued	
Command	**Purpose**
BLANK *<number>*	Table
BROWSE	Record
CALCULATE	Table
CHANGE	Record
COPY	Table
COPY STRUCTURE TO	Table
COUNT	Table
DELETE	Record
DELETE *<scope>*	Table
EDIT	Record
INDEX	Table
JOIN	Table
LABEL FORM	Table
RECALL	Record
RECALL *<scope>*	Table
REPLACE	Record
REPLACE *<scope>*	Table
REPORT FORM	Table
SORT	Table
SUM	Table
TOTAL	Table
UPDATE	Table

You can also release the lock on the table manually by choosing Table and Unlock Selected Record, or by pressing Ctrl+L when positioned on a locked record. Finally, you can use the command UNLOCK in the Command window to release all record and table locks in the specified workarea.

You can override some of the commands in Table 16.2 with the SET LOCK command. As you begin, locking is enabled by default. To use these commands, you must use the SET LOCK OFF command before going to the next command. When enforced, you may either enable or disable record locking.

The commands should be used with the SET LOCK OFF command. Locking affects some of these commands only when reading data from a table. When you write information into a table, the commands COPY, COPY STRUCTURE, INDEX, JOIN, SORT, and TOTAL automatically open the target table and set it to exclusive use. This is so the commands work without producing unpredictable results. These commands are as follows:

AVERAGE

CALCULATE

COPY

COPY STRUCTURE TO

COUNT

INDEX TO...

JOIN

LABEL FORM

REPORT FORM

SORT

SUM

TOTAL

Note

These commands work without locking, although data integrity cannot be guaranteed if the automatic locking feature is set to OFF.

After you finish using the table and record in question, the command UNLOCK releases the record. You also can use the commands CLOSE ALL, CLOSE TABLES, USE, CLEAR ALL, or QUIT to close a table:

- CLOSE ALL and CLOSE TABLES properly close all tables and the associated files that you have been using in an orderly fashion. This is the best method to use, because you are all but guaranteed that files are not corrupted.

- USE, when used in the phrase USE TABLE, opens the table, without assigning the controlling or master index associated with the table.

- CLEAR ALL releases any data fields from memory created by the SET FIELDS command.

- QUIT not only closes all database tables and their associated files, but also shuts down all dBASE processing and exits the program to the Program Manager icon.

Locking Related Tables

Because dBASE is a relational database-management system, it is almost a foregone conclusion that multiple tables will be open during an application's record update. It doesn't serve you very well to issue separate commands to lock and unlock myriad tables opened during an application; it is far better to issue one command that covers all tables and their records (shared or otherwise) in your application.

In the following example, a relation is set up between two tables. The first, CUSTOMER, holds all the client demographic information; the second, ORDERS, holds the records of customer purchases.

```
USE CUSTOMER IN SELECT() ALIAS CUSTOMER
USE ORDERS IN SELECT() ORDER ORDER_NO ALIAS ORDERS
SELECT ORDERS
SET RELATION TO INV_NO INTO ORDERS
SET SKIP TO ORDERS
SET FIELDS TO ORDERS->INVNO, ITEMS->DESCRIPT, ITEM->QUANTITY
BROWSE
```

This relationship describes a one-to-many operation among customers and their orders. As each record is selected for editing, dBASE locks the current record in the child table. When the user moves to the next record, the lock is released.

Processing Transactions

Whenever applications are forced into sharing their data across different users, it stands to reason that there must be some additional mechanisms within the table and records that are not the same as those applied to a single-user application on a stand-alone PC.

Transaction processing allows you to maintain the integrity of your data by instructing dBASE to verify the successful completion of an update before writing those changes to the hard disk. The results are an additional guarantee of the data's integrity and some acknowledgment that partial or incomplete updates do not corrupt your data.

dBASE for Windows operates under an event-driven mechanism for transaction processing. With this method, you may *commit* or *roll back* a transaction, making it easier to incorporate transaction processing within event-driven applications.

In dBASE IV, information was blocked or batch oriented. That is, blocks of information were written to the hard disk after each session completed. dBASE for Windows uses an event to write information out to disk. In such an event, transactions can be committed, or rolled-back independent of the utility or code that causes them to begin.

Three commands are provided for transaction processing in dBASE:

- BEGINTRANS(). Formally launches a transaction. The computer displays a .T. if the transaction begins without any problems. dBASE locks all records and tables until the transaction has concluded.

- COMMIT(). Ends a transaction, writing changes to tables and records to the hard disk, thereby making them permanent.

- ROLLBACK(). Also ends a transaction, but restores all the changes previously made to the open tables and records before any are released.

The following lines of code illustrate these three commands:

```
ON ERROR ROLLBACK()
USE ROCKER
IF BEGINTRANS()
    REPLACE ALL ARMS WITH GIZMO * 2.50
    IF .NOT. COMMIT()
    ENDIF
ENDIF
```

The following list illustrates the level to which dBASE tracks and stores all commands and functions used to update tables.

Command	Function
APPEND [BLANK]	BLANK
APPEND MEMO	INSERT
REPLACE	BROWSE
REPLACE MEMO	EDIT
REPLACE BINARY	@GET...READ
REPLACE OLE	RLOCK()
DELETE	FLOCK()
RECALL	

The following commands and functions are not allowed in dBASE transaction tracking; they alter tables.

Command	Function
BEGINTRANS( )	CREATE FROM
CLEAR ALL	DELETE TAG
CLOSE ALL	INSERT
CLOSE DATABASE	MODIFY STRUCTURE
CLOSE INDEX	PACK
CLOSE TABLES	ZAP
CONVERT	

Working with Non-dBASE Tables

Although this chapter has dealt mainly with dBASE-created information and those processes required to manage data-entry activities, there may be times that you have to handle non-dBASE information.

It may be that the information comes from Paradox for Windows or some other SQL table. dBASE enforces its table structure on these tables when they are opened with this program. As the table is opened, dBASE converts the data to a type that it can understand.

Once a database is defined, the command OPEN DATABASE establishes a connection to the database or its server. Then, the command SET DATABASE sets the database. You also can specify a location for a table within a database by prefacing the table name with the name of the database delimited with colons:

```
USE : FINANCEDB:ACKFIN
```

Caution

If a database or table is specified and cannot be located, dBASE displays a dialog box. Inside this box, you must enter your user name and password successfully before you are allowed to connect to that database.

Once a table is open, you can include either a .DBF or .DB file with a table name. If an extension isn't specified, dBASE opens a specific table by using the SET DBTYPE commands. You can override this command by specifying the TYPE options with the USE command.

The following sample code illustrates how dBASE opens a dBASE table called CUSTOMER.DBF and then opens two Paradox tables named ORDERS.DB and ITEMS.DB. The default is then changed to a Paradox table type, after which a Paradox table is opened.

When the command to open a Paradox table named ORDERS.DB is issued, Paradox doesn't recognize it; it fails equally in trying to open CUSTOMER in a Paradox format. However, when the CUSTOMER.DBF table is identified as a dBASE table, it is then opened. Finally, the dBASE table is copied to a Paradox table, and the ACKFIN database is opened in the FINANCE database. A DIR command lists the .DBF files. A SET DBTYPE TO PARADOX, followed by another DIR command, lists the Paradox database files.

```
USE CUSTOMER
USE ORDERS.DB
USE ITEMS TYPE PARADOX
SET DBTYPE TO PARADOX
USE ORDERS
USE CUSTOMER
USE CUSTOMER TYPE DBASE
COPY TO ONCEMORE
USE : FINANCEDB:ACKFIN
DIR
SET DBTYPE TO PARADOX
DIR
```

As you already saw, fieldnames in dBASE cannot include any spaces. Any spaces must by connected with underscores, as in FIELD_NAME. However, fieldnames in Paradox and other tables *can* contain spaces and other non-characters, such as brackets, the number sign, or parentheses. Therefore, when you use fieldnames not usually permitted in dBASE, you must delimit them with colons. The following example illustrates the point:

```
USE INVOICE.DB TYPE PARADOX
DISPLAY :Last Name:, Company,: Account#:
BROWSE FIELDS : Last Name:, Company,: Account#:
```

Using Data-Entry Commands

During normal dBASE data-entry operations, you can add, delete, or insert records anywhere you deem fit inside a table. However, in Paradox, and other non-dBASE tables, you can add records only to the end of a table.

Inserting Data

For the purposes of inserting data into a table, use the APPEND or INSERT command. You already know that using APPEND with a Paradox or other non-dBASE tables causes new records to be added to the end of a table, although the information always appears in the correct order in the associated index.

The command INSERT in a dBASE table allows you to force the computer to open a blank record in between two occupied records. Your new information appears in the correct order when the table is closed and updated. Use the commands APPEND or INSERT to accomplish this activity.

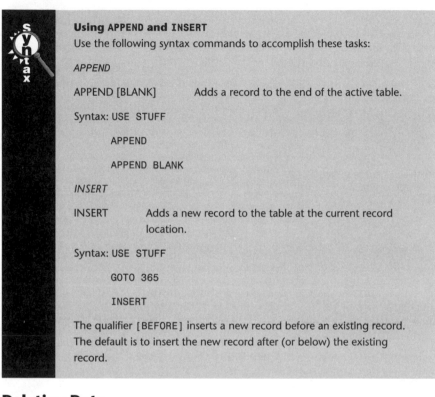

Using APPEND and INSERT
Use the following syntax commands to accomplish these tasks:

APPEND

APPEND [BLANK]   Adds a record to the end of the active table.

Syntax: USE STUFF

      APPEND

      APPEND BLANK

INSERT

INSERT   Adds a new record to the table at the current record location.

Syntax: USE STUFF

      GOTO 365

      INSERT

The qualifier [BEFORE] inserts a new record before an existing record. The default is to insert the new record after (or below) the existing record.

Deleting Data

Deleting records from within dBASE is a two-step process, similar to the discussion in Chapter 3. Recall that first, you delete the offending record with a DELETE command; this marks the record for deletion. Then you must PACK the database to delete it.

When you issue the DELETE command in Paradox, however, the record is immediately purged from the table. A deleted record cannot be recalled—it is gone forever!

In Paradox, the command DELETE RECORD 49 immediately deletes that record from the table, such that it may not later be recalled. The same command in dBASE only flags the record for later deletion. If you decide that you want to recall the record, you can do so with the command (as in RECALL RECORD 49). Deleted records are not gone forever in dBASE until you PACK 'em!

Validating Data

You can issue validity checks for each field within Paradox and SQL tables. Such checks verify that the data in the field is acceptable. They usually specify a minimum, maximum, or default field value. For example, if you had a fieldname called DATE and defined it to accept only date information (as in 10/14/55), the computer is expecting that you will type in only the numbers 10, 14, and 55. It provides the front slashes as you proceed.

A validation check here allows you to type in numbers, but it might not accept any year before 70. If you attempt to put anything earlier, the rule is violated, causing a prompt, or other arrestor to appear. As you continue, a validation checker also makes sure that only numbers will be accepted: You can't put alpha data into a date field. Similarly, a logical field expects to receive either a Y or N as acceptable input. Anything else that you might type in there is rejected.

Paradox validity checks are stored in a file with the same name as the table and a .VAL file extension. When you open a Paradox table, dBASE automatically opens any existing .VAL file. Consult the Paradox manual or other manuals to determine the specific type of validation checks that are provided, as well as how they should be created.

Summary

This chapter discussed ways you can use transaction processing in data-processing activities to ensure data integrity. Methods such as file- and record-locking were discussed, and workarounds for non-dBASE tables, such as those existing in Paradox, were examined.

Using dBASE III and dBASE IV Applications

A plethora of databases has been created by thousands of people over the years using dBASE III, dBASE III Plus, and dBASE IV program packages. Indeed, you might be using some of these even as you read these words. If you are musing over whether to convert these various files into dBASE for Windows format, ponder no more! You can, you probably should, and this appendix shows you how.

Most of the tasks inherent in the conversion effort are based on finding those files on your hard disk, and then updating their catalogs. There are only a few rules to observe in this task:

- Make sure that you move (or copy) only those files that dBASE for Windows needs: some are now redundant, and even though disk space may be less expensive than last year on a dollar-per-byte basis, there's still no point in cluttering your hard disk with superfluous files.

- There might be occasions when you need to update the directory paths of these catalogs so that the computer can access them. When you make the formal conversion, use only the dBASE File Viewer to open these catalog files.

Files formerly used in dBASE III and dBASE IV fall into three main camps when applied to dBASE for Windows: those you need; those that you may use after conversion; and those that you don't need.

Files You Need

Table A.1 shows the status of the files that you need and their resolution in dBASE for Windows. Unless specifically noted, all these filename extensions are interchangeable in dBASE for Windows.

Table A.1 Files You Can Use Directly with dBASE for Windows	
dBASE Filename Extension	**Purpose**
.CAT	A catalog file keeps all of the files associated with a particular application together.
.DBF	Database files, now known as tables.
.DBK	Backups of database tables; similar to .BAK files. They can be renamed to .DBF files when needed.
.DBT	Database fields used for holding memo text.
.FMT	These files house source code for screen formats (.SCR). This code should be updated to accommodate dBASE for Windows by redesigning the screens which, when saved, upgrade the code in the new format.
.FRG	These files house source code for reports. This code should be updated to accommodate dBASE for Windows by redesigning the report through the Report Designer.
.LBG	These files house source code for labels. This code should be updated to accommodate dBASE for Windows by using the Report Designer.
.MBK	These files use spare copies of .MDX files created when a table was modified in dBASE IV. If the file is renamed with the .MDX extension, you can use it in dBASE for Windows.
.MDX	Multiple index files are available for normal dBASE for Windows use.
.MEM	Both variable and array memory files work in dBASE for Windows. However, these files don't work in dBASE if they contain multidimensional arrays or other specialized memory objects available for the first time in dBASE for Windows.
.NDX	Index files.
.PRF	These files house the printer settings as established in the Control Center Print menu of dBASE IV. Such references may be made using the _pform system memory variable. Be aware, however, that the codes used in today's state-of-the-art printers can be quite different from those available during the dBASE III or dBASE IV tenure. In other words, technical obsolescence may require you to start over.

dBASE Filename Extension	Purpose
.PRG	These program files contain all of your textual lines of code in ASCII text format. Although these files are usable in dBASE for Windows, you might consider changing the code, or using the dBASE design tools to upgrade existing programs quickly.
.QBE	Query-by-Example files previously created using the Create/Modify Query command. These files contain information for record filtering. Any binary information from dBASE IV files is ignored.
.QRY	This extension is applied to files created with dBASE III Create/Modify Query commands. These files contain source code for filtering records. Any binary information that exists from dBASE III files is ignored.
.TBK	Database memo backup files are an additional spare copy of .DBT files. These were created automatically when dBASE IV tables were created or modified. If you rename these files with a .DBT filename extension, you can use them safely in dBASE for Windows. If this method is employed, use care not to overwrite existing files.
.UPD	These Query-by-Example files were generated by dBASE IV. Although they may be used in dBASE for Windows, you improve your speed and flexibility by using the Query Designer to create new queries prior to running dBASE for Windows.
.VUE	View files generated using the Create View command in dBASE IV can run unchanged in dBASE for Windows. Although they may be used in dBASE for Windows, you improve your speed and flexibility by using the Query Designer to create new queries prior to running dBASE for Windows.
.WIN	Not to be confused with any Windows program manager, these are dBASE IV window definition files. Although they work unchanged in dBASE for Windows, any screen forms and windows created in dBASE for Windows are saved with a .WFM file format.

Files You Don't Need

Table A.2 shows the status of files that you don't need in dBASE for Windows. Before you delete them from your hard disk, however, you might consider backing them up on disks just in case.

Table A.2   Files You Don't Need in dBASE for Windows

dBASE Filename Extension	Purpose
.$$$	Temporary files that, incidentally, don't just apply to dBASE for Windows, but can appear scattered throughout your entire hard disk structure. Some are zero bytes, but all may be deleted.
.$AB	These are interim file storage files and are not used by dBASE for Windows.
.ACC	User count files in dBASE IV.
.APP	Application design object files created by the Application Generator in dBASE IV.
.ASM	These files used assembly language to create binary files in dBASE IV. They were formerly used to support external subroutines and are not used in dBASE for Windows.
.BAR	As the name suggests, these files are used when creating horizontal bar design object files. These files were used internally by the template language compiler, but they have fallen into disuse in dBASE for Windows.
.BCH	These batch process design object files were used by the Applications Generator in dBASE IV. They do not apply to dBASE for Windows.
.BIN	Binary files. These were probably used in external subroutines in dBASE IV. They are not used by dBASE for Windows.
.CAC	Proprietary memory caches are not used in dBASE for Windows.
.COD	Not a saltwater fish, but the template language source code that was formerly used to create template files. Such files controlled the way source code was outputted to the dBASE IV Control Center's code generators. Because dBASE for Windows no longer employs templates to generate code, you can delete these files.
CONFIG.DB (File)	The old configuration file in dBASE III and dBASE IV, it was used to control screen colors, automate commands, and help provide program status. Because dBASE for Windows now uses the Windows DBASEWIN.INI initialization file for such configurations, this file is no longer used.
.CPT	Encrypted database memo files formerly created in the dBASE IV PROTECT command system. These files do not replace the unencrypted .DBT files. Consider bringing decrypted .DBT files from dBASE IV with you to the dBASE for Windows format.

dBASE Filename Extension	Purpose
.CRP	A second set of encrypted database table files. These were also created in the dBASE IV PROTECT command system. Again, these files replace the unencrypted .DBF files. You may want to consider bringing decrypted .DBT files from dBASE IV with you to the dBASE for Windows format.
.CVT	Originally, dBASE IV's CONVERT command added a _dBASElock multiuser record-locking field to a table. In so doing, a duplicate spare of the original file was created. dBASE for Windows can use this file, but the .CVT file—the spare copy—isn't needed.
.DB2	These files are veterans of the dBASE II program. Although dBASE for Windows doesn't utilize these files directly, a conversion program is available for those purposes in dBASE IV.
DBASE.VMC	A virtual memory configuration file from within dBASE IV Version 2.0. It doesn't apply to the Windows environment.
.DBO	These files were used by dBASE IV to create a database object file from a program file. The .DBO files work only in dBASE IV. dBASE for Windows creates its own set of unmodifiable object files from existing .PRG files that you copy into the program.
DBSYSTEM.DB DBSYSTEM.SQL	These two files are *encrypted:* they contain user profiles, including password information. dBASE for Windows doesn't use a schematic of this nature for security purposes.
.DEF	These files were used internally by dBASE IV's template language compiler.
.DOC	Documentation files created by the Application Generator in dBASE IV to document your applications. They are not used by dBASE for Windows.
.ERR	The error log file. These were created by dBASE IV to log and track errors in code compilation. They are not used in the same manner by dBASE for Windows.
.FIL	dBASE IV's Application Generator used this file extension as an organization tool. It does not apply to dBASE for Windows applications.
.FMO	The screen format object files work only in dBASE IV. dBASE for Windows can compile source code in screen format files from which the .FMO files were created.

(continues)

Table A.2 Continued

dBASE Filename Extension	Purpose
.FNL .LNL .SNL	These files are employed only by DGEN and DEXPORT.
.FRM	dBASE IV alone uses these report design files. dBASE for Windows can use these files in a report format (.FRG) from files generated from .FRM files. You must use the Crystal Reports in dBASE for Windows to convert these files to .RPT format.
.FRO	dBASE IV used these report form files. dBASE for Windows can use these files in a report format (.FMT) from which the .FRO files are created.
.FW2 .FW3 .RPD	These files represent old Ashton-Tate *Framework* or *RapidFile* files. You cannot use them in dBASE for Windows.
.GEN	Generated files from dBASE IV. Because dBASE for Windows now generates its code without using template files to control code creation, these files are obsolete.
.KEY	These file extensions were a dBASE IV Control Center mechanism. dBASE for Windows employs a Windows Recorder to create the next generation of macro files.
.LBL	These were label files in both dBASE III and dBASE IV schemes. They work only in dBASE IV's Report Designer. dBASE for Windows can use the code used to generate the old files, but saves your file using an .LBG file extension. If you insist on using the old system, first import the files into dBASE IV, and then add them to a catalog in the Control Center. Then open them in the Label Designer from the same Control Center. Generate an .LBG file containing the source code for dBASE for Windows. You will be more satisfied, however, if you create a new label file in dBASE for Windows by using the Report Designer. You must use the Crystal Reports in dBASE for Windows to convert these files to .RPT format.
.LBO	These files accompanied the label files. They work only in dBASE IV. As with the label files, dBASE for Windows can compile source code in label format files from which the .LBO files were created.
.LOG	Transaction log files served the beginning and ending of transactions in dBASE IV. dBASE for Windows uses transaction processing only in SQL data in a client/server environment.

dBASE Filename Extension	Purpose
.NAP	Network Access pack file lists are used only in a multiuser dBASE IV arena.
.PIF	The dBASE IV Program Information File allowed Windows users to use non-Windows applications. dBASE for Windows doesn't use this specification.
.POP	Popup menu design objects were used by the dBASE IV Applications Generator. They don't apply to dBASE for Windows.
.PR2 .PR3	These are Windows printer drivers and devices. None of the dBASE DOS-based printer drivers applies to dBASE for Windows. (See .TXT.)
.PRS	Commands for SQL commands and procedures work only with dBASE IV. Although dBASE for Windows can access SQL tables, it still needs the correct SQL drivers.
.PRT	dBASE IV used printer-output files created by the REPORT FORM command. The resulting output contained little more than a report's contents in text format. They were output to disk as text files, embedded with printer control codes. A new format produces these .PRT files with the REPORT FORM command in dBASE for Windows.
.QBO	The old Query-by-Example format in dBASE IV does not work in dBASE for Windows. Use the Query Designer in dBASE for Windows to create new QBE file queries.
.RTM	This doesn't stand for *read the manual*, but are runtime list files. They are unsupported in dBASE for Windows.
.SCR	The (old) screen form design in dBASE III and dBASE IV. These files hold much the same information that dBASE for Windows needs, and thus you can run them directly in the new system.
.STR	These structure list design objects used by dBASE IV's Applications Generator. No utility exists for them in dBASE for Windows.
.T44 .W44	These two files were used as Interim holding areas for database table indexing and sorting activities. No utility for them exists in dBASE for Windows.
.TXT	Textual data is sent to a filename with this extension. Use the REPORT FORM command in dBASE IV or dBASE for Windows. As before, none of the old printer drivers— including the ASCII.PR2 driver that was typically used by this activity—are required because printer control codes are no longer embedded in text files.

(continues)

Table A.2 Continued	
dBASE Filename Extension	**Purpose**
.UPO	dBASE IV alone uses these Query Update Object files. Use the Query Designer in dBASE for Windows to recreate queries.
.VAL	The dBASE IV Applications Generator used these values list design object files. dBASE for Windows does not use them.

Files That You Can Convert

You can use some files formerly encrypted using the dBASE IV PROTECT command in dBASE for Windows. Typically, the PROTECT command was used to enforce security: a user wanting to employ a PROTECTed file had to enter a password to gain access to that database/table. This system was also used to protect data from simultaneous, multiple read/writes and file-locking scenarios.

Note

If you want to employ a similar type of system in dBASE for Windows, your file(s) must be decrypted before use.

The following procedure describes what you must do to utilize file-encryption schemes effectively in dBASE for Windows:

1. Make a full backup of all the data you are about to modify. Then make sure that you have EXTEND, DELETE, and UPDATE privileges for the files that you want to access and modify. You must also enjoy FULL field privileges for each field in each file. Therefore, you must have two distinctly different accesses; having one without the other doesn't work!

2. Find the required files on your hard disk. Enter the dBASE IV database program and get to the dot prompt. Type the command SET ENCRYPTION OFF.

3. Issue the command USE *<filename>*, substituting the name of the file that you want to decrypt.

4. Issue the command COPY TO *<filename>* WITH PRODUCTION, where *<filename>* is your new file. Always use a different filename to avoid

overwriting your existing data. dBASE IV creates a decrypted copy of your encrypted table, along with an associated memo file (if it existed originally) and the table's production index.

5. Close dBASE IV.

6. Copy the new files to the appropriate subdirectory (wherever you keep your applications software). Or you can set the file location icon after launching dBASE for Windows.

7. Enter dBASE for Windows and modify your file location in tables to view the new files. They should be fully accessible.

Summary

This appendix showed you which of your preexisting files you can use from the dBASE III and dBASE IV versions, and which ones you can delete once you make the switch to the new version. A mechanism to translate encrypted files was also discussed. Now you are ready to dig into dBASE 5.0 for Windows!

Index

Symbols